Out of the FIRE

The God That Does Not Fail

James Pemberton

Vladimir & Val.
May God's Best!,

[signature]

© Interior & Cover Designs by Cindy Bauer

ISBN 13: 9781791806682

2nd Edition

Printed in the United States of America

Dedicated to our Blessed Savior
and Lord, Jesus Christ with special
thanks to Him for His faithfulness.

And

Special thanks to the many friends
who have allowed me to share their
testimonies for the glory of our Lord.

And

Special thanks to my wife
and love of my life, Elena.

INDEX

The God That Does Not Fail

His Voice

I understand that a subject such as "His Voice" would immediately be controversial but let me start up front with an explanation of what I refer to as "His Voice." For most of my life, when facing a stressful situation, or when perplexed, or when just in need of advice about a decision, a voice from within has addressed me with words of wisdom, words of encouragement and/or instructions. The only explanation that I can accept is that it is the voice of the Lord. It has never been an angry voice. It is always patient, it is always kind and informational; it is always soft but rational and logical. It has always made sense and appeals to my sense of logic.

I do believe that caution must be exercised when a voice is heard in the head, as is frequently reported by people who are psychotic. If it is an audible voice, heard in the head, it must be rejected quickly and firmly. I believe when the Lord speaks to us, it is as a "still, small voice" and comes from deep within our very being. Sometimes, it wouldn't be characterized as a voice at all, but rather a sudden understanding or sudden burst of knowledge that develops and consumes, like "seeing something for the first time," and we just know that we know. Several references to hearing the Lord's voice are found in His word, Ps 95:7, Heb 3:7 and Rev 3:20 as well as other places.

I believe He addresses most people the same way, but most people have never recognized it, or they minimize it as "something said to me" or the "voice of reason," or some similar explanation.

7

The Lord has spoken to me at times when I was going through obvious stress. He has also spoken to me at times when there has been no apparent stress, such as the freeway incidence that I will share later in this chapter. Whether powerful or low key, many of the occurrences will stay with me all my life—both, the situation I was in at the time, as well as the words spoken to me. My memory of the words is pretty close to verbatim. As I grow older, many incidents that have happened throughout my life become lost to memory. But those times when the Lord has clearly spoken to me are as fresh in my mind as if they had been spoken just moments ago.

I still recall very vividly an occurrence from when I was about 12 years old—the first such that stands out in my mind. My parents had punished me for some reason. I don't recall why, and the reason is no longer important.

I was walking down a country road that led from our house to a barn about a quarter mile from our house. I was going to the barn for a breather and to dissipate some of the hurt that lingered. I was downcast because I felt that I had been wrongfully punished for something that one of my brothers had done. As I walked, I thought, "Maybe I'll get back at my parents by leaving home. I could go to an aunt's house about 40 miles away and spend a few days." I didn't want to go far nor stay very long, just a few days to let my parents worry a little for unfairly punishing me. Anyway...

As these thoughts filled my head, I know to this day that the Lord spoke to me and said, "You are much too young to do such a thing. The time is not right. To do so would unnecessarily hurt you and your parents. Just bide your time and there will come a day when you will leave home properly and the timing will be right. Your parents will release you with their blessing. When you do leave, you will not come back again for any length of time during the remainder of your life."

To this day, I remember that I felt so much better. Not because of what was said, but because of who said it, even though I was much too young to understand much about it at that time. I knew someone was watching over me and that thought instilled tremendous peace.

I never considered running away from home again, nor was I ever bothered by any decisions made by my parents. I realized that my parents were human, and humans everywhere make mistakes. They tried very hard to raise their children as best they could. They understood things like discipline and, as parents, it was their call. There was even a time when an older brother was critical of something they did, and I became offended and informed him, "No one is interested in what you think about choices or decisions they make."

When I was 14, we lived in a village that had numerous rocky cliffs nearby populated by shallow caves in the hillsides. It was common for young people to skip school and go to the cliffs to spend the day, always unchaperoned.

On one spring day, it occurred to me that the weather was much too beautiful to spend all day in school. So on impulse, I decided to go to the cliffs. Because I was alone, that decision nearly cost me my life. After exploring a number of small caves, I noticed one that appeared to go back some distance into the cliff. As I bent over and peered in, it looked as if it had a very narrow entrance but opened into a large roomy area within just a few feet of the entrance. As I lay on my stomach, I could barely squeeze into it. After pushing myself in for a couple feet, I could also see that it dead-ended a short way in and there was no room to turn around. I had made a mistake in my perception of a large roomy area in it.

As I attempted to wriggle myself back out, the bottom of my coat balled up around me and I became wedged. I could move forward okay, but no matter how I tried to squirm backward, the coat would tighten around me and

I became wedged again. My arms and hands were extended in front of me and there was no room to get them to my side to smooth out my coat as I tried to back out. Panic set in as I realized that I was helplessly stuck, and no one knew that I had gone to the cliffs today. Even when someone started missing me, they wouldn't know where to look for me.

Because I had plugged the entrance, there was no longer light ahead of me and my mind started playing tricks in the darkness. The air in the cave was damp and cool, but I began to sweat profusely as claustrophobia enveloped me, and I could feel various small, long-legged insects crawl onto my head and face. I knew it was common to find crickets and something that we called "Daddy Longlegs," a spider-like insect, clinging to the roofs of these caves, but I had no idea what else might be there. It was torture to have these things crawling on me and my hands pinned in front of me where I couldn't reach to knock them off

The next couple of hours were probably the worst two hours of my life even though I prayed a lot. After awhile I began to calm somewhat as I realized that I would have to get out of there on my own if I was to live. As calm returned, I began working my body methodically in and out of the opening, in and out, each time gaining a little. Perhaps an hour later, my coat torn and my body bruised and lacerated in several places, I felt myself break free from the confines of the rock and relief swept over me as I made my way off the cliff.

Upon my arrival home, my mother wondered if I had been in a fight or had been wrestling with one of the farm animals. To this day, I cannot have my arms or hands pinned or restrained without feeling claustrophobia. I did return to the caves many times after that incidence, but never alone, and I stayed away from tight places.

I felt so stupid about going there alone and then getting stuck, I was embarrassed to share the experience with but a few people. Yet the Lord knew and etched the experience in my memory as a reminder that when we feel bound by things in life, we will make it through if we don't flounder or give up. Life is not for those who give up but for those who place their faith in Him and then watch Him move the mountain. For all I know, He may have stretched that cave opening that day allowing me to be released. This lesson in my early life would help me at other times later when I felt bound or pressed by other situations that I've gone through.

I turned 17 years old in March of 1959 and joined the Army immediately. Upon completion of Basic Training I was sent to Alaska for two years. There God continued His influence on my life. I quickly located a good church in a nearby village and, along with several friends, attended regularly. Sometimes, I, or a friend, would check out vehicles from the post motor pool and take a number of others from our barracks to church with us.

In October of that year, a fellow soldier asked me if I would like to accompany him and another on a moose hunt, and I quickly accepted. Since I didn't have a rifle, I would check out a three quarter ton military vehicle from the post motor pool and drive the others to and from the hunting area about 25 miles down the Alcan Highway. We left the Alcan at milepost 1416 and navigated tank trails for about 30 miles back into the brush country. There were only two roads in that part of Alaska at that time. The Alcan ended where it joined the Richardson Highway at a village called Delta Junction, near our military post. The Army used their vehicles where no roads were, leaving "tank trails" crisscrossing hundreds of square miles of government land.

Upon reaching the proposed hunting area, I parked on a slope while the others moved to an observation point nearby. Not a single moose could be seen, so we got back into the truck to move to another site only to discover the truck would not move. After it was all over, we were told to never park this particular model on an incline while in four-wheel drive because it had a history of the transfer case locking when parked in that manner.

Right then, we were in a potentially very serious situation. People disappear in the brush country of Alaska all the time. We were aware of many stories where people, found weeks or months later, told of just walking a few feet from the road and becoming disorientated and not being able to find their way back to the road.

The temperature was around zero degrees and a fire would feel pretty nice as the truck cab cooled. So we built a large fire to keep away marauding animals. Wolves were plentiful and we knew they were creatures of opportunity. In addition, there were wild bison. Even though bison are herd animals, if frightened, a herd can flatten anything in its path. There were also lynx and bears that could become threatening.

With the fire roaring, the decision had to be made about who was going to walk out to get help. I insisted that I would do that. I don't know why; maybe I was just naïve and didn't realize the danger. It may have been because I was the youngest and thought I was in the best shape. In any case, looking back, I realize it was not very smart.

The oldest guy in our group handed me his 30.06 with three shells. That was all he had with him. Our best guess put us at about 25 to 30 miles from the nearest road with dozens of crisscrossing tank trails between it and us. I would need to select the right one (several times) or I could be wandering for days.

I set out full of confidence, and within a quarter mile met my first challenge. I had to make my first choice which tank trail to follow. It would be like completing a 30-mile maze with only one possible exit before I finished.

I felt the hand of the Lord on me all the way. Sometimes I made choices about taking certain tank trails, pretty sure that I had made the right decision, only to start experiencing a bad feeling about it. I would retrace my steps to where I had made the choice and choose another. It wasn't a voice, but a feeling pressed into my spirit. I was new at sensing that the Lord was trying to guide me and it wasn't till later when I had the time to look back, that I was able to see his footprints alongside mine.

It was dark throughout the entire trek area this early fall night, but a foot or more of snow brightened the sub-arctic night. The trail that I was traversing crossed an area that forest fires had cleared in earlier years, and a low ridge was on my right. Suddenly I heard a low rumbling noise from the vicinity of the ridge. Paying close attention in the low light, I could see shadowy figures emerging from the brushy timberline on the edge of the burned area. As I watched, these figures melded into a large clump and I realized that it was a heard of bison, apparently startled, on the run and generally heading my direction.

As they came closer, I fired one of the three bullets from the 30.06 into the air to spook them, hoping they would divert away from coming straight at me. It was a relief to see them angle a little away from me and move down the slope to my right.

I never knew what had spooked them into stampeding, but I guessed it was wolves, which was also a little unsettling.

At one point I thought I could save a little time by cutting through a low area to the tank trail on the ridge on the other side. I didn't realized that wind had filled the low area with snow several feet deep, and I floundered repeatedly as I tripped over underbrush and pitfalls hidden by the deep snow. Once on the other side and discovering that it had taken considerable more time as well as energy to make the "short cut," I made a mental note to not do that again.

Eventually, I stepped out of the brush and onto the

pavement of the Alcan Highway just several hundred yards from my pastor's home, which I had set as my goal. After leaving the few villages along the Alcan, homes become few and far between. If I had missed my target, it would have required additional miles to get to another house. It had taken over ten hours but I was still in good shape after covering the approximately 30 miles.

I used the pastor's phone to call the Military Base to have a tow truck sent to me and then I rode with the crew back into the brush, directing them through the maze of tank trails to where I had left the others. The guys I had left behind were in a panic by the time we reached them because they were wrestling with the idea that I had not made it, and were trying to decide whether to try to make it out themselves. They embraced me as well as the tow truck crew. After that experience, anyone from the post planning hunting trips encouraged me to drive for the group even though I most often declined.

In retrospect, Gods hand was on me. I would have never made it relying solely on my natural sense of logic or instinct. I was only a 17-year-old boy at the time, green to the ways of the Alaska wilderness which, I came to realize in the two years that I was there, was a killer for careless or green individuals who are not wise to, or respect its ways. There were so many places where I could have—no doubt, would have—made the wrong decision, or floundered in a snowdrift, or injured myself, and no one would have found me. I had pushed the envelope just about as far as it would go. I later become convinced that had God not placed His hand on me, I would have never made it.

Months later, I checked out a military vehicle for recreation and, along with a couple of guys who went to church with me, decided to go to the Black Rapids training site, about 60 miles from our post. This place was used to train troops coming up from the lower 48 states for arctic training on a rotating basis; usually a group was there for about two months before rotating back to the lower states.

We decided to drive from the camp up to where soldiers were learning to ski on the ski slope. To get there required driving about a mile, mostly uphill on a precarious road that ran dangerously close to a ravine about 30 feet deep with about two feet of snow, mostly compacted on the road. As we drove parallel to the ravine, the road became pretty steep and my vehicle, even though in four-wheel drive, lost traction and started skidding backwards. After skidding for some time, I was worried about going into the ravine. I had turned my steering wheel sharply so the front wheels entered fresh snow on the side of the roadway, giving them limited traction. This compelled the vehicle to spin completely around so it started heading down the hill forward. This also increased my ability to control the slide and bring the vehicle to a stop.

As we surveyed the skid marks afterwards, we realized that when the vehicle went into the spin, the rear end had jutted dangerously close to the ravine. Tire marks indicated we were only inches from the edge. That's when we really got scared. And again, I felt that God had His hand on our lives and had spared us serious injury.

In the early spring of 1960, the same three of us were again at Black Rapids. This time, we were out to do some hiking and climbing in the rough country surrounding the training area. After several hours we decided to return to where we had parked the truck, only to discover that we had to either go around a rather steep ridge or go down it. After some debate, we decided to go straight down the slope; honestly, risk or possible danger wasn't even a consideration. I think we were simply not smart enough to consider those things, so we proceeded down, oblivious to any possible danger. We safely made it to our truck and returned to the post.

Next day, we were astounded to hear that the military had taken eight guys on snowshoes over this slope after we had gone down it, and an avalanche crashed down and buried everybody. It took several days to locate and excavate the dead. There were two survivors. While feeling dismay and concern for those lost, we also were in awe that God had protected us from the same fate.

As I look back on such events in my life, I can't help but feel that God has set me apart for some reason. Yet I also understand that He is an all-loving God for everyone. During the three years that I was in the military, even though I didn't completely surrender my life to Him, I attended church regularly and desired to walk with Him continually. He kept His hand on my life and protected me so many times I don't have the room or the time to tell of every occurrence.

Later, I was stationed in the Pacific Northwest until discharged. Job opportunities were pretty good in that area at that time, so after a three-month illness/convalescence in Kentucky, I returned and have lived there ever since then. It is some 2,600 miles from where I was born and raised, and first heard His voice.

Immediately upon being discharged from the Army, I returned to my parent's home to visit with my family, intending to stay only a couple of weeks then return to the Pacific Northwest where I had been discharged. It was strictly an economic decision because of the better job market.

I arrived at my parents' home and become very ill the next day. I had a few hundred dollars in my pocket but I didn't want to use that for medical assistance. Besides, I thought the illness would pass in a few days, and I would be all right. After all, I had been sick before, and always was fine in a few days.

After several days, my Mother was becoming very concerned and continually pressed me to allow them to take me to a doctor.

The pastor, whom I had known from my youth, came several times to pray that God would heal me. I recall the last time he was there. The voice had come to me again and told me, "It is important that I go through what lies ahead, I must pass through, I would not die, but would have a very tough time before it was over He would not heal me at this time but would go through it with me."

I informed the pastor that he should not pray for God to heal me, but rather pray that God will see me through. I shared with him what I believe the Lord had told me. At the time, I could not have imagined what lay ahead.

I was having frequent bouts of delirium, so he may not have believed me because he continued to pray for my healing. After some time of intense prayer, as if puzzled, he said to my mother, "I don't understand. When I ask the Lord for Jim's healing, it's like heaven is brass. My words bounce back at me."

I don't think he returned after that.

After the fourth day of high fever, my Mother entered my room and this time she didn't ask me to go to the doctor; she told me that she had called an ambulance which would arrive shortly.

Everything from then on became very fuzzy. I became comatose and drifted in and out most of the time while in the ambulance. I learned later that the driver first took me to a local hospital where my temperature registered 108 degrees. That hospital refused to take me, knowing that I was just discharged from the Army, not knowing if I was connected with Viet Nam war and because of concern that I might have jungle fever or something worse. They were afraid I might start an epidemic in the hospital. The Vietnam War had started a few years earlier, and while I was never there, I was in contact with soldiers who were going to, or coming from there.

The ambulance driver didn't know what to do with me. He couldn't just dump me on the street. Realizing that I was recently discharged, and that Fort Campbell was about 120 miles from where we were, he decided to carry me there. That decision probably saved my life.

Several hours later, we arrived at the Fort Campbell hospital where an initial check by emergency medical staff diagnosed pneumonia. Because of my recent discharge, military authorities agreed to accept me in the base hospital and informed my parents that in a few days I would be as good as new and they could come to bring me home.

My recollection of the admittance process is very hazy. I remember that, when awakening briefly I was so incredibly thirsty; I thought I was going to die from thirst. I begged a nurse to give me something to drink, and then drifted back into unconsciousness.

While in the coma I became aware of a sensation similar to a floating feeling, as if I was drifting off and out somewhere. I was not in my body, but was being pulled along through a tunnel. I could feel no actual pull on my body mass as I was out of it, yet I experienced a feeling of motion and understood that I was moving. Gravity seemed to have no effect on me.

At some point, I could see a light ahead of me, not as a bright light, but as if the tunnel widened into a lit area. I knew that I would soon move into this lighted area and that the presence of the Lord was there. Fear gripped my soul. I knew that I was not ready to meet the Lord. Even though I had not been a bad person per se, there were some things of which I felt a need to repent—probably mostly just having not made the Lord the Lord of my life. The fear that I experienced was not natural, but supernatural. Most fear humans experience is a result of physical stimuli received by the brain from one of the 5 or 6 senses that might indicate danger. I cannot find words to describe the fear I felt. It tore at my insides and I wanted to heave, but couldn't. It was somewhere in my soul and I was in anguish, yet I had no power or will to resist the direction that I was moving.

Somewhere, way off in the background, I began to hear someone call my name. As I concentrated on it and wondered who might be calling me, my movement began to reverse. I returned to my body to discover the nurse shaking me and very forcefully speaking my name. I didn't realize that, after asking her for something to drink, she waited until the doctor approved it and then returned with a carton of milk. The timing was perfect, and I remembered the Lord's promise that I would not die at this time.

The diagnosis of pneumonia had been premature. I was in a solid coma for the first week, and off and on the second while my situation began to slowly stabilize. The doctors had discovered an abscess on my right lung, but couldn't determine what was causing it. I was given massive doses of Staphcillin and Streptomycin, normal treatments for pneumonia, but didn't respond very quickly.

In an attempt to identify the problem, doctors extracted bone morrow from my chest, which showed negative from any known problems. They then performed a lung biopsy and a liver biopsy, but found nothing. I was awake during both surgeries, responding to questions, sometimes fighting with staff, all the time in great pain as these medical procedures/surgeries were all without any form of sedation but included several hospital staff holding me down. I begged for sedation, but was told that local (shots) would not work as there were no nerves to sedate in the areas where the surgery would be performed and they didn't want to put me to sleep because of the possibility my lungs may collapse and should that happen, they wanted me awake so I would resist or fight against the collapse. After the lung biopsy, I lay with a tube in my chest for a week to prevent fluid build-up in the right lung.

The fever had subsided, but my weight had dropped from 160 to 98 lbs., and I just didn't seem to be mending. My lungs were continuing to accumulate fluid. The left lung had been tapped five times to remove fluid using a hypodermic needle, and the right one once before the tube was inserted after the lung biopsy.

The lung tap process involved pushing a needle, without any form of sedation and as I recall, the needle seemed to be about the size of a standard pencil, between my ribs into the lung cavity, high on my back and to the left of my backbone about three or four inches. It was excruciatingly painful. The first few times, I was so sick the doctors could have probably done anything to me and I wouldn't have noticed, but by the last time, it was terribly painful. It lasted for about ten minutes or so.

At six weeks, the lung cavities seemed no better, and the doctor indicated he must repeat this procedure again the following day to remove fluid that was building up on the left side. I would rather he told me he was going to shoot me. I just didn't want to go through the pain again.

That night, I called out to the Lord and reminded Him of his promise to see me through, wondering why it was taking so long. I promised Him that if He would just heal me and get me out of there I would re-commit my life to Him and yield my future to His will. I knew exactly, at that instant, He touched me. I didn't glow, I didn't feel anything significant, there was nothing that I could label that happened, but I know He touched me and that I was healed. It was an assurance. Faith swelled within me and I felt I could walk on water. I barely slept that night because of the excitement that was building in me. At the time He touched me, He impressed upon me from within, that in addition to healing me, He will add 20 years to my life which I understood that as I was 20 at the time, He would bring me home at 40 and that impression stayed with me as I neared 40, I stressed a little thinking my time has come but I sailed through my 40th year without anything happening so I tried to put it out of my heart yet it remained there so I accepted that I didn't know for sure how to understand it. Later in life, as I neared 76, I received several comments that I looked 20 years younger. After a few such comments, it hit me what the meaning of the "additional 20 years" meant. I am convinced that He was telling me that He would add 20 years to my life span. Out of the 11 children my Mother had, currently, I have lived longer than any of the others as all but two have already deceased.

Anyway, the next morning, the doctor entered my room to repeat the painful lung tap process. Knowing that God had touched me, I asked him before he started the tap if he would just take a moment to check me first.

The check consisted in using his knuckles to thump me on the rib area, much like thumping a watermelon to see if it's ripe. As he was checking me, a puzzled look came over his face and he said to me, I don't know what's happening, but you seem to sound a lot better. Maybe we will wait until tomorrow for the tap and check you again. I shouted inside but I didn't tell him that God had touched me and that I was convinced He had healed me. The following day, it was the same story. By the third day, and after several additional tests, all positive, the hospital agreed to release me. I was anxious to get out of there, feeling that I had overstayed my time. Doctors were concerned about me leaving by myself because I had lost so much weight and still appeared weak, but I convinced them to release me.

I remember my final conversation with my doctor. He said, "We never identified any bacteria or virus that would have caused the illness, and have no idea what made you so sick, and have no idea why you suddenly improved so quickly."

I was too shy to tell him that I knew why I healed so quickly. Anyway, I walked away on my own strength, caught a bus, and returned the 120 miles to my parents' home.

After convalescing for another 6 weeks at my parents' home, I was relaxing on their front porch when I was joined by my mother. Her demeanor suggested to me that she had something serious she wanted to talk about so I invited her to share what was on her mind and as she did, to this day, I remember the solemnity and exact tone of her voice and noticed her holding back tears as she told me that she had sensed that I should not remain in this place. That my future was not here but was out there somewhere and that I need to go and find it. That she would miss me terribly but even if she was to never see me again, as long as I was fine and doing well for myself, she could be satisfied. Within a week, I had made plans to return by Bus to the Pacific Northwest. I recall as I boarded the Bus, mother told me to just board and don't look back, to continually look forward toward my future but after I was boarded, I leaned down and looked through a window to her and it was so clear why she had ask me to not look back as she was crying profusely. I understood her so did not attempt to go to her.

I have remained in the Northwest part of the United States ever since. However, the reality and the focus of those dark days and the near-death tunnel experience and my departure have remained as real as if it had happened only yesterday.

In 1964, living in the northwest, I was employed as a pond man by a large timber company. My job was running a log bronco (a small boat designed especially for a log pond) sorting and moving logs around on the water. It was easier to move logs while they were in water than on dry land. I would sort them after they were de-barked, for species as well as quality, and after they were penned and sorted, move them around the pond to the mill, about a half mile away.

For several months, I had increasingly become annoyed if things didn't go the way I expected. Even little things would bother me. One day, I was trying to nudge a log into a pen. After several tries, it just didn't seem to want to go in. I was quickly getting frustrated when, from deep within me there was His voice again saying, "If you don't get control of this anger, it will get control of you."

Not necessarily profound words, but it was like a dam burst within me and a river of understanding swept over me as I realized He was telling me the truth. It seems to me, when hearing an audible voice through the head, a person can rationalize it away, but when it comes through the heart, it carries tremendous personal impact and you know it's true and exactly for you.

I answered, "I understand," and immediately decided to work to control my emotions from that moment on. To this day, if I feel anger or annoyance arising within me too frequently, I remember His voice again as it came to me on that log pond almost 50 years ago.

In a separate chapter I will relate the 1970 incident where God spoke to me in the darkness of the night, "Stand aside and see the glory of the Lord," after having been laid off from my job. In that same chapter, I relate how a Christian friend had called my wife and gotten her worried, precipitating a crisis situation between us. This friend happened to be our pastor. He told her that he had not gotten a green light from God concerning my plans to go to Bible School. I informed her, "God was speaking to me about it, not my pastor. I am on speaking terms with God myself."

This somewhat diffused the situation.

Analyzing the whole thing a few days later, I caught myself thinking, "How is it possible that God could use such a person, who would call a guy's wife and get her all upset like that?"

The Lord heard my thoughts and responded with the following allegory.

He said, "I am not necessarily agreeing with you that he is as you think, but remember, I once used a donkey. I didn't change him into a glorious creature of light or anything. I used him as he was. He was a donkey before I used him, he was a donkey while I was using him and he was a donkey after I got through with him. Sometimes, I have used people even if they make a donkey of themselves."

How can I argue with such logic? I have since come to realize that everyone, including myself, is susceptible to doing something, or saying something that, afterwards, may seem foolish.

During the mid-1980s, the Seattle area was experiencing out-of-control political protests, including mobs on the freeway stopping traffic and creating confusion all around the area. I remember saying to myself one day, "My God, what's this world coming to?" I wasn't particularly talking to the Lord, but I very clearly heard Him say, "Wait a minute; what you just said implies that I am no longer in control, but I am. What you see happening, must happen. The world you have known must change as it moves toward the time when I will come back."

Since that time, I have also observed the decline in moral values, destruction of the family, increased stress in our culture and many things that God's word says would happen before His Son's return (Matthew 24:37-38). When I see these things happen today, I am reminded of what He shared with me at that time.

It also seems that the whole world is returning to one basic language. To be a part of the global economy today requires knowledge of the English language. As new markets open around the world, companies scramble to provide English instruction or recruit English-speaking employees. I'm aware that in Russia, for example, there is a rush to teach, as well as learn, English, as it is a ticket to prosperity. As the world reverts to one major language, the cutting edge of technology advances so fast that retailers can't keep up with it.

At the tower of Babel, God confused the tongues to prevent technology increases, (lest man become as us, Gen 11:1-9). Yet today He is allowing it to increase rapidly. We are so far ahead technologically from where those folks were. To me, that may be the most compelling sign of the Lord's soon coming.

Today, we are also pressed on all sides by sexual perversion and rarely hear a church leader anywhere speak out against it. When you do hear a lonely voice in the wilderness, he is quickly ostracized and made to look like a fool by the left-leaning media. Believers should hope that the lonely voice would become like a trumpet blast, rallying every Christian around the world to lend support until it became a mighty voice saying. "Enough!"

You would think, given the push by deviates in recent times, that every pastor in the nation would be in the forefront leading the church against the acceptance and tolerance that is undermining the very principals of the Scriptures, as well as destroying lives and bringing God's punishment on our nation and the world.

Fundamentalist churches across the nation should be uniting against the onslaught, including calling the church to concerted prayer to push back this spiritual battle. Yet it seems they are anesthetized or numb to what is happening.

Judges across the nation uphold same-sex liaisons and elevate them to the level of marriage. Some states have enacted laws granting the status of marriage to same-sex couples, and it seems only a matter of time before it becomes legal on the federal government level.

The only voices we hear are ungodly proclamations from old-line, spiritually powerless and bankrupt churches previously written off by the fundamentalist churches. The broad acceptance of this perversion across our nation and around the world is another strong indication to believers that Jesus is coming soon. I don't expect matters to improve, but to increase as we near His coming.

My wife shares with me that, as a young person growing up in the former Soviet Union, she was shielded from the damaging effects of pornography and the filth she sees everywhere today. America, with its technological advantages, began dumping its filth in the third-world countries coinciding with the breakup of the former Soviet Union. Since my first visit to Russia in 1999 and my recent visit in the fall of 2006, I could hardly believe the depth of depravity on TV programming and other media garbage available to the folks over there. And, sadly, the majority of it is made in America, or influenced by American products. These folks, because they have been lacking in strong Christian values, become an immediate gullible market for our sewage. God's Word tells us that, "even so, when we see these things happening, you know that the kingdom of God is near" (Luke 21:31 [NIV]).

Into the mid-90s, I continued to enjoy the blessings of God. I became quite successful on my job while earning numerous awards from my employer. We raised four children. The Lord blessed me, usually in spite of me. I have always thought that He loves me more than anyone else because He has been so good to me (of course, this is not true, He loves everyone the same), even though I feel as though I am the least deserving in the world.

My goal and my heart's desire are to be like Him. I feel all Christians should try to reflect Him in all their ways, and others ought to be able to see it. None of us is perfect, nor will we ever be in this life. We must be declared perfect by Him, after His blood has washed us from sin. And we need to be careful that our experience with Him doesn't drift into just a religious experience. If Christ lives in us, and we have given Him control of our lives, the things we do should please Him as well as reflect Him to others.

The Most Successful Year

On January the 5th, 1970, my family's financial security collapsed with notification that I would be laid off from my job in the aircraft industry. We weren't totally unprepared mentally because I had known for a few months that it could happen. But from a financial position, I was completely unprepared. We had no reserves to draw from, and I had $400 in monthly obligations, plus the personal expense for a family of four.

The lay-off was effective on the 19th of January. I spent a few days looking for work of any type, only to wind up frustrated. After about a week of futile searching, my frustration gave way to desperation. One night I was awakened suddenly from my sleep with a terribly depressed feeling sweeping over my body, coupled with worry about the situation that I was in. This lasted for a minute or so and then God spoke to me from the darkness, and said, "Stand aside and see the glory of the Lord!" It was just as clear as any voice I've ever heard, and a supernatural peace swept over me. I immediately went back to sleep and slept like a baby for the rest of the night. Little did I know that His same voice would come back to comfort and assure me in the days ahead.

The local economy, including the job market, became so bad that sometime later, a billboard was erected at the edge of Seattle saying, "Would the last one out please turn off the lights." There were complete blocks of houses in many areas of town where only a few remained occupied. Real estate became so cheap that many of those who had money picked up homes at perhaps, 70% of their value.

Two days later, my wife went to the hospital with sudden medical problems. The next evening, I was preparing to visit her, feeling low because of the job situation and knowing our kitchen cupboards were empty. I was trying to decide whether to buy a few groceries with the meager dollars that I had, or save them for a day or so. While I was pondering the situation, the doorbell rang. I opened the door, and to my surprise, there stood two families with their arms loaded with sacks of groceries. I again heard His voice speak to me, "Stand aside and see the glory of the Lord!" Such a wonderful feeling of gratitude and assurance swept up from the depths of my soul.

Word had spread among the church folks about my wife being in the hospital, so when I eventually did get in to see her that night, her room was full of folks who had come to pray with her and cheer her up. After I informed her about the groceries, I think she was feeling well enough to come home, had the doctor allowed.

During February, I was hampered from looking for work by a respiratory illness that created an asthmatic effect even though I wasn't sick enough to be confined to bed. Allergy tests later showed my problem was caused by a reaction to pollen from a tree species found mostly in this area, but I wasn't to find that out till several years later.

I was receiving $42 a week from unemployment compensation and qualified for $108 a month in food stamps. Not nearly enough to meet my obligations, except for the grace of God.

Several times a week, some Christian brother or sister would approach my wife or me and push money into our hand, saying that they felt led of the Lord to give it to us. One dear lady approached my wife one night and pressed $50 into her hand. As my wife protested, the lady stated that the Lord had allowed her to sell a painting and she had promised God that she would give half to us. I had already learned that you don't ask God to meet your needs, than refuse it when it comes. We accepted the money and praised God for it, and asked Him to especially bless this lady.

The first of March came and I still had no job. I heard of several job vacancies but they were all taken by the time I applied.

In late March, a younger brother who lived in the area with his family was traveling to Kentucky and invited my family and me to join them. Since there was no significant cost to us and I hadn't seen my folk's in several years, it seemed like an opportunity, but...... the illness had become more acute. Even minimal physical effort would trigger near collapse with coughing and choking. I was afraid the condition could easily develop into pneumonia with the change of climate I would experience on the trip. We took some time praying about it, and after doing so we felt God wanted us to go.

The first day of the trip found us leaving the damp coastal areas where the culprit trees grew, for the higher, dryer part of the state. The coughing became uncontrollable but the condition seemed to be breaking up, and by the second day I was feeling better than I had for a month. After a couple more days of driving through the worst blizzard conditions that I've ever seen, and a couple near mishaps, with God's hand on us we arrived in Kentucky.

We didn't realize it, but God was setting the stage so He could reveal Himself to my sister and her family. On previous visits, we had always stayed with my parents in their home. This time, it was different. They had moved into a small house and didn't have extra room. But my sister had plenty of room, so she invited us to stay with her and her family.

Thank God it worked out the way I feel He planned. We were getting ready to attend a local church service the first Sunday there and invited them to join us. I never pictured them as having an interest in going to church or in the things of God, so I played it kind of low key. To my surprise, they agreed. And that day, "Praise God!" my brother-in-law gave his heart to the Lord. The following weekend, their two teenage sons gave their hearts to God. Upon our return home, we learned that my sister had surrendered her heart to the Lord and my Father come back to the Lord right after we left. In awe, we say "Praises to God!"

By now, it was getting into late April and still no job. My unemployment compensation had increased substantially, but it was still far from meeting our needs. The crisis reached a new peak around the first of May. We had gotten behind in our utilities and owed $78. It was necessary to pay that amount within a few days or suffer the inconvenience of having things shut off. We had no idea where we would get the money and after a few days of worrying about it, as an act of faith, we put it before God in prayer and then expected Him to provide it within three days. God had been so giving to us and so good to us, I just knew He would give me the desires of my heart as well as our needs, and would do it within the three days that I had set.

To my horror, three days passed and nothing happened. I couldn't believe it! I returned to the bedroom and, kneeling by the bed, I remember telling God, "You sure blew it this time. I trusted you to answer my prayer and as an act of faith, even believed you would do it in three days. Now you have let me down and it looks as if I may lose my house and everything else."

His response will stay with me as long as I live. In that calm, reassuring voice He asked, "Do you really trust Me?"

I mumbled, "Of course. That's why I am here crying out to you."

He then said, "If you really trust Me, you must trust because of who I am, not for what I do. You will get up and go back to the living room and stop your crying. Also, you will never worry about this thing again. But remember, you would have a complaint only if you had actually lost something. Until then, you can't worry or complain just because it looks as if you might lose something."

I was stunned by His truth. I understood so well what He was saying. In fact, the force and dept of the understanding that swept over me after His voice is indescribable. It was like a fountain that burst forth within and sprayed into thousands of little bits of understanding.

I realized that faith in Him is not dependent of whether

THE GOD THAT DOES NOT FAIL

He performs for us. True faith trust in Him even if He does nothing, because it assumes He knows what is best for us and that He is in charge. Romans 5:3-4 (NIV) asserts that "troubles produce patience, and patience produces character, and character produces hope."

"In all things God works for the good of those who love Him, and are called according to His purpose" (Rom 8:28 [NIV]). We had been tested and had failed. I do not believe for one minute that God needs to test us. He already knows the outcome since He knew us even before we were born and knows our life and everything that will happen in it.

I do believe we need to be tested, and as we pass certain tests, we grow spiritually. He knows this so He allows certain things to come into our lives for that reason. It also seems to me that if you flunk a test, you will go through it again and maybe again, until you learn from it.

I was reminded of the Hebrew young men in the Old Testament, when about to be cast into a hot furnace, said, "We believe God is able to deliver us, but even if He doesn't, we will still not bow down to the king." Their faith was not predicated on whether God performed. They assumed that if God allowed them to burn, then it must be His will and then, so be it.

He had been so kind to us. We had begun to perceive Him as if He was no more than our genie in a bottle. You know, rub the bottle and get your wish. We were like spiritual babies. Now, it was time to develop our spiritual walk. I understood that it was time for spiritual growth in our lives and from here on it would mean a real exercise in faith. We must learn that our faith must be something to stand on even if everything around us washes away.

I wiped my tears, ask the Lord to forgive us, got up from my knees and returned to the other part of the house, purposing in my heart not to mention the need to Him again. I was a much smarter young man for that experience.

The following day, a Christian friend who knew that I was out of work, but did not know I had a specific need, approached me and told me that he felt impressed by God to give me $50. Later the same day, an unsaved person who also knew that I was out of work, but did not know that I had a need, handed me $30. Praise God, I paid the utilities and had $2 left over!

May gave way to June, and our financial situation had not improved. But we were coming to know God in a way that we had never known Him before, and it was absolutely wonderful! Oh, there were times when we would become discouraged and would go to our knees and cry out to God for relief for our souls. He was always there and would lift our spirits.

It was just such a time when God spoke to us special words of encouragement. We had visiting relatives in our home when we felt the need to pray, so excused ourselves, retired to the bedroom and sought God for answers. We prayed for about fifteen minutes, but not wanting to leave our guests alone very long, we prepared to return to the living room. The Spirit of God was so very real and near to us as we left the bedroom. About half way across the living room, the Spirit seemed to settle on my wife and she fell to her knees. Weeping and praising God as He spoke to us through her, saying, "My children, lean not upon your own understanding, but cast yourselves upon Me. I am your God. Keep your hand in mine and I will lead you through all this." Praise His name!

Two to three times a week, we had also been getting together with other Christians for prayer and Bible discussions. On occasion, there were as many as 35 or 40 present and everyone would have a blessed time.

It was sometime in June that I felt God was speaking to me about going to Bible college. Several times within the past few years I had talked about it, but I never really gave it any serious thought. I started making plans to attend a local Bible school in September, and immediately ran into opposition from some of my closest friends and relatives. Most of them thought I was stupid for thinking of school instead of concentrating my efforts toward finding a job, even if it meant leaving the local area, and generally I agreed. But I knew only that I had to do what I felt God was wanting, for my future. However, it was a personal conviction that only I could feel, and I could not communicate it to them. So, of course, they could not understand.

As summer progressed and the registration date drew near, I knew that I must make some serious decisions about my future. After carefully praying and putting it before the Lord, I decided God was in it and I would go. Immediately, opposition increased tremendously. So many times, I thought of dropping my plans, but I would go to God and He would lift my spirit.

On one such occasion I was directed to James 1:5-8: "If any of you lacks wisdom, he should ask God, who gives generously to all without finding fault, and it will be given to him. But when he asks, he must believe and not doubt, because he who doubts is like a wave of the sea, blown and tossed by the wind. That man should not think he will receive anything from the Lord; he is a double-minded man, unstable in all he does" (NIV).

That was my answer. I had already made up my mind to go to school. I had set my course. I would not turn back except God should direct me to in no uncertain ways.

Our crisis reached a critical stage about a week before school was to start. I did not have the funds and it didn't appear that I would get them. My oldest son was to start first grade in a few days and needed some additional "things." I had been out of the home most of the day. When I returned, I found that a number of well-meaning friends had called my wife and firmly expressed their belief that it was wrong for me to go to school instead of seeking a job. Though not as strong as I, she had always shared my desire and was pretty much in agreement with me. But of course, she could be influenced under the proper circumstances, causing her moments of anxiety or discouragement.

That night was one of the times. She told me on no uncertain terms that she thought I should drop my plans. I could sense a showdown coming. Aware that the next few moments might be the most crucial in our lives, I thought about it for a moment before I responded.

I carefully explained that "I cannot give up what I feel so strongly God has for me and my family, and that I had resolved to go to school. I cannot—will not—turn back.

"You had better be right!" she replied. "Because if you are wrong and the situation doesn't work out and we lose everything we have, I'll take the children and leave you." There it was. Everything I had was on the line.

"I care for you and the children more than I ever have in my life," I said. "I understand how you feel but I must do what I know God would have me do. I've prayed about it, thought about it and I am convinced in my heart that my decision is the right thing to do. I do not know how God will work things out for us, but I know He will."

We prayed about it and in a few minutes we both felt better. (We later lost our home, but that's another chapter)

The next week, we lived it a day at a time and God met our needs as they came up. The day before my son started to his school, a Christian friend brought him some things and they were just exactly what he needed. To my knowledge, that friend knew nothing about him needing anything.

I registered for the fall quarter at Northwest Bible College of the Assemblies of God in Kirkland, Washington, and began classes, still not knowing how my needs would be met, but trusting God to work things out as they came up. And that's just what He did.

After the peak in the crisis just before school started, our situation didn't really improve but our perception of it changed dramatically. Instead of fixing our eyes on our problems, we tried to keep them on Jesus. And our problems always worked out even though there were many times when it didn't appear to the natural mind that it would.

It was about this time that the Lord shared something with me that I have shared with many others since. He impressed on me the illustration that our walk is much like swimming a river. In most rivers you can find debris drifting downstream. If we are to get across the river, we must be very careful not to take our eyes off the other side. It can be easy to fix our sight on this debris, but if we do, we probably will follow it downstream, and may never get to the other side. The debris can also temporarily block our vision of the far shore and we can become disorientated. We know the shore is still there, but we can no longer see it, so we lose our vision. We must let the debris pass before our eyes, then affix our eyes on the other side again. Keep in mind that when you are swimming, you are up to your eye level in water and even small debris can look large and can block your vision. Through it all, if you are to get to the other side, you must keep your eyes on it and face that direction.

It was around Christmas; I'd finished the fall quarter at school and was looking forward to the winter quarter, when I became aware of a feeling within me that God would soon give me a job. A few days later, a friend informed me of a job vacancy so I took the necessary test and applied for it.

Winter quarter started shortly after the first of January and I returned to classes, even with the feeling that I probably would not be able to finish because God was about to give me a job. A job that would most certainly interfere with my current class schedule.

I had attended school two weeks when I was called in for an interview. I learned that, including myself, seventeen applicants interviewed for one position, yet I got the job. I would be working the early morning hours so I had to drop my class schedule. I didn't mind too much because by now, I knew that God knew what He was doing and if He intended for me to continue, He would work out my schedule conflict for me.

I went to work on January the 19th, remember this date? It had been exactly one year to the day, since I lost my job.

I was later able to work out a new class schedule around my job hours, and continued attending School for the next four years.

Reflecting on that one year, it probably was the least prosperous in terms of material gain, but without question, it became the most prosperous spiritual year of my life.

Something of Value

In September of 1971, while working to develop the bus ministry for our church, a friend and I selected a certain area of our town and proceeded to knock on every door. After spending a few hours each day for several days and reaching about 50 homes, not gaining even one person for the bus route, we concluded that the residents of this area were not too concerned about spiritual matters. So, we left the area discouraged, little realizing that God was not finished with it yet.

After my decision the preceding year to go to Bible college, two very clear issues arose. One was that I needed to move closer to the college, and the second was that we could not afford to keep the house that I was buying at the time since my payments were in the $190 per month range. We had lived there for about three years and had built up about $5,000 in equity. The local economy was very poor, so the likelihood of selling it was zero. But I didn't want to lose my equity. $5,000 was a lot of money and I could use it to help out over the next few years with school and other necessities. The best answer was to quit deed it back to the bank and move on with my life, but I would lose my equity. That was hard to do.

I turned to the Lord about my concern. In His calm voice, He reminded me that when I had moved into the house, I had dedicated it to Him, "Right?" My squeaky voice: "Wellll, yes."

Then does the house belong to Me?"

"Wellll, yes."

"Then there's no problem, because I am losing the house, not you, and I can afford to lose $5,000 if I want to."

I had no argument. I understood that everything we have has been given to us to enjoy or make our lives more comfortable, but they still belong to the Lord.

The Bible often speaks of giving back to God a tenth of our goods, and we are taught that we should also do that. Yet we should understand that everything we have belongs to God, and we need to remain detached from it so that if He ever calls it back, we can separate from it without destroying ourselves. A tenth is a minimum and an expectation, but in reality, all belong to Him. He seldom requires His people to give up everything, but sometimes He does. If He asks us to give up everything, we can be sure He will give back better and more than before, if we can separate from it without destroying ourselves.

If we can appreciate how much He loves us, we will also know that He is in control of our lives and knows what is best for us. We will put our faith in Him as a child would their parent. It's an accepted truth that when He calls us home, we will separate from all things physical. We are just travelers in this world and we will not take home any attachments. Over the next few days, I quit deeded the house over to the bank, rented a three-bedroom house in Bellevue (about three miles from the college), and made plans to move.

The Bellevue house was very adequate. However, in time we learned that my wife was pregnant with our fourth child. Another baby would pretty well cramp us in this house, and my wife had a lot of concerns about that.

With the doctor's confirmation that she was pregnant, the Lord had given her the assurance that He would work out the housing problem when the need came.

Nearing the middle of November, with a week and a half before the baby's due date, we had not been able to locate a larger rental home. To buy a home at this time just wasn't one the things that came to mind, as it had not even been a year since we had quit deeded the last one back to the bank. We also didn't have the money for a down payment.

Just before I arrived home from work one evening, my wife had picked up the local newspaper and thumbed through it. Immediately, the Lord said to her, "Look in the homes for sale section."

Not realizing that it was the Lord's voice, she argued with herself, saying, "But we are not looking for a house to buy." However, the insistence was so strong she gave in with a "Well, okay," and immediately felt a sense of relief. Glancing over that section, her eye fell on an ad that very briefly said "4-bedroom, tri-level, assume payments."

Again, that voice spoke to her and told her that we should call about it. She circled it, and when I arrived a few minutes later, she shared her feelings with me and encouraged me to call about it. While I don't normally jump into anything without some discussion, I sensed something in her voice, and without saying much I picked up the phone and dialed the number.

To my surprise, I learned the house was located in the area where there was so little response to our church outreach. I was even further surprised to find that I could purchase the home with very little cash outlay, and that we could move in immediately. The owners were intending to move to South Dakota and would let the house go back to the bank if they didn't find someone to assume their loan quickly. To say the least, I was stunned by the rapidity with which the situation was changing. As I've mentioned, I never jump into anything. But when we drove over to see the house, the Holy Spirit witnessed to my heart that this was okay, that He was in it, and I got that special feeling again.

Since the owner was leaving the state within the next few days, we quickly made arrangements with the mortgage company to assume their loan, which required paying closing costs of $270. I would pay them a hundred dollars in a couple days and the remainder when the deal closed. While trying to shuffle my budget to find the $100, the carburetor went out on my car. After replacing that, I was $30 short on what I needed to start the deal. I called the mortgage company and told them that I would be in by Monday evening to give them the hundred dollars, or I would forget about the house.

On Monday evening I had not been able to get in touch with them before they closed, and a little later I went to a Bible study at a friend's house. After having been ministered to by the Holy Spirit that night, I was more concerned about seeking the will of God in our lives than anything else.

My wife, realizing that something would have to be done the following day, and knowing we didn't have the $100, asked me, "What are we going to do about it?"

I replied, "Since we don't have the money, there's nothing we can do."

If it was true that God was opening the deal for us, and we had both felt from the start that He was, He would meet the need by the next day.

To be honest, I must confess that it was strictly a matter of fact rather than a statement of faith on my part. If He did not provide the money we would presume that it was not His will for us to get this house, and He had other things in mind for us. We would walk away from the deal.

My wife had been attending a ladies Bible study with a time of prayer and share on Tuesday mornings. That Tuesday morning, she shared with the group what God had been doing in our lives, and the situation concerning the house. She requested they pray with us about the matter. When she finished, one of the lady's present presented $100 to my wife, explaining that she had come into possession of it a few days earlier, and the Lord had told her that the money was not for her but for someone else whom He would reveal to her soon. As my wife talked, the Lord spoke to her heart and instructed her to give it to my wife. Overwhelmed by the goodness of the Lord, my wife could only weep.

When I came home from work later and she shared with me how the Lord had met our need, I wanted to weep also. Praise His name!

Remember the house that I quit deeded back to the bank, on which the monthly payments were around $190, and I had felt bad about losing $5,000? I discovered that with this house I would pick up the previous owners' equity of about $5,000, and, my payments would be $112 per month, and, it was a four bedroom where the other had been only three, and, it was situated where we had a territorial view of the mountains in the background with a huge lake in the foreground. It was so much bigger and better than the one I thought I had lost. Only God can bring things together like this.

Needless to say, we made hurried plans to move on Friday. I contacted a couple of guys to help me move, and I prepared to do most of the packing because my wife was near childbirth by then. A friend of my wife called and volunteered to clean the carpets in the house we were moving into. As it turned out, I worked later than anticipated that Friday so I had to call my help and cancel plans for that day.

However, just before noon, two ladies from a church about fourteen miles away, who had met my wife on only one occasion a couple of weeks earlier, phoned and offered to help move some things. They were fantastic is all we could say! They removed items from the cupboards and closets and packed them in boxes. Using a pickup truck, they made three trips and unpacked everything at the new house and put everything away. They left before we could even thank them. We didn't even catch the name of one. In final analysis, we concluded that they were two angels, sent there by the Lord to help.

When I finished work that day, a Christian friend approached me and inquired about the status of my move. When I told him that I had cancelled because of concern about imposing on friends with such a late start, he informed me that he had recently purchased a truck and would be glad to come and help, and stay till it was finished. I was not aware at that time that the two ladies had moved most of the boxed stuff.

When I arrived home, I learned that another friend was driving over to help after he finished work at his job. We finished about midnight. Our hearts were so thankful as we rejoiced in the Lord for His goodness and kindness toward us by orchestrating everything so well. Over the next few days, a number of friends whom the Lord would send came to help out. Most of the unpacking and arranging of the furniture was done by Christian friends. Some brought over dinner or baked items—whatever the Lord would lay on their heart. Words cannot convey the appreciation and gratitude we felt toward the Lord for manifesting His love to us through these wonderful people. With a great sense of humility, we look to God and say, "Thank you!"

I had paid the initial $100 at the time we moved in, but after two months living in the house, the loan was about to close and we had to pay the remaining $170. That was not a problem because the Lord had provided me overtime on my job, which brought in the extra money. However, the mortgage company informed me that their calculations now reflected an additional requirement of $140.

That put a strain on my fledging budget for which we had not planned. Again, we went to the Lord, having no idea where we could come up with that amount.

Two days later, we were called to the mortgage company office to sign the final papers. I informed them that I still did not have the additional $140. They assured me not to worry about it because there was exactly enough left over from the former owners' reserves account to cover it, and he had released it to our account. God is so good!

Even though we may worry about things months before they happen, the Lord is never late. But sometimes He waits until right up to the time the need emerges.

We had been in our home only one week when my wife felt the time had come for her to deliver our baby.

I had obligated myself to speak at a service in Seattle that night, and after an unsuccessful attempt to locate a replacement speaker, I decided to attend the speaking engagement. Although feeling a deep sense of responsibility to my wife at the time, I decided that since the Lord had given me the opportunity to speak, I would. I called one of my wife's friends who agreed to come over and stay with her. As I left, I committed everything to the Lord and felt a sense of peace.

The turnout at the service that night wasn't so great, but Jesus was there and the presence of the Holy Spirit was so sweet as He moved on our lives. About halfway through the service, I received a call from the friend who was with my wife indicating she was going to take her to the hospital. She also said that just before the decision was made to take her, another couple just stopped by and wanted to take my other three children on to their house for the night. It was so beautiful how He worked everything out.

While she was in the hospital, a number of Christian friends came by with dinner for my children and me. Some would take the children to their home, as I had to work and take care of other things.

When my wife came home from the hospital with our fourth little boy, we learned that a number of ladies had decided to bring in dinner for us for five evenings while my wife had time to recuperate. Others came to help her with housework. The most beautiful part was the way people responded spontaneously. When we had a need, the Lord would send someone at just the right time, and often without prior arrangements. Some, we didn't even know beforehand. Some we still don't know. They would leave before we could get acquainted.

We are again reminded that in Christ Jesus there truly is something of value in that He takes care of His own. It's as we surrender our lives to Him and leave our problems with Him that He will show forth His love toward us in such a manner that we stand in awe of such a mighty God.

It is not my intention to seek glory, or to attempt to make ourselves seem religious or have special favor with God. Rather, I seek to uplift and glorify out Lord and Savior Jesus Christ, for truly all honor and glory belong to Him. I hope to share the value of a relationship with Him, knowing that it is not as the world would assess value, for they cannot perceive things of a spiritual nature. Religion? It kills, as demonstrated by those in various places of the world where people are being killed in the name of some religion, including Christianity. A relationship with Him saves, heals, restores, and promotes acceptance of others.

We had lived in our home about six weeks and had not been able to obtain a kitchen stove. Shuffle our budget as we would, we just couldn't seem to come up with the extra money. We finally located a used one for $35, and were to have it delivered within a few days.

Our home was plumbed for an extra bath, so my Father-in-law had brought a commode over for me to install. But after attempting to install it, we found it didn't fit very well.

That week at her Bible study, my wife learned of a family that had need for a commode, so we gave it to them and I offered to install it for them. As I was leaving, the husband pressed a check into my hand for $35. Although I protested, they insisted because they felt the Lord had told them to give me that amount. They were not aware of the stove deal.

We were thankful to the Lord because we thought He had provided the money for the stove since it was the exact amount. By next morning though, I began to feel something was wrong, as if the money was not ours, almost as if it was stolen or hot money. I can't explain just how I felt. I didn't share this with my wife because she was rejoicing that God had given it to us and she would have a stove on which to cook for a change. Anyway....

At work, the feeling intensified until I was miserable. By noon, I realized that the money was not for us. I surrendered it to the Lord and asked him what I was supposed to do with it. He quickly spoke to me about a minister friend of mine whom I had not seen for six months, and had no idea about what his needs might be. Since he lived some distance from me, I told the Lord that I would try to get up to his place in a few days to give it to him. The Holy Spirit prompted me to go there immediately after work. That left me no choice.

I stopped by home to pick up the money and share with my wife what the Lord had instructed me to do. Her reaction was pretty predictable. She didn't feel what I felt, and she didn't know where or when we would get the money again for the stove, but if I was sure that the Lord had spoken to me about it, of course, I must obey. I wrote out a check and left right away.

While driving to his place, I was fighting a battle within myself. I told the Lord that I would arrive at their place and find that they would accept the money, but there probably would not be the real need for it that I have, and I would make a fool of myself. Nevertheless, the Lord was patient with me.

Upon arriving, I entered his home and quickly produced the $35, and gave it to him with a little speech that I'd prepared on the way up. Handing the money to him, I told him that I didn't know if he had a need for it or not. I just knew that I was supposed to give it to him. He could tear it up for all I cared; I'd obeyed the Lord in giving it to him. He had relatives from out of town staying with him at the time and didn't really have the opportunity to confide to me in their presence whether there was a need or not. Since we were going to church later, I left quickly.

Driving home, I wasn't quite satisfied with their reaction, and was telling the Lord how He really blew it this time, and how I could have used the money better. Again, His patience and goodness showed forth.

The next day, my friend's wife called my wife and told her that they had not had a significant income for several months (he was going to Bible college also) and didn't expect to receive any for several weeks. Due to the relatives being there, the situation had been compounded and they were earnestly praying that God would meet their need. She was so thankful to God and excited the way it had come about. They both had a good cry.

We already were committed to buying the stove though, so it was delivered a couple of days later. I informed the deliveryman that I didn't have the money to pay him right then, but would drop by his office on my payday and give him the money. Imagine my surprise when he replied, "Don't worry about that, I received a call just before I left my store from someone who wished to remain anonymous, telling me not to take money from you but that he will pay for the stove."

I could only respond with a subdued, "Please tell him, 'Thank you' for me." Inside I was having a meltdown, remembering how I had chided the Lord about the money. It never fails to amaze me how the Lord will bless us if we will just obey Him. We had simply been messengers to deliver the money from the one party to the other, and by our obedience to the Lord He provided money for the stove anyway. Praise the Lord! Isn't it wonderful how the Lord works things out to both bring honor to Him, and at the same time maturing our spiritual perspective?

The first year of Bible college was the toughest. By the second year I was actually working full time, going to school full time, had a part-time business selling and installing carpet, and was a supply sergeant and unit recruiter for the US Army Reserve. Some nights, I managed to get only a couple of hours sleep.

In late September, after finishing I was approaching my car to return home when I had the strongest compulsion to locate a fellow student. I tried to shrug it off, but could not, so I set out looking for him. I knew there was a good possibility that he had already left, so after trying the snack bar and wandering around the campus for a half hour or so, I shrugged and headed back for my car.

I again felt a strong urge to look elsewhere for him, and by then I was convinced the Lord was trying to tell me something. As I listened in my heart for that still, small voice, I understood that I was to find Jim and give him some money because he was in need. I ran my hand into my pocket and came up with a little less than $20. With that in hand, I set off to find Jim.

I was rationalizing all the way, and was somewhat convinced that Jim had left campus, so I told the Lord, "I will go to check the library, the only place that I had not yet been, but if he isn't there, then I will dismiss the feeling and go home."

Entering the library, I spotted Jim right away, sitting at a table. I approached him and handed him the money and told him that the Lord had instructed me to give it to him. Tears welled in his eyes and he asked me, "Why did you take so long?"

I asked, "What are you talking about?"

He responded, "This morning, when I left home in Seattle [perhaps 10 miles away] I knew that I didn't have enough gas to get to college and return. I told the Lord that I will go, and trust Him to provide the gas for me to get home afterwards. Class is now over and I have no money for gas, so I decided to go to the library and wait on the Lord. I've waited about 30 minutes for you to obey the Lord."

We rejoiced together at the Lord's goodness, and we both grew spiritually as a result of the experience.

One year after moving into our home, we felt led of the Lord to give a $100 to a family in the church we attended. We were timid about it because this family had not indicated to anyone that they even needed a $100. But feeling a strong witness of the Spirit about it, we followed through. I put it in an envelope and slipped it to them after the service because I didn't want to elicit a conversation that might reveal their surprise or that there was no specific need. Presenting it to them, we exited quickly from the church building.

The next day, the wife called and shared that they were also trying to buy a house and the money would allow them to complete the purchase. They were praying that God would provide. Praise His name!

Special Witness Opportunities

Late 1969, I was working at my job with an old fellow whom I hadn't known previously. We were working alone, that is, at a considerable distance from other workers. This old man seemed to me the angriest person I had ever met. Most of the day, he was swearing at everything and everybody, including me, which made him a difficult person to work with.

I usually try to stay away from this kind of person, and even in the best of situations I don't like just arguing or playing mental gymnastics with people. I always want to give a person something meaningful to think about or challenge their logic. This requires proper timing, which only the Holy Spirit gives.

The Lord gave me peace and compassion for this old man. When he expressed himself in strong expletives, I would suppress the urge to engage him in a conversation, but rather just give him my best smile while remaining focused on my job. As we neared the end of the shift, he mentioned to me that I was different in some way because of the way I had responded to his behavior.

That was the opening I had been waiting for. I responded, "I'm a Christian."

Before I could say more, he went into a rage and through clenched teeth, hissed at me, "I know all about you Christians, your prayers don't get any higher than the ceiling, and it's all a joke, and all Christians are hypocrites."

When I could get a word in, I replied, "I have listened to you all day, and thought a lot about what you have been saying. I have decided that if someone were to write a book about your life, a good title could be, how not to live a life."

I had his attention immediately. "Oh," he replied in a subdued tone, "why would you say that?"

I told him, "You haven't shared with me, but the Lord has revealed to me that at one time in the past you have known the Lord, but now have gotten away from Him. Your family has left you and you will probably die a bitter, broken old man. If anyone attends your funeral, it will be to spit on your grave."

It was as if I had hit him with a club. His whole

demeanor crumbled and he began crying.

He then shared with me that he had been a pastor in a church in Arkansas in times past, and that he did go through a divorce, that he had grown children and that they didn't care anything about him. He had not seen any of them in years even though some live nearby.

I shared with him that he must understand the Lord had not turned from him but, rather it was he who had turned from the Lord. Jesus was still facing him with outstretched arms to receive him back no matter what his problems were. All he had to do was turn toward the Lord and embrace Him again and He would forgive him and help straighten his life out and heal his family relations. I emphasized that God had known him even before he was born, and knew all the things that he was to go through in his lifetime, and even if he would come back to the Lord. I shared with him that it was no accident that we had been put together at this time, and that the Lord was dealing with him about his soul. He was receptive but did not make an outward indication that he had turned around.

The work shift closed and I never saw this old man again. In retrospect, I feel the Lord set the stage for me to encounter this person and then gave me the wisdom to break through his hardness. I only trust that something in our discussion touched him and that before he died, he surrendered his life back to the Lord.

Early in 1970, I was able to obtain a job at a local lumber mill, pulling lumber from a green chain. The green chain is a conveyer that green lumber moves along, and employees remove it at different positions, depending on the type and measurements. I remember there was a young man working with me named John who was constantly exclaiming "Jesus" as a swear word. On the third day, I had enough. So I asked him if he was a Christian. He replied, "You mean like Mary and church and stuff like that?"

I said, "No, I mean like accepting Jesus as your personal Savior and letting His Word guide your life."

"No, I've never heard of anything like that before," was his response. I told him, "Then I need to talk to you."

At lunch, we sat together and I explained to him more about accepting the Lord Jesus. I told him that I sensed I would not be seeing him anymore, so it was imperative that he listen to me and consider very seriously what I was saying.

After lunch, as we were working, I pulled on a large piece of lumber, and as I did, it twisted against my stomach where I had an old surgical scar. The scar tore and I left to seek medical attention and never returned, nor did I ever see the young man again. My prayer is that someone after me watered the seed of the word that I had planted in this person's heart.

In 1976, I was assistant pastor at an Assembly of God church in Spokane, Washington, when I got word that my Mother had passed away in Kentucky. Of course, my wife and I went there to attend the funeral.

While there, a number of people, both relatives and non-relatives, shared with us an unusual event that occurred as she was passing away.

Mother had been in a coma for about two weeks. She was diabetic and her kidneys had shut down leaving acid in her blood stream. The acid perforated her veins causing blood to seep from her skin. She seemed only to occasionally recognize who was with her.

Seconds before she died, she sat up in the bed and fixed her eyes on the ceiling. She began smiling as if she was seeing someone whom she knew, then slumped back on the bed with a smile on her face and went to be with the Lord. She was buried with the same smile on her face and I don't recall ever seeing such a smile for as long as I had known her.

No one in the room saw anything, but everyone is convinced that mother saw someone. There was a presence there that everyone felt but no one could explain. One nurse, who as far as I know, didn't know the Lord, told me that she fell across the bed weeping even though she couldn't explain why. She said, "It was just the presence of something in the room" that brought her to tears. No one described the events as a negative experience. They were unanimous in that they felt it was the Spirit of the Lord.

We returned to Spokane by way of Chicago where we laid over for eight hours. I was emotionally drained from the prior few days and just wanted to sit by myself with my own thoughts. A lady came and sat by me, and honestly, I just didn't want to become involved in a conversation with anyone. Yet I knew she was about to engage me in one. I turned my back to her as I turned toward my wife. It didn't matter, in a few minutes, she was asking me something. Just small stuff, nothing earth shattering. Finally she asked where we were coming from. I casually mentioned that we had been to Kentucky to attend my mother's funeral, but I was trying to send strong signals to her that I really didn't want to be bothered.

She said, "I'm sorry about your mother," implying it may have been a negative event.

I cannot explain what happened next. I found myself explaining about how mother, being a Christian, was ready to meet the Lord. I told her how mother had gone home, and how I was happy for her because she was laying down her old broken body for a brand new one that was perfect. I spoke of how she will live with the Lord forever and, even though I felt a tremendous sensation of separation from her, I can be happy for her, knowing she is having a homecoming in Heaven.

For whatever reason, she mentioned that she was returning to Spokane from Florida, having attended an American Legion meeting there, and wasn't feeling well. She lived in a little town near Spokane called Coulee City and even told me that her name was Janet Rice, which is incredible because no one ever tells another at the airport their names. But...

We never saw her again after boarding the plane. The next morning, having arrived at Spokane late in the evening, I picked up the local newspaper, and to my absolute surprise, I saw the headlines, "Local woman dies of Legionaries Disease." I read the story and learned that Janet Rice from Coulee City had arrived in Spokane the night before after attending a convention in Florida. Feeling ill, she went directly to a local hospital and died hours later with what was diagnosed as Legionnaires Disease.

My heart tore as I realized that God had given me an opportunity to share Him with a stranger just hours before she was to die. I understood why she had shared her name and where she was from. Had she not, I would not have had a confirmation about our encounter. I felt ashamed before God that I had trivialized such an opportunity. I was too wrapped in my own situation that I had been insensitive to an opportunity. I had shared, but she had literally extracted it from me. I purposed in my heart that in the future, with God's help, I would try to allow the Holy Spirit to increase my sensitivity to His guidance and try to treat every opportunity as a divine encounter. We meet perhaps thousands of people in our lifetime without knowing how many are just a few breaths away from death.

Again, I must trust the Lord that some little thing we talked about sparked hope in her heart that may have caused her to call on the Lord in those moments before death.

I am human. I can still get so involved with the physical aspects of living that I may miss opportunities. But my prayer is, "Lord, keep me sensitive to your Spirit."

Out of the Fire

Prologue

God has blessed me by allowing me the privilege of assisting in various ways, perhaps fourteen thousand immigrant families, most from the former Soviet Union, who have immigrated as refugees to the Puget Sound area of Washington State. To immigrate to the United States on refugee status, the pending immigrant must convince embassy and Immigration Service officers that religious or political persecution has existed in the past and most likely will continue in their home country. It's a frustrating process that can take up to five years or more to complete. Many people do not qualify after investing considerable time and resources in the process, if they are not able to produce convincing argument or evidence to an Embassy Consul Officer.

It has been such a blessing and a privilege to be able to assist these very unpretentious folks with relocation concerns as they adjust to a new culture and the variety of problems that arise as a result.

Some families have now been here since 1988. Each time I see one of them, there is a story that comes to my mind involving that family, etched in my memory forever, concerning the hardships they endured and stressful situations they had to deal with upon their arrival.

I share not only my experience, but include a compilation of stories related to me by those who experienced them. I was blessed by the opportunity to have known and befriended these people after they were released from the Soviet system or elsewhere and allowed to immigrate. I offer only a sampling of my own experience, because there have been so many that I couldn't possibly capture all, nor do I remember all. Weekly, I am approached by people whom I have long forgotten, who refresh my memory of a time past when the Lord allowed me an opportunity for Him to touch their lives

As I stood near them and listened to their stories of not only physical, but spiritual survival, I felt I was standing in the presence of spiritual giants, and my life will never be the same. It seemed in some cases, the person had such a compelling need to share their experience that, provided with a listening ear, those experiences gush out as from an uncapped fountain.

It is my hope that this writing will inspire and encourage the reader, just as the real events have done for me. The stories related here are true to the best of my remembrance, translation problems notwithstanding. To do less would dishonor the tenacity, the strength, and the dignity of these spiritual giants.

Everything shared is for the purpose of showing the Lord's grace and compassion for His own, and to allow the reader to reflect on the blessings that we in this country enjoy. We often don't realize that we are a blessed people and usually do not understand that our own future could easily include similar persecution.

Today, I typically can have around three thousand people through my office annually. In the past three years they have come from 140 countries, representing most major religions. If given an opportunity by the Holy Spirit, I engage them in a conversation about the Lord and share with them experiences from my own life intended to reveal Him to them. I have had a surprising interest from some whom you would think might even get offended.

The Immigrants

In early 1989, I had reached a place in my life where my children were approaching the time when they would be leaving home. I had enjoyed a successful career as an industrial engineer with the Boeing Company, but was finding myself with a lot of after-hour extra time on my hands. I had heard that there were in the area, immigrants (technically classified as refugees by the U.S. Immigration and Naturalization Service) from the former Soviet Union. Most were Pentecostals, along with a few Baptists, some Armenian Orthodox and a few Catholics. I knew that it must be difficult for them, coming into a new culture.

With a heavy heart, I remember saying to the Lord, "I have all this extra time and I know there must be some of those folks who need help, perhaps desperately. Please Lord, somehow, let me be able to use that extra time to help those who need it."

Within days, things began to happen in my life, but it wasn't until later that I was able to look back and see it.

First, my son had been transporting food for local food banks. This involved picking up overstocked items from a local bakery and distributing them free to several apartment complexes in the area. One day there were problems with his truck, so he called me and asked if I would use my truck to cover for him for a few days. It wasn't something that I was excited about, but I agreed to do it.

During those few days, my wife and I met some of the tenants and discovered they were refugees from the former Soviet Union, mostly from Ukraine. They were very

55

kind and hospitable people, and a few families invited us to their home for dinner. As we met with them, we discovered there were problems, little things, paperwork problems, problems with neighbor children, landlord problems, things of the nature with which we could help. So we started doing what we could. Word spread among the families that we were willing to help, so it didn't take long before many families were calling us.

Viktor and Valentina had five children when we met them. The children ranged in age from very small to about 14 years old. The three oldest were Oksana, who was 7, Lyudmila (Luda) who was 12, and Sergey who was 14. I think they may have been the first family that we became acquainted with.

They invited us to their home for dinner, and a strong bond formed quickly. Since the area where their apartment was located was in a very poor part of town, it was not a very attractive place to live. There were gang fights, problems with neighbor children trying to shake their kids down for money, and minor vandalism against their apartment.

Several times Valentina called to ask if I could come to their place, once when neighbor children sprayed water from a hose into their windows and wet everything down. I went to the neighbor's apartment to speak with the Mother about it, only to be informed that she was a working mom and could not watch over her kids when she is working. I assured her that if we continued to have a problem, I would have to involve the police. A couple weeks later, they were evicted from the apartment complex for other reasons.

Another time, Valentina was upset because she thought a local store checker had cheated her in her return change after a food purchase. I spoke with the manager and he gladly returned to her the amount that she felt she was shorted.

We got into the habit of bringing the three oldest kids

to our place on weekends to give their parents a breather, and also for their help on household deliveries to other families we helped with interpreting issues. Over the years, the kids were at our place often and became very special to us. The family eventually moved from Seattle proper to the suburban city of Kent, and the environment changed for them. Today, Sergey has a business, Luda is married with four children, and is employed as a dental hygienist. Oksana is now married, has two children, and lives in Missouri where her husband is employed as a medical professional.

We were visiting Viktor and Valentina when we heard that the husband of a neighbor family, also immigrants (Russian), was bedfast with a heart problem. We met the family and prayed that the Lord would touch and heal him. Mikhail got up from the bed while we were there and we had a nice visit. We were at their apartment several times after that because they were having problems with young people from the neighborhood throwing rocks into their open slider door. We developed a strong appreciation for Mikhail and his family. As far as I know, he has not had recurring problems with his heart. Today, he is the pastor of a local Slavic church of several hundred. Every Christmas for the last 29 years, he has never forgotten. He always appears at my front door with a "Merry Christmas" and a box of candy.

We also met Aleksandr and Cladiya, a couple from the city of Chisinau (pronounced "Ke-she-nev") the capital of Moldova. They have a large family with 10 children, varying from a small child to the oldest who was about 17.

Aleksandr shared that the Lord had spoken to him back in the 1970s and told him that he and his family would eventually immigrate to America. Immediately after receiving this promise, Alek went to the local body of believers where he and his family worshiped. He shared the news, only to discover they did not believe him.

Within days, there were ugly rumors that he and his family were a little crazy. To appreciate this incident, you must remember that, at that time, the possibility of anyone emigrating from the USSR to America was next to nothing. Even though many shared this dream, it was considered just that.

Not long after, members of the local KGB office started visiting him at home to interview family members with suggestions that Father must be "koo-koo," and to interrogate Alek about any possible American connections. They produced a statement that his local pastor had written for the authorities indicating his belief that Alek was mentally ill. This form of abuse went on for nearly 15 years with Alek unswerving in his belief that God had promised that he and his family would come to America.

Eventually, He and his family were treated as outcasts. Fellow Christians and friends no longer came to them and even avoided them outright. This was especially hurtful. They had come to expect this kind of treatment from people outside of the church, but when those who are supposed to be Christians turned on them, it was very hard for them, and they felt very alone. Yet Alek never let go of God's promise.

In 1988, to everyone's surprise, Alek received an invitation for an interview at the U.S. Embassy to determine eligibility for immigration to the United States. As a result, he was provided refugee status. He could enter the U.S. as soon as he wished.

It was then that local folks started beating a path to his door. Many wanted to know how he got permission to leave, while some came to apologize, others to wish he and his family well in their new country. The pastor who had written the statement for the authorities came to apologize, and explained that the authorities had threatened to harm his family if he did not write the letter. Some of those folks eventually followed him to the

U.S. also.

They did not leave right away, though. There were things to sell or otherwise dispose of, since they were limited to only three pieces of luggage that could be carried out of their country.

They arrived in the United States in 1989, and the Lord gave me the honor of assisting them with their needs. With that, they blessed me with their friendship. Months later, their apartment unit burned and the Lord gave me the household items they needed to set up a second time. I will never forget some of those rich experiences that we shared in their early years in America.

The children are now grown. Some live in the Pacific Northwest, while Alek, his wife, and the younger ones— who are also now grown—moved to Tennessee. There they purchased a home and property to pursue the American dream. I recently heard that Alek went to be with the Lord within the last couple years while some members of his family still live in that area.

An ethnic Russian family from Batumi, (Soviet) Georgia, approached me soon after, interested in renting a home that was available next door. I didn't own the house, but I was taking care of it while the owner was overseas serving in the military.

Unsure that I could speak with them about the things expected of a tenant, I was hesitant about renting it to them. At that time, they could speak no English, and I knew absolutely no Russian. After praying about it, the Lord assured me it was okay, so they moved into their first American home. During the six years they lived next door, we came to accept and love them like our own family.

It was a large family with several older boys, including one named Andre who was about 26 at the time. Shortly after moving in, they took me to meet another refugee family from the Ukraine. I was moved. Aleksandr (Sasha) and Yekaterina were such nice people with two children, but they had very little furniture and the children were sleeping on the floor. They appeared very content with the situation they were in, but I felt bad about it. The next day, I went to a local furniture store and bought a bunk bed set for the children. I also found some excess furniture stored in my garage. Over the next few days, I asked others who might have furniture they didn't need or want, and soon had the family in pretty good shape.

When we finished with the furniture, Yekaterina insisted that we have lunch with them. The food was delicious. She had boiled some whole potatoes until they were soft but not mushy; she quartered them, then deep-fried them in oil till they were a golden brown, then served them with a side dish of garlic juice. We learned that you use a fork to break the potato then dip it in the garlic. I had never thought of garlic as tasty, but these potatoes were possibly the tastiest things that I had eaten in a long time.

The next day, there was another family, and then another. I soon realized that without help from others, I could not afford to spend the money required to get the things these families needed. I started visiting garage sales and asking for donations, as well as asking local thrift shops for items they couldn't sell. Local newspapers heard of our effort to help these folks, and over several years they printed favorable articles, which also helped spread information and generate additional household items.

Over the years, St. Margaret's Thrift Shop (manager, Joann Able) in Bellevue would funnel enough household items to set up some 45 families. If we had families who needed clothing or personal items, she let them go through the store and select what they needed and never charged them anything. She was just an angel. She was always open to helping with other problems also.

Valentina had come to the U.S. for a visit, then applied for asylum. When I met her, she was awaiting an answer from the INS. She had no job, no family, no place to stay. And I had no idea how to help her. The day after meeting Valentina, while at Joann's store picking up some items, I mentioned Valentina to Joann. She responded that she might be able to help, and would contact me the next day if her idea worked out.

When she called, she told me that in her church there was a single Mother who worked as an airline stewardess and who was gone from home for several days at a time. She had a young son whom she was having trouble getting someone to watch for her while she was working. Joann had proposed that she let Valentina live with her and it would solve everyone's problem. That way, Valentina would be with her son while she was out of town and the arrangement would cost only her room and board for another person. The lady agreed, so Valentina moved in the next day.

A year or so later, Valentina got a job in Seattle where she met a nice young American man. She is now married, and an American citizen herself. She has two children and is living in Kirkland. She is quick to give God the glory for the way her life has been blessed after coming to the United States.

At the time, I had no idea that over the next ten years I would obtain household items for approximately 2,500 families. Some weeks, I worked 40 hours at my job and 60 hours helping new families. Some months, as many as 25 families (more than that arrived each month, but I didn't get involved with all who came) would arrive with only what they could get into a couple of suitcases. In addition, I would have an opportunity to assist several thousand other families with a variety of problems, including numerous young people with their own types of problems. I prayed with them about varied needs, and in turn, many people prayed for me when I was in need of the Lord's help.

The families were always very hospitable when visiting

their home. This included an invitation to eat something with them. It didn't matter what time of the day you were there, it could be late at night or very early, a plate was always set and you were expected to eat. One day we stopped by four homes and ate four times. We didn't know enough Russian or Ukrainian to explain that we had just eaten, and we didn't want to appear impolite by refusing, so would try to eat something.

In the area were a number of local apartment complexes that welcomed the rush of new families. About a year after I became involved with the refugees, I had picked up a load of donated furniture and brought it to one of these complexes where several new elderly families had just moved in and were in need of household goods.

It was early afternoon before I pulled into the parking lot. I asked some of the refugees who were already settled, for physical help in moving the furniture to those families with needs. It may have been the hottest day of the year. I was hot, sweating and tired. The first people I contacted told me they could not help because they were getting ready to go to the lake with others so didn't have the time.

I remember very well the thoughts that came to my mind: "I must be very stupid trying to help people who will not help their own people; I could and probably should be going to the lake myself."

Immediately following these thoughts though, there came peace as the Lord reminded me that He had not asked these people to do the job for Him but had asked me to do it. I understood that an immigrant could never locate the things that I had, or be in a position to pick up and deliver it. The Lord had asked me to do that, and He always provided the resources to get the job done. I have learned that the Lord expects obedience from us, as He was obedient to the Father. Even though He lived a perfect life, He was perfected in the death that He died. He was obedient unto death in that He laid down His life. He will require few of us to give our lives, but He does expect us to be obedient.

With this peace also came other individuals who gladly pitched in and helped move the furniture. I do not recall ever, experiencing discouragement after this time.

Mid-summer of 1991, there was a new family, Zanic, Lydia, and three children, for whom we had been successful in getting most of the things they needed, but who were still in need of a sofa. After several days, we decided to look around at garage sales; maybe we could talk someone into selling one to us at a reasonable price. I might say that with all the assistance that I was blessed to be able to provide, there was never an offer of financial assistance to me from anybody nor did I ever solicit any. The Lord provided as the need arose.

After two days of looking with no success, I remember the Lord speaking to me and saying, "You're going about this all wrong. You are worrying about something that you should let Me worry about."

Of course, He was right. I told my wife, "We'll go home and wait for the Lord to bring us the sofa that we need."

I knew there were a lot of items out there, and people who were willing to donate them, but just didn't know who, or how to get it to those who needed it. The Lord could easily get my phone number into a donor's hands.

We went home and I even put the cordless phone near me so that when I got the call, I wouldn't have to go to the other room for it. About 30 minutes passed before it rang. I grabbed it quickly and said, "Why did you wait so long to call?"

The party on the other end was very surprised that I answered that way, but informed me that she had a sofa that she would like to donate, which I gladly accepted.

After hanging up, my wife and I marveled, but praised God for His faithfulness. We left quickly for the sofa. It was beautiful, in excellent shape and a hide-a-bed—just what these folks loved. It may have been the best sofa ever donated to us. We delivered it to the family that afternoon without the family ever knowing the miracle that the Lord had performed for them. (I couldn't speak enough Russian to explain it to them.)

Late one evening, we were in Kent checking with new families when, on impulse, we decided to stop for a minute to visit Alek and Lyubov. They were a new family we were trying to help. Within minutes of arriving in their home, we were told that Alek's mother, who was elderly, was very ill in the bedroom. I asked to see her. She appeared to be having a heart attack. I called 911 and Medic-1 responded. Indeed, she was having a heart attack, so the Medics took her to the hospital where her condition was stabilized. Weeks later, she went through open-heart surgery. I know it was God's timing that we arrived there just when we did.

Stepan, the husband of the lady with the heart problem, told of events that happened to them while in the former Soviet Union. He had been a pastor of a Pentecostal group in the Ukraine. They met in homes, partly to maintain a low profile, but also, they were not registered with the government so could not obtain facilities for a proper church. As such, they were considered an illegal religious group by the government. Authorities repeatedly raided the homes to disrupt and threaten the people with jail if they continued to meet.

After a year or so, they arrested Stepan, processed him through court, and sentenced him to 12 years confinement at a prison camp in Siberia, near Lake Baikal, about 4,000 miles from his family.

To be near him, his wife moved to a village near the prison. Because he was not properly fed, she raised a vegetable garden and brought food to him in prison daily. Stepan surprised the authorities though, because he continued preaching and witnessing to the prisoners as well as the guards.

He eventually was released in 1988, as a result of a negotiated package deal between President Reagan and

Soviet President Gorbachov involving political and religious prisoners. After being released, and before immigrated to the United States, he stayed near the prison, visiting daily, preaching, witnessing and ministering to the prisoners. He even managed to get a few pictures of himself baptizing some of the prisoners in water.

Anatoly

Anatoly shared a similar story about serving time in a Siberian prison as a result of his testimony. His family was also in the Ukraine, about 4,000 miles from his prison. He was assigned to a logging crew where they cut wood all day. The wood was then loaded on skids and pulled by mules to a railhead some miles away, where it was re-loaded onto trains and carried to cities to be used as fuel.

The crew was expected to walk miles every day from the prison camp to where they cut the wood, then walk back to camp at the end of the day. Winter temperatures were often below zero, and frequently there were readings of 50 or 60 below zero. Most of prisoners were malnourished because of poor diet and inadequate meals. Meals usually consisted of bread and water unless someone was fortunate enough to catch a rat or other small animal.

When making the daily march to or from the woodcutting area, all prisoners were expected to keep up the pace. If any were ill or exhausted and fell out, the guards simply left them there to freeze to death. As bodies accumulated, other prisoners were pressed to pick up the bodies and dispose of them. Even now, Anatoly has large spots on his body where he was exposed to frostbite, and he has been told that they will stay with him forever.

There was a time when Anatoly became very ill, so he was able to obtain the proper permits that excused him from the daily regimen, essentially, allowing him to remain in his bunk at camp. He was sick for several days, had eaten nothing, and was nearing unconsciousness when he became aware of a young man standing near his bunk.

This person was offering him a loaf of bread. Anatoly was struck by his appearance. He obviously was not one of the prisoners because he was wearing fine clothing, was healthy and clean. Anatoly's immediately thought it was some kind of trick by the guards, so he pushed the bread away. But the stranger protested, saying, "I know who you are," and called him by name. "I have been sent here to give you this bread. It will restore your health."

His voice was persuasive so Anatoly took it, and as he ate some, he marveled at how strength flowed through him.

He quickly raised himself to thank the stranger, only to realize that he was no longer there. Anatoly got up from his bunk and made it to a window where he could look out, but the stranger had disappeared. This was an armed camp with wire around it; it was not a place where a person could just come and go as he pleased. To this day, Anatoly is convinced that the Lord sent an angel to him when he was in great need.

Peter

Peter was a professor on staff at L'viv Poly Technical Institute in the city of L'viv, Ukraine, when he accepted Christ as his personal Savior. His wife and family immediately rejected Christianity, and after complaints to the authorities, he was arrested and committed to a mental clinic where he spent several days. He was given shots of several types of drugs and was constantly encouraged to abandon his beliefs. It didn't matter that some of his art was, and is to this day, on display at the Russian National Gallery of Fine Arts in Moscow. He was subjected to what amounted to torture. His wife divorced him, then she and the children abandoned him.

Peter didn't recant, and after several years of frequent

forced visits by authorities to the clinic, he was released to pick up the pieces of his life. The Lord was faithful to him and he later married a Christian lady. Today they reside with their two children in a suburb of Seattle. They are happy and attend a local fellowship. Sometimes Peter will speak at the service, as no one loves to talk about the Lord more then he, and will witness to anyone at anytime as the Lord gives him boldness. He has continued his interest in art and has held numerous shows at different galleries in the Seattle area.

Slavic and Maria

I received a call from Slavic and Maria's family. It was a Saturday. One of the children could speak a little English and was trying to ask me about something. After several minutes, I determined that Maria had been walking across the parking lot at the apartment complex where they lived, when a neighbor child ran into her on his bike and cut her leg. I could not determine how serious it was, so I drove out to their place. One look at her leg and I could see very quickly that she must have medical help.

They thought all doctors' offices were closed on Saturday, and didn't know about the emergency admittance at the local hospital. An older daughter put her in a car and followed me to the hospital where Maria got the injury sewn up. The gratitude expressed by the family made it well worth the trouble it caused me to help out. Slavic, the Father, even though ill for several months, presented me with a special engraved plaque for my fiftieth birthday. Within a month he died of a stroke. This family also became very special for me over the next few years.

One day, while visiting them, we were discussing the fact that I had four sons and no daughters. Svetlana, the second to the oldest, quickly said, "No problem, I will be your daughter."

I later discovered that since I had trouble remembering

the young people's names, if I called the teenage girls "Daughter" and the younger ones "Princess," it didn't seem to matter that I couldn't remember their names. I eventually picked up many "daughters," but I always considered Svetlana number one because it started with her. She is now married with two children, and her husband has a local business. I see them from time to time.

Another time I stopped by, Lucia, the youngest daughter, had been working at her first job for 90 days and was facing a test which would determine whether she continued working with this job. If she passed, she would also receive a raise in pay. We joined hands at the table and prayed together that God would give her a clear mind and help her with the test. She called a few days later and announced to me that she had passed. Today, she has a good job with the local hospital, is married and has two children.

Later, another daughter of Slavic and Maria, Lyuba, and her family came and we have also become very close with them. She is now working at Sea-Tac Airport, so when she learned that I intended to go to Florida in November of 1999 she presented me with a buddy pass issued by her company entitling me to reduced fare. This entire family has been such a blessing to me.

Lyuda

The phone rang one evening about 11:00 pm. It was Lyuda, and she was crying. It seems her husband and a friend were delivering a bed to another family and become lost. They had pulled into a vacant area near a junkyard and were trying to understand a map, which, of course, was in English. Someone from a nearby business noted their vehicle there and alerted the police. The police responded and the immigrants could not explain what they were doing. Unable to understand Russian, the police took the two to jail and charged them with criminal trespass.

Lyuda had received a call from them at the jail, but she didn't know where the jail was or how long they would be there. Nor did she understand the charges. I called around to the jails in the area and located them at Auburn where the person on the other end of the line explained everything to me, as they understood it.

The husband and friend would be released the next morning on their own recognizance. I called Lyuda back and explained all I knew to her and tried as best I could to calm her. She, like most of the people, was very fearful of authorities since where they came from, family members and relatives who were jailed often disappeared. Over the next few months, I took time off from my job to accompany them through two or three court sessions. There wasn't much I could do, but Lyuda insisted, and it seemed to make the families more comfortable being with someone they trusted.

Charges were eventually dismissed. I was to receive a number of calls over the years about family members being jailed for different reasons—young people for speeding or driving with no licenses, that kind of stuff. Nothing serious, and in all cases, they were released the next day on bail or to their parents.

Orest

Orest was about 14 when he arrived in America with other members of his family. Someone had given me a bicycle and I had passed it on to him.

A couple months later, I heard that while riding it, he had been hit by a car. I stopped by a couple of days later to see just how bad off he was. He had bruises all over his body, and his face was covered with abrasions, but didn't appear to be seriously injured; he just looked terrible. His folks had not taken him to a doctor because, among other reasons, they couldn't afford to. We offered prayer for him to God, and spent a little time with him.

While we visited with his family, his Mother related a story concerning an incident that had happened to him before coming to America. Orest had been riding the train to a neighboring city when some young men who knew him accosted him. They taunted him for some time about being a Christian and being from a Christian family. The encounter escalated until it got out of control and the assailants succeeded in throwing him from the moving train.

For some time, he lay by the tracks injured before a kindly person found him and helped him get to a hospital. He was in the hospital for several months with his face swollen beyond recognition. He withheld his name from the hospital staff out of fear they would stop treatment knowing he was a Christian.

During this time, his folks were frantic. They had no idea what had happened to him. When local police were asked for help, either they weren't interested or couldn't help.

For several months his folks spent hours praying that they may learn his whereabouts and/or what had happened to him. Eventually, the hospital released him and he returned home to a joyous reception where his folks learned about his events. Evidently the police never took an interest in it even after it was known what actually happened.

I didn't see much of Orest for several years. Then early one morning I received a call from his mother. It seems he was about 17 at the time, had his driver's licenses, and was returning home about 2:00 A.M. from work at a local McDonald's. Police stopped him for doing 75 in a 50 MPH zone. For some reason, which was never clear to me, the police took him to a juvenile detention center and towed his car. His mother asked if I could locate exactly where he was, and help find out where the car had been towed to. It was cleared up over the next few days.

Today Orest is married and doing very well.

Bogdan

Bogdan came to this area in 1991, after about a year in the eastern part of the United States. We met him and his family after being notified that they were in need of furniture. They had three beautiful small children. We knew them about four months when his wife Lyuba called me one evening around midnight.

When I answered the phone, she said, "Jim, my Bogdan is dead."

I was in total shock for a few minutes. They had been in our home just a couple days before. He may have been 27 or 28, and was a big, strong guy—the picture of perfect health. The two of them seemed to really love and respect each other.

I got out of bed, dressed and went out to their place. Friends were also coming to her. As the story unfolded, I learned there had been a quarrel and she had taken the children and gone to friends. Bogdan had dealt with an anger problem for the better part of his life. Knowing this, Lyuba had asked his Father, who was visiting from the Ukraine at the time, to go to their home and try to reason with him. After some time in their apartment, Bogdan, still very angry, grabbed a knife from the kitchen and stuck it into his chest, hitting his heart. He immediately tried to withdraw it but fell onto a TV set, causing it to fall to the floor and break. He was rushed to a hospital but died a short time later.

When the police arrived, seeing the broken TV and thinking there may have been a fight between him and his father, they immediately took the father to jail until they could rule out any possibility that he actually had killed Bogdan.

The next day, I contacted the police department that was holding him, and they asked if I would agree to act as liaison between the police and the family (because of the language problem). I agreed, and late the next day I went to the jail to assist when he was released to his daughter

Lysa, whose family also lived in the area.

When I met the father in the jail building upon his release, it's my impression that he may have cried the whole 24 hours he was there. He came right to me and embraced me for the longest time while sobbing. My heart went out to him, as I understood losing his son, but also the trauma of going to jail and knowing that he was aware that where he came from, people go to jail and stay there, or disappear. Back then, as I have previously mentioned, most new refugees were terrified of authority figures.

I took time off from my job for several days and went with Lyuba to help her make funeral and burial arrangements, providing as much moral support as I could. I remember trying to think of something really meaningful to say, something that might touch that inner person that resides in all of us, something to help her lean on the Lord and absorb His strength, but I fear my attempts came up short.

In any case, the families somehow made it through the next few days. The father returned quickly to the Ukraine since his wife, Bogdan's mother, was there, going through a terrible time as well. In time, Lyuba married an American man and now seems to be very happy; the children seem to have gotten over the traumatic experience and are doing very well in their American school.

Several years later, Bogdan's father and Mother came to the United States as refugees. A couple hours after arriving, the Mother was at the daughter's house and complained that she didn't feel well, so was going to lie down in the bedroom for a while. The daughter checked on her in about an hour and discovered that she had died. The Mother is now buried beside Bogdan in a local cemetery. This family has experienced a double tragedy in this country.

Valentina

Valentina contacted me, worried about a young person who was in the city jail and needed $500 to post bail before being released. She asked, if she gave me the money, would I be willing to go there and bail him out. I cautioned her that it might not be wise, but she assured me that she knew the person and was convinced that he had not done anything wrong. I finally agreed, and arrived at the jail about an hour later. I had never met Pavel before, so when I paid the bail and he was released, we talked for just a few minutes and he left.

I learned a week later that he had been stopped in his car for some reason, and when the police ran his ID on the computer they found that he had an outstanding traffic fine against his record from a state back east. After his release from jail, he went very quickly and got a receipt to prove that he had indeed paid the earlier fine, so the local police dismissed everything and Valentina's money was returned to her. I thought the story ended there, since I didn't see Pavel again for about two years.

The next time I saw him, he supplied details to the story after he left me at the jail. Unknown to me, while he was in jail his family was conducting an ongoing prayer meeting. They were praying that, somehow, God would get Pavel released from jail. Remembering from where they had just moved, to them a trip to a local jail could create fears that we can't even imagine.

Anyway, Pavel told me that he arrived home and knocked on the door only to have it answered by a little girl. Rather than unlock the door and let him in, she returned to where the prayer meeting was and told those people. They had been praying for God to release Pavel, but when the little girl told them "Pavel is at the door," they didn't want to believe it. Finally, someone did go to the door, and then there was rejoicing among the group. When he related to the group how he was released, they became convinced that Pavel has an angel out there somewhere named "Jim" because of the similarity between this story and the one where the angel released Peter from jail as related in the 12th chapter of Acts. My heart melted at the possibility that God had allowed me an opportunity to help one of His.

Vladimir

I was returning home one Saturday evening when I felt that I must stop by and see Vladimir and his family. I had only a little time, but had heard that he had recent surgery and felt I should check on him. He appeared to be doing fine. We discussed some of the problems facing him and his family since they had been in the country only a couple of months. His car had broken down and needed repairs. We took the time to pray with him, and I mentioned that I had had the same surgery a few years back—sort of a run-of-the-mill conversation, and maybe even less. Because he couldn't understand English and I knew very little Russian, I soon left, and the incident escaped my mind as I busied myself with other families.

I didn't see him again until a couple of years later when he was much better at his English. He related to me that I will never know what that visit did for him. He was in a strange country, couldn't speak the language, no job, car wasn't running, and maybe the worst thing of all, the surgery had left him worrying about his ability to deal with anything. He was quite depressed and on the verge of just giving up.

After sharing with him that I, too, had the same surgery and was now lifting furniture and doing everything that I wanted to do, and more. I am not sure what I may have said to him, but as he tells it, I told him, "Stop feeling sorry for yourself, get your carcass out of bed and get started on what you must do."

I doubt that I said those words; it's not my style. But that's what he heard, and he said that it worked magic on him. He did get up, and within a couple of days he was repairing his car. Whatever happened, we both acknowledge that God was in the timing for us to stop that day, and certainly it was the Lord who moved on his spirit to motivate him to pull himself together.

Vladimir also shared with me about a time when he was living in the Ukraine. He was very sick and had a high fever for several weeks. He realized that he was leaving his body and could see his wife, Daria (pronounced, Da dy a), leaning over him on his bed. As he left this scene, he became aware that he was in the most beautiful, most comfortable place he had ever experienced. He felt as if this was what he had been originally created for and it was if he had been waiting all his life for this moment.

He also became aware that there was a being with him. He didn't recognize it as an angel, but later realized that it must have been one. He could hear a lady's voice way off somewhere crying and recognized it as Daria's. He turned to the being beside him and said, "Please, can I just go to her and explain everything?"

The being smiled and nodded his head knowingly, but at the same time, without saying a word, he also conveyed to Vladimir that he would not come back. If he returned to his wife, he would stay. Vladimir nodded agreement.

He could actually see himself coming back down to where his body was and re-entering his body, then waking to explain to his wife who was crying because she knew he was dead. The thing that he did not anticipate was the depression that he experienced upon re-entering his body. He explains that it was as if he had been free and was now again in prison and his body felt very heavy and awkward. He smilingly admitted that he was irritated at his wife for crying and causing him to come back to her.

Irina

Irina came to my door after someone told her that I might be able to help with her problem. She was a Gospel singer in her country of the Ukraine and had traveled much of her country as part of an evangelistic singing group. Even though the Soviet System had collapsed, animosity against Christians remained very strong. At almost every service her group performed, she and the group were heckled, sound equipment was unplugged, fights would break out and pushing and shoving by radicals was becoming normal. She tolerated it as pressure from the Devil until she started receiving threats against her life. Those, she took very seriously, knowing she could not count on local authorities for help. In fact, she suspected they were often behind her problems. About that time, she was offered an opportunity to come to the United States and minister to the local Slavic churches. She quickly accepted, believing it was the Lord's will for her own protection.

About five months in the United States, her visa about to expire, she was struggling with the possibility of asking the Immigration and Naturalization Service to grant her religious asylum, which, if approved, would allow her to stay here permanently. She was very concerned for her personal safety if she were to return to her home country.

After our initial discussion, she returned several days later to ask if I would help her complete the application, which I agreed to do. Little did we know the long and anxious journey that lay ahead of her.

After completing her applications and submitting them to the Immigration and Naturalization Service, I assisted her in locating a local immigration attorney who agreed to handle her case. She waited for about two years before she received an interview appointment, and her request was promptly denied. The attorney appealed and she had her day in court. I was allowed to testify on her behalf because I had worked with so many refugees, and the court allowed that I would know something about the things the Ukrainian Christians had endured and what they might expect if they returned.

Shortly after the trial, Irina moved to California. Within a year she married a naturalized citizen, Sergey, who had immigrated to the U.S. several years earlier. She was unaware that as a result of her trial, she was again denied asylum and was ordered to leave the U.S. within 30 days or be deported. Her attorney could file another appeal, but he temporarily lost contact with Irina. An appeal must be filed within 30 days, so, consequently, no appeal was initiated.

After about two years, Irina, with a ten-month-old child, tired of waiting, approached the Immigration and Naturalization office in her city to inquire about her status. She was promptly arrested, handcuffed, put in leg irons and taken to a prison about 90 miles from her home. Her husband, obviously distraught, could only watch in horror.

Word immediately went out to all the Slavic churches in California as well as in Washington State. Thousands of people knew Irina, as she had sung in most of the churches. Many organized around-the-clock prayers. Several led groups to protest and picket at the State Capital in Sacramento. Some politicians promised to try to help.

It would be three weeks of hell for her before she would be released to her family and friends. I and others petitioned several congressmen and senators.

This family had become special to me. I quickly joined them in Sacramento to provide moral support and anything else that I might be able to do. Really, I didn't have a clue when I left, but while there I wrote letters to anyone who might be able to help, even President Bill Clinton.

In May of 2000, Irina was again granted a new trial. This time, to God be the glory, she was offered an application for permanent status in the United States. Today, there is joy in her camp; she and her husband have three children and are looking forward to a bright future, believing the dark days are over. She is now an American citizen and her parents have joined her on a family-based visa and live nearby.

Viktor

Viktor recently sat in my office and shared with me an occurrence that happened in 1994. He had arrived in 1993 and had not found any work. It was a hard time for his family since they already had two children and his wife was expecting a third. I had met him when he arrived in the U.S. with his family, and had helped them with household items, but had not seen him very often since.

The Lord had brought us together again in 1994, and he shared with me that he really needed a job. I couldn't give him any hope, but after returning home, I couldn't get him out of my mind. At the moment, I knew several men who were out of work and I also knew these men make excellent workers if only I could find an employer who would give them a chance. Since they could not speak English very well at the time, it would have to be an unskilled job, but something that would pay enough for them to support their families.

The Lord gave me an idea. An acquaintance of mine was a foreman for a company that installs and repairs roofs, so I contacted him to ask if he needed any help. He informed me that, with the kind of work he does, he always needs help. I arranged to have him come to my home and meet some of these people. There may have been eight people show up that night including Viktor. Three or four were actually hired, and one of those was Viktor. The next day, I was involved with other things and soon forgot about this situation. I saw Viktor off-and-on over the next few years and knew he was doing well with the job, even breaking from the original company and starting his own roofing business.

Now he is sitting in my office with his wife, Valentina, with tears in their eyes, sharing with me the faithfulness of the Lord and recounting that meeting which turned his life around. He has purchased a home for his family and is living the American dream.

I feel a great sense of humility as I realize that the Lord has allowed me to be a part of something that had such a major impact on the life of this family, and I rejoice with them.

Bogdan and Galina

Bogdan and Galina were in this country for a few weeks before I could arrange to meet them. We learned at the first meeting that Galina had already taken x-rays and a sonic test for gall bladder problems at a hospital in Seattle, and they revealed an enlarged gall bladder with stones. The diagnosis indicated she would need surgery to remove them.

My wife and I had been attending a weekly Bible study at that time so we invited Galina to accompany us to the next one, and she accepted. The lady leading the study that night, asked if anyone would like to be prayed for. We urged Galina to allow her to pray for her and she agreed.

We saw Bogdan and Galina off-and-on after that, but it wasn't till about eight years later that we had a real visit with them, and by then, they were speaking English very well.

Galina reminded us of the prayer that the lady had offered up for her. She related that when she had seen the lady, she didn't believe God would use her because she had make-up. At that time, the Ukrainian Pentecostals were not using make-up, but nevertheless, Galina had agreed to allow her to pray for her. The lady had anointed her with oil before praying, and after she went home that evening, she didn't particularly feel any different.

She was scheduled for surgery a few days later and didn't think to ask for a repeat on the test, but went directly into the surgery.

The team of surgeons later told her they were very surprised to find only a small piece of tissue where the gall bladder should have been, so, worried that the gall bladder had burst, they widened her incision so they could look further into her stomach cavity for remnants, only to find nothing. The chief surgeon indicated to her that throughout his career, he had never seen another case like hers.

She then realized that God had indeed touched her and healed her when the lady prayed for her, and if she had only believed, she would have requested new tests before surgery and found surgery unnecessary. I've also noticed that Galina now uses some make-up and she looks nice.

Aleksandr and Valentina

In 1994, I was informed that a new couple, Aleksandr and Valentina, who had arrived a few days earlier, was in need of household items for their family. They had already rented an apartment but did not have any furniture. Immediately after being told about this family, the phone rang and a lady was offering her entire house of furniture to a new family. I expressed gratitude to her and mentioned that I was not feeling well; by tomorrow, I would feel better and would come for it.

She said, "Oh, but that's the catch, you must come tonight because tomorrow, my family and I will move to Hawaii, so it must go tonight."

My son volunteered to help, so I told the lady that I would come right away. I remember it was January, very frosty out with the temperature at about 15 degrees. I made two trips that night and took the furniture directly to the new family.

I finished quite late, and after returning home I

developed a very high fever. My son took me to the hospital where I lay for about four hours while hospital staff fed me medication intravenously. I may have gotten four or five hours of sleep that night, but by mid-morning the next day, I was feeling fine and was going in another direction to pick up some furniture for yet another family.

Chang

Chang was different. As he sat across from me at my desk, I took a moment to size him up. He was obviously not of Slavic decent but appeared possibly Chinese or Vietnamese. A local organization, World Relief, had referred him to me and had called before he got here so I knew a little about him.

He was seeking help in completing an asylum application and was interested in bartering information about three American soldiers buried in his home village in North Vietnam in exchange for remaining in America on asylum status. His story began in 1966 when, during a heavy wind and rainstorm, a U.S. military plane with three people aboard crashed near his village. His people, fearing the militia would come looking for it, buried the bodies and pushed what was left of the plane over a cliff into the ocean below.

Chang was later sent by the communist government of North Vietnam to the Ukraine to be educated and politically groomed in a communist culture. But after three years he decided to defect to that country. He eventually married a Ukrainian lady and they had several children, but because of his race, he was never completely accepted by that culture. The basis of his request for asylum was discrimination based on race and he told of many things that might have qualified him.

He was interested in revealing the whereabouts of the graves to American authorities if he received approval of his application. I contacted the State Department to see if they were interested, and was told very quickly that, they "don't buy that kind of information. If, on the other hand, his application was approved on its own merit, they would certainly like to talk to him." I relayed this information back to Chang and provided him with the name and number of the State Department spokesman. After assisting him with his initial application, I never saw him after that. I don't know if his application was approved or not, or whether he gave anyone the information about the MIA's.

Aleksandr

Aleksandr may have the most unusual story, if not even a little bit exotic. He entered the United States on a seaman's visa and approached World Relief for help with an asylum application. They in turn, referred him to me.

He was from Russia Far East. His home was in Magadan, a city on the Pacific Coast. He was officially a fisheries inspector for the Soviet Union, later, Russian government, and worked much of the time in support of KGB activities. He even had a government plane at his disposal anytime he needed, as he would often fly out over the sea and rendezvous with ships of the fleet.

In the early ninety's, He committed his heart to the Lord in response to hearing the Gospel, without much immediate thought about the impact on his life relative to his profession. Problems started immediately. He found that many of his job activities that did not bother him before, now left him with emotions that he had never experienced. For the first time in his life he was experiencing misgiving about some of his job responsibilities.

Over the next couple of years, he tried to untangle himself from his profession and resign from his job, only to discover that it was difficult. Attempts to resign only brought threats of bodily harm to himself and family members. He was told, "You don't quit this job unless you die." In time, his wife, who was a policewoman in the city, and his son, also accepted Christ as their Savior.

About two years after he gave his life to the Lord, and enduring numerous threats and losing most of his job responsibilities, there was a knock at his door. When he opened the door, several people pushed inside and grabbed him, his wife and teenage son. The wife and son were not harmed, but the intruders proceeded to beat Alek for some time in front of his family while making many remarks about him being a Christian. Bruised and broken, barely conscious, he was held by one intruder while another cut his throat before leaving.

Friends and family members managed to get him into a hospital, and after convalescing for nearly a year and maintaining a low profile, he saw his chance.

With his previous position, he had become acquainted with many ships' crews. Through one of these contacts, he was able to attach himself to a ship coming to the Seattle harbor.

Upon arriving in Seattle, he heard that World Relief might be able to help him, who, as I have mentioned, referred him to me.

When he came to me, he had already contacted his family and made plans for them to join him here as visitors because of concern that when it became known that he might stay here, there may be retributions against them and/or they might never be able to join him.

The scar across his throat corroborated his story somewhat, but I wasn't sure about this one. He presented what appeared to be many sensitive documents, which also helped to corroborate his story. Still, I was a little uneasy about everything. It occurred to me that he could have been sent by the KGB to establish himself in the local community in order to gather information or who knows what?

He gave me the name of a local Russian evangelist with whom I was much acquainted. When I contacted Pavel, he told me that he was in Magadan when Alek gave his life to the Lord, and he urged me to help him if I could. I told Alek that I would agree to help him if he would agree to go with me to the FBI with his story. The FBI didn't show much interest in him but eventually did agree to interview him, then turned his case over to Naval Intelligence. Anyway, I felt better about the whole thing.

I've now known Alek and his family for several years, and they regularly attend local fellowships. The Lord has continued to change and bless their lives as they adapt to their new country. He and his family are still full of enthusiasm about serving the Lord. He recently contacted me to inform me that they have been approved to remain in this country on asylum status, the first step toward becoming an American citizen.

Vadim

Vadim is Ukrainian, from Eastern Europe, but he had made his way to Russia Far East and hired out as a crewmember on a fishing boat in the early 90s. Because he is a Christian, it didn't take long for him to fall into disfavor with shipmates. The ship had a Political Officer (PO), who was placed there by the government to make sure that no one usurped the prevailing communist philosophy. All ships had these officers and it was generally assumed that they were operatives of the KGB. After several interviews in the PO's office concerning rumors about Vadim's Christianity, and enduring verbal threats, he found himself accosted and threatened by other crewmembers.

The PO was in a position to offer incentives to other crewmembers who did favors for him, so Vadim's life had become miserable. He had no one in whom he felt he could trust. After several weeks of threats, he was assigned to work only in the hole of the boat, with brief moments topside, scrubbing and cleaning the deck, always with the promise that if he recanted his Christian faith he would be reinstated to the full rights of a

84

crewmember and would be allowed to work outside of the hole.

By the time the ship arrived in Puget Sound heading for Seattle Harbor, conditions had become intolerable for him. He was restrained from coming up to the top deck by deckhands assigned to guard him. As night fell, he managed to slip past those assigned to watch him, made it to the top deck and dropped over the side into the water.

Fear engulfed him immediately because it was dark, the water was very cold and he wasn't sure how far it was to shore. Nevertheless, he struck out, and with incoming tide giving him an assist, he swam ashore near Everett, Washington. He was surprised to reach shore in about 30 minutes. After shivering in the night air for a while, he started running on the beach to bring up his body temperature.

After several days of wandering through the suburban area, he came upon a lady whom he overheard speaking the Ukrainian language. He learned through her that a Ukrainian church was nearby, where he made other contacts, one of whom agreed to bring him to me for help. I assisted him with the completion of an Asylum Application which was eventually approved. Today, he is married to a local Ukrainian girl. They and their children still live in the Everett area. I understand he has become a strong pillar in the Ukrainian fellowship where he attends. See his story elsewhere under Vadim.

Ivan

Ivan stopped by my office to inquire if I might help his family bring their youngest son from the Ukraine. While still living there, he had submitted an application to the US Embassy in Moscow for refugee status. As is normal, it took several years to process the family application, and during this process time they had an additional child—a boy. Of course, this child's name did not appear on the original application, so when they were eventually provided an interview, they discovered all the names but the youngest were approved to emigrate. This created a predicament for them.

Upon receiving their exit visas, they must leave the country within a year or lose their opportunity. But the baby would not be able to leave. They waited almost a year and the child still did not have its exit visa. So, they made the decision to leave the baby with his grandmother and come without him. They prayed that God would expedite the baby's approval, allowing him to join the rest of the family in the United States as soon as possible.

More than a year later he was in my office asking if I could help. He said his wife is so stressed, leaving her crying every day. This was a very different situation than I had faced before.

I contacted Senator Jennifer Dunn's office for help. Her associate, Keith Kosik contacted Homeland Security in Washington, DC. After doing so, he called me back to inform me that I needed to complete a Humanitarian Parole application for the family and told me where to send it. This would allow the child to come here and wait while his immigration application was being processed. We quickly complied and the child arrived about a month later. That has been a few years ago, but this family is still praising God even today for His assistance.

For several years, In addition to picking up furniture from all over the Puget Sound area of Washington State and delivering it to approximately 2,500 new families I was also asked to assist in planning weddings and funerals, finding suitable places for worship, writing business letters, helping with immigration problems and applications, assisting with landlord/tenant problems, co-signing for housing rentals and sponsoring relative families in need of a sponsor, as well as assisting in locating legal or medical help for a variety of needs. I sometimes amazed myself with the variety and nature of problems that I found myself agreeing to help with. I never turned any one down unless it required specific legal counsel. Then I referred them over to an appropriate attorney.

Through all these years, I have seen the hand of the Lord in so many situations affecting so many families that I stand humbled and offer gratitude of praise to Him. The impossible so many times has become the possible.

Tanya

Tanya was fourteen when I first met her and she was experiencing a lot of problems with her family. They were enduring a great deal of stress from moving here and trying to reestablish themselves but were not doing a very good job of handling it. Her father had turned to alcohol in an attempt to deal with the stress. But as usual, it created more stress, at least for other family members, and manifested itself in the form of spousal abuse.

For a couple years, I met with Tanya about once a month at a local fast food place for a couple of hours, just to talk. I would always try to take time to pray with her and assure her of God's love and that I was praying for her.

Because of all her parents' problems, she felt that they, and specifically her father, had no time for her at a time in her life when she desperately needed direction, advice and interaction from them. During those two years, I watched as she fought for some hope in life, sometimes succeeding, other times, giving up. I sensed hopelessness from this little girl and felt tremendous compassion for her. But I realized that all I could do was pray for her and provide a listening ear and an encouraging voice.

I spoke to several local Slavic pastors about her and, in general, the problems that the young people were going through. For the most part, I was met with denial. It's my perception that the churches are interested only in those folks who can maintain the appearance of being spiritual.

(If they have any kind of problems in their lives, just keep it hidden and in the family). If a person had a problem and others knew about it, the traditional church, to avoid controversy, distanced itself from that person. Many young people fell into that category.

The Lord revealed a truth to me a long time ago about the Church (I speak not of the building, but of the body of believers) while I was mulling over something about some folks that I knew. He created the Church perfect; unfortunately, He staffed it with imperfect men. Hence, those problems that we encounter with individuals in it, or those dirty spots that we read about in the media or hear about from others in the community, are all caused by individuals who are either misguided, or are not living up to the level that God desires for all members of His body.

I asked Tanya several times for permission to discuss the issues with her father since I knew him, but she would panic at the suggestion. I was aware that if I violated her confidence in me I would lose her.

I tried to reason with her by suggesting that she take him aside, give him a little embrace and tell him, "Papa, I know there are so many things competing for your time, but please, I need just a little time with you."

One would think that any father would immediately set aside time for a daughter, but she rejected that suggestion quickly for concern that it would just embarrass him, and that could cause him to get mean with her.

I haven't heard from Tanya for several years now. The last time I saw her, she shared with me that she was into alcohol, drugs, prostitution, and was part of a strip show in Seattle. My heart aches every time I think of her. She was such a nice little girl, and had she gotten the proper help at the right time, her life could have been salvaged.

Yet I know that, as long as one has breath, one is still salvageable.

Nadiya

She was 19 and had become involved with a much older guy who had become abusive and threatening toward her. It was complicated and potentially serious. She told me a little about the guy, and from those things, it seemed to me he was schizophrenic. Knowing that schizophrenic people are often afraid that authorities are looking for them or watching them, I had an idea.

First, I went with her to the police station and helped her apply for a no-contact order against him, even though I knew that if he really wanted to harm her, he would.

Within minutes of meeting him, he proceeded to ask me a number of questions. I carefully mentioned that I had worked with a number of problems involving the police and had even worked with a couple of situations involving the FBI. He immediately became very uncomfortable and left within minutes.

Within the week, he left the area to return to California, and to my knowledge he never returned to the Northwest.

Nadiya is now married and lives with her husband in the local area and is doing just great.

Maria, Lysa, Natalya and Vasiliy

Three children in particular became very important to us over the years. When we met them, Lysa was 9, Natalya was 7 and Vasiliy was 6. There were other, younger, children in this family but we rarely involved ourselves in very young children because it would quickly turn to babysitting.

But one of the younger children, Maria, touched my heart when I first saw her. She was three at the time. Maria was such a beautiful little girl. She looked just like a little doll. It was also quickly obvious that she had a potential problem. Her legs were so bowed that when she walked, she waddled from side to side.

When I met them, I received permission from Maria's parents to try to get her some medical help, so the next day I called Children's Hospital in Seattle.

After explaining the problem, and that the family has no money, the hospital agreed to see Maria at no charge to the family. I set them an appointment for a couple of weeks later.

Mikhail, the father, took her to the hospital, and was glad to learn that the problem was caused by malnutrition. With proper diet and a large supply of special vitamins, she should grow out of it.

Today, you should see this little girl. She is a young adult, and there is no indication of her ever having a problem. She is now married, has two children and her husband is the youth Pastor at his father's church in Tacoma, WA. When I see her today, I am so proud of her and in my heart, I praise God for her good health. I understand that, unfortunately, it can be very difficult for someone with a disability to rise to the level of acceptance that others enjoy.

Children learn English very quickly, so I found I could use them to interpret for me when discussing something with the older people. They would often ride on the truck with us to help with the language problem. We were careful to stop by a fast food place before we returned them home.

Over the years, these three sisters became like our own kids and were often at our house. In 1995 we flew to Disneyland and took Lysa and Natalya with us for five days. They were such nice kids, so well mannered, and they had a great time. I videotaped the trip to give them a copy, which I understand they still have even though they are now grown.

Several times a year, we went to the mountains for a hike or picnic, and they went with us. On one such occasion, other picnickers noticed and approached with compliments on the behavior of our kids.

Eventually, Lysa brought a young man to us and announced that she was getting married. Of course, she invited us to the ceremony. We talked for a long time about all those times when she was growing up. It seems incredible that this little girl we used to know was now grown and about to be married. I was so happy for her, and also very proud of her. They have been married now for several years and have three children of their own.

Natalya is also married and has her own children. She has a bright future ahead of her as a medical professional. She recently visited my office to give me a photo of her and her family and made me tear up a little by telling me "thanks" for being there for her when she was little.

Vasiliy is also married now. It's hard to believe that the little ones grow up so quickly.

Olga

We met Olga when she was 19 and quickly accepted her as a daughter. At 30, she approached me for help with the application process in getting a young man over from the Ukraine. She had visited there and fallen in love with him, and now they planned to marry. Today we know him very well and think she could not have done better. Olek and Olga, now have two teenage children and we get together often and love them as if they were our own. Olga and my wife Elena get together at times as very close friends. I feel the Lord has honored us by allowing us to know these young people.

Oleg

I first met Oleg when he was about 12. He also rode with me and helped deliver furniture and translate. Today he is married, has three children, and lives about a block from me.

There must have been hundreds of kids that we have met over time. I often see young people who know me, but I have no idea who they are. When I inquire about their name, I discover that I had met them when they were very young. And even though I have forgotten, they have not. When I last saw them, they were very small but today they are as tall as I.

The Lord is raising a movement within the immigrant community that is considerably successful in reaching many of these young people. I have lost the contact that I had with them through Nadiya as they have their own families. Some have moved out of state, and all have developed their own lives, so I am not sure about the magnitude of the problems the immigrant young people are going through today. I continue to pray that God will provide caring ministry for them.

I bow my heart before God in gratitude for those many children and young people who the Lord has allowed me the opportunity to influence for Him. Those who were just children when they came to America will remember little acts of kindness long after the Lord has taken me home. Even if they don't remember a name, they will remember that when their family arrived, an American came alongside them and helped. This recent Christmas, a young man now married and with two children, visiting from Florida stopped by and we talked of times when he was young and events in his life that the Lord had allowed me to participate in and he had not forgotten.

Nothing is more thrilling for me today as when one of these young people, most now in their 30's and married with families, take the time to stop by and say "Thanks" for being there when I needed it.

In my own life, I recall an incident when I was about seven years old. I had walked with older brothers to a country store that may have been three miles from my family's home. It was a typical summer day for Kentucky, very hot, and I was so tired and so thirsty. Being from a poor family, we had no money other than the money given by Mother to make her purchases.

There were several farmers at the market, just lingering a little and enjoying a cold drink before returning to the fields. One must have taken pity on us because he approached us

and asked if we would like a soft drink. It was an offer that he did not have to repeat. We accepted, and you can never imagine just how good that drink tasted.

To this day, I do not remember his name or even his face. He would undoubtedly be dead by now, but that little act of kindness will stay with me as long as I live. He set up a memorial to himself in my memory that outlived him.

Amusing Moments

Some of the more amusing moments might be the time a new immigrant asks about a certain brand of canned tuna, "Why do they call it 'Chicken of the Sea' when it's actually tuna?"

A young boy's first morning in America, upon hearing a dog barking, exclaimed, "Oh Mom, that American dog can speak Russian!"

While dining with my wife and a little girl of about five-years-old, the little girl was asked if she would like a corn dog. She didn't understand much English at the time so we tried our best Russian and used the Russian words for corn dog. (Cucurosa Sabaka) She laughed for a long time. We later found out she was looking for a dog made from corn.

One teenage girl told me that she thought the large spoiler on the back of a sports car was a "handle."

One immigrant lady, using an automatic dishwasher for the first time, put far too much liquid dishwashing detergent in it (instead of powder) and soapsuds emerged from around the door and all over her kitchen floor, creating considerable consternation for her.

There was the incident when an elderly immigrant had a dental appointment, and, knowing very little English, asked a teenage daughter of a friend to accompany him to interpret. After x-rays and a thorough check of his teeth, the dentist asked the girl to explain to the man that all his teeth were bad and should be pulled. The girl thought he said that one of them should be pulled and relayed this to the patient. "Of course, no problem," the immigrant replied, not realizing that he was agreeing to have all his teeth pulled.

You can imagine how bad he felt when he left the dentist office with no teeth. I think he was still upset a couple years later. It was amusing to everyone but the patient.

One lady shared with me that she had discovered some most delicious canned food at the store, only later to discover it was dog food. She now laughs about it.

One grandmother received a letter from her apartment manager but couldn't read it. The following day, her seven-year old grandson was visiting so she asked him to read it and translate it for her. The letter was asking the lady to come to the manager's office to sign something, but the little boy translated that she must come and sing something. After several days of worrying about what she must sing, she finally got it translated properly.

An apartment manager contacted me and asked if I would please help her communicate to one family that the apartment swimming pool was not intended for children to swim in fully clothed.

Then there was the time another manager contacted me about a small child living on the second-floor urinating on the deck and it falling onto the tenants of the first-floor deck.

There were so many situations that today produce smiles from those involved when the incidents are mentioned.

Terror in Baku

"Nella"
(Tulaunt)

Azerbaijan is a small country that was a former republic of the Soviet Union. It is bordered on the east by the Caspian Sea, on the south by Iran, the west by Armenia, and the north by Russia. The capital city, Baku, is located on the shores of the Caspian Sea.

Over the years, Armenian people had migrated to Azerbaijan with huge numbers immigrating as refugees from the war that swept Armenia in the early part of the 20th century. By 1989, a community of approximately 400,000 had accumulated, mostly in or around the city of Baku. By then, most were born there and thought of themselves as citizens of Azerbaijan. There was a major difference as Armenians were generally Orthodox Christians and Azerbaijani people were Moslem. Over the years, the Armenians and the Azerbaijanis tolerated each other pretty well, with only an occasional dispute between individuals. As a republic of the Soviet Union, tight controls had been maintained over the country. As the Soviet Union began to disintegrate, a wind of nationalism swept the country. Many Azerbaijanis saw it as an opportunity for the ethnic cleansing of non-Azerbaijani people from their country.

In early 1989, tension was mounting between the two groups. Open hostilities were becoming common, and occasionally a fatality was reported. Still, most Armenians living in Baku were not unduly alarmed. After all, they had lived here all their lives and most had substantial investments in the economy as well as the culture.

In early January, uneasiness settled over the city. Daily, there were disturbing rumors about mobs injuring or killing Armenian people. Rumors also abounded about ultimatums to the Armenians to leave the country within hours or risk being shot. Some were intimidated, and slowly a trickle of Armenian people started showing up around the Moscow, Russia, area, declaring themselves refugees from Azerbaijan.

About 7:00 P.M., January 13, 1989, Nella, her sister, her sister's husband, and their 87-year-old Mother were at home. There was a noise at the door, but before they could answer it, the door was broken down and about twenty-five radicals poured into their fourth-floor apartment. Nella and her family were unaware that, minutes earlier, the Armenian lady occupant of the apartment across the hall had just been strangled and her body placed in a canvas bag.

For the next forty-five minutes they were bound with their hands behind their backs and with rags stuffed in their mouths. They were beaten with whatever the perpetrators could get their hands on. They were cursed and threatened with death. At the same time, their apartment was systematically stripped of anything of value and passed to members of the mob. Once the apartment was stripped, the radicals pushed and shoved the occupants down the four flights of stairs to the entrance level.

On the street, they were dumped into two waiting cars and driven into the countryside. Nella remembers that they were gagged and couldn't speak, and were wedged close to each other in the car, trembling with fear. Feeling death was eminent, she locked her eyes on her sisters and they said a silent "Goodbye."

After what seemed like an eternity, the cars stopped and they were pulled from them, forced to the ground, then doused with gasoline and pushed down an embankment. At the bottom, they were horrified to see the body of their neighbor lady, but even more horrified to see one of their antagonists light a match and throw it at them. Immediately, they were engulfed in flames.

Nella relates that horrific incident: "We were crying and praying, the terror and pain was unbearable. By some miracle of God, my hands became free and I tried to tear burning clothes from my body while some of the people tried to prevent me from doing so."

Burned over fifty percent of her body, she managed to separate herself from the fire and turn her attention to her sister who sustained about seventy percent burns before the fire on her was out. Checking her Mother and brother-in-law, she discovered they had died as a result of their burns. The surviving sisters then tried to climb the bank to the roadway above, but the perpetrators, watching from above and realizing they were not dead, started stoning them. Nella lost consciousness when a stone struck her on the back of her head.

While Nella was unconscious and unknown to her, the commotion had caught the attention of a group of Russian soldiers who were in the area who moved closer to see what was happening. When they did so, the radicals became nervous and got into their cars and fled, although it's likely that the soldiers didn't actually intervene.

Sometime later, Nella awoke and discovered she and her sister were still alive. They were in very bad shape, and she realized that if they were to live they must get to the road above and try to get help.

It may have taken an hour to ascend the bank; she doesn't know. She only remembers clawing at the hard soil with her fingers for what seem like an eternity, enduring the pain from her injuries and burns, encouraging her sister to keep trying.

On the road above, they tried to signal passing motorists for help, only to discover the people passing were either afraid to help or didn't care. After some time, a young ethnic Russian saw them and took pity. He stopped and told them he could take them to the nearest hospital but would discharge them a block from it and they must walk the rest of the way. For his own safety he didn't want to be seen helping them.

Arriving at the hospital, they entered the emergency room and discovered the hospital was staffed with people who were not sympathetic to them and were not interested in helping "Armenian's." One doctor tried to reason with the rest of the staff, but was overruled, and a decision was made against helping them. As Nella tried a weak protest, a nurse grabbed a teakettle full of hot water and smashed it into her mouth, breaking most of her teeth and leaving others crooked. She took her sister's arm, and together they staggered into the night.

Some distance from the hospital, they encountered a group of Russian soldiers who were trying to locate Armenian people to evacuate them to boats tied up at the waterfront. As she was escorted across town, Nella couldn't help but notice the piles of bodies being soaked with gasoline and burned.

The boat they were put on already contained about 200 people fleeing Baku, most of whom were injured. They were ferried across the Caspian Sea to the Republic of Kazakhstan, another former republic of the Soviet Union, where arrangements were made to transport the more seriously wounded to hospitals in Moscow. While crossing the Caspian, near panic swept the boat when rumors passed among the injured that an earlier boat, making the same trip, had been purposely sunk, drowning all passengers by the Russian operators after receiving incentives from the Azerbaijanis.

Over the next three days, Baku's Armenian population was reduced to practically nothing as hordes of people took to the streets. Anyone who couldn't prove their Azerbaijani nationality or whose name sounded Armenian was beaten to death or shot, then piled and burned. Their property was confiscated. It is estimated by survivors that thousands of people of Armenian descent were killed, thousands of others injured, some barely managed to escape, and many others simply disappeared. There has been no attempt by any country to calculate and document the amount of human suffering that occurred in Baku during that week in January of 1989.

Nella spent about a year in Moscow before getting clearance to immigrate to the United States as a refugee. Much of that time in Moscow included treatment for her burns. The sister whom she saved was to stay in the hospital for about two years before she was considered well enough to immigrate.

Now living in Seattle, Nella is 69 years old and enjoying life very much. Her sister has also joined her after the long stay in a Moscow hospital. When asked if she has any animosity against the people who harmed her, she flashes a quick smile and responds, "Absolutely not! The people who did those things to me were spiritually blind people who didn't have the capacity to assess what they were doing. God will judge, and His judgment is fair." She continues, "Life is too short to carry extra baggage around with you."

Her outlook on life and her positive attitude is a blessing to everyone she meets.

The following is an account in her own words as recorded in her original petition to the United States for Refugee status.

"I was always an optimistic person, and though I'm over 60 now, I'm still full of energy and desire to work for people, to be useful for them. I'll be simply happy if you allow me to enter your great country and become a merited member of your society. The conditions of refugees from different republics of the former Soviet Union here in Moscow become worse and worse every day as the flood of refugees is greater, and the conditions of life get worse, not from day to day, but moment to moment. Though we did not get a positive answer from you yet, we still hope that your great country will once more display its humanism and mercy for all those suffering and enduring all the difficulties and troubles with dignity. God Bless You!"

Nella is very quick to give God the glory for sustaining her through it all, and eventually opening the door for her to come to the United States.

Rafael

Throughout my entire life, I have been subjected to inhumane treatment, harassment and racial discrimination because of my nationality and religious beliefs.

I was born in 1957 of Armenian parentage in Baku, the capital city of Azerbaijan. At that time, while Azerbaijan was a republic of the former Soviet Union and under the Soviet regime, our lives were at least tolerable; discrimination from the ethnic Azerbaijanis was subtle.

In 1988, conditions changed quickly as the Soviet Union fell apart and Azerbaijan became an independent republic. Ethnic cleansing is the term that best describes the situation in that country as it struggled for a national identity. Even though generations of non-Azerbaijanis had lived peacefully in this country, many, primarily ethnic Armenians, became targets of anyone, including authorities. Ethnic Armenians are of the Armenian Orthodox Christian faith, while ethnic or native Azerbaijanis are Muslim. All Armenians were immediately subjected to harsh discrimination, and often brutalized to the point of death. Thousands died and hundreds of thousands were driven from Azerbaijan, winding up in any country that would accept them, most going to other former Soviet republics.

In early 1989, while at my place of employment, I was beaten then fired. Over the next several months, my family and I barricaded ourselves in our home to protect ourselves from attack. When we ventured out for food or other necessities, we were subject to threats of bodily harm. On occasion we actually were attacked and beaten, always with the message, "Get out of Azerbaijan!" Eventually they came to our home and set it on fire. We barely escaped with our lives, losing everything we had to the fire. We decided to run for the airport and, upon our arrival, friendly Russian military who was evacuating refugees assisted us in booking passage on a plane to Moscow.

Without money or the means of earning money, and without government-required documents or ID papers, we were forced to live in a refugee camp on the outskirts of Moscow. Even though we were thankful that we had escaped Baku with our lives, we were now in a miserable situation, living like animals in a zoo. We had no medical care available, there were no schools for our children, we were living on meager subsistence and we felt no sense of a future. We were again foreigners, as local Russians saw us as a threat to their livelihoods and a drain on their resources, preventing acceptance.

Authorities told us that we must work our own way out of the camp because they could do very little for us. Attempts to locate outside housing resulted in frustration as locals would not rent to us and often met us with open derision. Because we were not Russians by birth, we could not register and take required and necessary identity cards. We were in effect, stateless. Ventures onto the city streets would result in harassment by locals as well as by the police and militias. By late 1989, we decided that it might be better for us to leave this area, so my family and I moved to the Caucasus region of southwest Russia.

We settled into Stavropol where local Armenians who had come earlier provided us with a little assistance. To our horror, we discovered the local citizenry and authorities viewed us much the same as those near

Moscow. We couldn't obtain necessary registration papers there, so it was impossible to get employment. Life was again miserable for us. A local ethnic group known as Cossacks now threatened us. We had to be very careful on the streets as we were called vile names and threatened with bodily harm if we didn't leave their land. Eventually, my father and I borrowed some money from people in the local Armenian community and opened a little shoe repair shop where my father and I succeeded in making a small amount of money. But we were under constant threat as we were illegal immigrants (not registered) and therefore our little business was illegal. To prevent legal action, physical abuse or physical damage to our shop, we succumbed to offers of protection for a monthly fee, from both the Cossacks and the militia, which amounted to extortion. Life was so dreadful; we lived from day-to-day in constant fear.

In 1991, Cossacks burned our shop and told us that we must leave the area or they would return for us. We reported the incident to the militia but they appeared to have no interest in our compliant. Returning home, we were again attacked by the folks who had burned our store. We struggled to survive until 1992 then made the decision that we would move to Tashkent in the former Soviet Republic of Uzbekistan, where my sister lived. We put our future into this move, expecting to find a peaceful life.

Arriving in Tashkent with nothing but the clothes on our backs and a little pocket change, we attempted to start over again. Since we were not allowed to register for ID papers, we could not get employment and had to depend on the measly resources of my sister for a year and a half. Finally, after paying a bribe, (borrowed from my sister) I received my papers.

Uzbekistan is a Muslim country. As Christians, we were not free from our problems. With our papers, my father and I could now accept a job. So we took one that no one else wanted. It was very dirty but paid a small wage. However, we were treated as loathsome outsiders and were kept separated from fellow employees. We were constantly subjected to cruel remarks about our race and religion; we tried to clench our teeth, ignore their taunts and provocations and hope things might change for the better eventually.

In 1994, we borrowed money from relatives who had been fortunate enough to immigrate to the United States. We rented a small space from the Tashkent authorities, where we opened a small retail business. The space was run down and had been neglected for years, so we spent time and resources making it presentable. This effort required considerable bribes for approval from the authorities. Again, after a brief period, we were required to pay protection money to the local militia. However, in May, within months of opening the business, the same people who rented the property to us, told us to vacate. I insisted that I had signed a four-year lease and had spent my own time and money for renovation, so would not vacate. I was then told that there had been numerous complaints that as an Armenian, I was not a suitable person to operate a business in this town. I also learned there were local Uzbeks who wanted to take over my store property. I started receiving harassment by phone; unknown assailants assaulted my family and me in our apartment, always demanding that we leave town. My complaints to local authorities were to no avail.

In June of 1994, I was arrested in my store by an obvious set-up. While other customers were present, a customer offered to purchase items with US dollars, which is illegal in that country. I refused to accept them and insisted that the purchases be paid in Uzbek currency. About 10 people who identified themselves as tax authority officers, accused me of making illegal currency transactions. They immediately surrounded me. I was taken to jail where I was mistreated for two months

104

and forced to confess to the crime. With such confession, I was released on bail and went to trial in late August, receiving a guilty verdict and sentenced to two years in prison.

My family sold everything of value to obtain money for an attorney and to bribe the judge who suspended my sentence for two years on condition there would be no more problems. The corruption of this system took everything from my family, and the stress was so hard that I developed a congestive heart problem.

The president of Uzbekistan was a carryover from Soviet times, and even though he was making convincing positive political statements to the world about broad acceptance of minorities in his country, the contrary was actually happening. In order to assuage the anger and unrest of the people, the government chose to increase the power of its position by beginning a program of extreme nationalism, which resulted in race and religious discrimination. They promised a return of the country to its Muslim roots, which stirred up the majority population against minorities. Ethnic Uzbek's then began openly mistreating us and trying to force us to leave. The situation was rapidly becoming similar to the atrocities that we had endured in Baku.

Under these circumstances, some progressive Uzbeks formed an opposition party and opened it to minorities such as us. I now suspect it may have been a plan to identify minority leaders or those of stature so action could be taken against them individually. In mid-1997, hoping to work for legislative change, my father and I joined this Democratic Party and actually attended a few meetings. In December of that year, there was a meeting held near the Presidents Building and we were warned by the militia to leave the area. We didn't, so were attacked immediately by a group of Army Special Forces that forcefully removed us. In the process of doing it, they beat many of us unmercifully. My father and I received severe beatings with clubs and batons. Four days later, my father died of the injuries.

In August of 1998, I was arrested on the street and taken to the police station for interrogation. I was given no explanation for the arrest. I was interrogated about my work, my general attitudes about the government, and any political opinions. I was reminded that because of my previous currency exchange conviction, they could find any reason they wanted to charge me and then I would be put away for a long time. After this encounter, I was virtually under surveillance constantly by the local militia.

By September of 1999, after constant altercations involving a member of my family, we placed our two children with relatives and came to the United States to request asylum and pray constantly that God would favor us with an approval of our request.

To return to any of the former Soviet Union republics would be to accept a life of misery as abuse on the basis of nationality and religion is commonplace. In Russia, because of ongoing problems with the Republic of Chechnya, anyone with dark hair is automatically considered to be Chechen and is spit on, accosted on the street by police and local people alike, and denied life's essentials from authorities simply because they appear to be Chechen.

Margarita

I was born and spent all my life in the country of Azerbaijan, in the city of Baku. I am ethnic Armenian and of the Orthodox Christian faith. Azerbaijan is primarily Muslim.

In early 1989, the Soviet Union had collapsed and nationalism was strong in all the former Soviet Union republics. All ethnic Armenians living in Baku were killed or driven out of the country at risk of death. I fled the country of my birth to the neighboring country of

Armenia, thinking that since I was also Armenian, I would be welcomed with open arms. That was a mistake.

Upon arriving in Yerevan, the capital city of Armenia, my husband and I, and my daughter and her husband, were assigned living quarters at a refugee camp composed of dilapidated buildings that were on the verge of falling down. These buildings had no running water or heat. My husband has since died, but my daughter, son-in-law and I have lived in these quarters since, trying to obtain permanent housing and acclimate to the native culture with hope of becoming productive members and citizens of Armenia.

The people of this country have never accepted us even though we are ethnically the same, share the same religion and have most things in common. We have been constantly taunted and told by natives, "We never asked you to come here. If you aren't happy with what we've provided, then go back to where you came from."

Our living facilities weren't fit for cattle, much less humans. We asked not that anyone give us anything other than just a chance to make a living like others, and to live in peace with our neighbor, and God will prosper us. To remain in Armenia is to commit to a life with about as much as a prisoner might expect from life.

In 1999, and continuing into the year 2000, a local individual approached those of us living in the refugee camp and demanded that we leave immediately as he held the title to the property the camp was on, even though the camp and its dwellings were designated by the government as a official refugee camp, intended to house those refugees arriving from Baku. There was nowhere to go except the street. No one moved out, so this person took the case to a local court, and the judge ruled in his favor. Even though this decision was illegal under Armenian law, it seemed to no longer matter. It appears that this country has enough loopholes that a judge can make such a decision without fear of reprimand. It is usually influenced by bribes.

I eventually managed to get a low-paying job, one that no one else was interested in. I can go for months before getting any pay from it. If I want to keep the job, I don't complain. And as it offers a little hope to my family, I continue to go there every morning.

We are now living in makeshift shelters, wherever we can find scrap material, usually living on the ground like animals. The nights can get very cold when the winds blow off nearby Mt. Ararat. Time is measured from day to day, and we constantly pray that God will take care of us and deliver us from this terrible life.

Daily, we are subjected to open criticism, taunts and harassment, on the job, on the streets, and while shopping. My complaints to authorities result in them telling us to go to Azerbaijan as I have no rights here.

This testimony was submitted by Margarita O. who is currently still in Yerevan, Armenia. I maintain contact with a son who lives in Bellevue, Washington. He tells the author that the conditions are deteriorating for the folks still in Armenia while they wait for any country to accept them as refugees. Many submitted applications through the United Nations High Commission on Refugees as long as fourteen years ago. Most do not have any hope now of leaving.

Farida

My name is Farida. I was born in the city of Baku, in the country of Azerbaijan, a republic of the former Soviet Union. Azerbaijan is predominately Moslem even though a few Orthodox Christians, ethnic Armenians, may remain there today. To my knowledge, very, very few ethnic Azerbaijan people ever become Christians. I was an exception.

The first information that I remember receiving about God came through my grandmother even though she cautioned me to never make the mistake of discussing it with anyone, not even best friends. At this time in the Soviet Union, all religious books were forbidden. If found, they were confiscated and destroyed. People could easily disappear, and did, for simply mentioning the Lord. Grandma continued to teach me from the Bible about the Lord's teaching and biblical principles, but we maintained our silence outside the home.

I accepted Jesus as my Savior in 1980, and even though I was attending school for advanced musicians, I shared my testimony with no one. I would have been immediately discharged.

Later, I met a young man who, I thought, shared my life's goals, I shared my faith with him before we were married and he reacted very negatively. Because we shared strong musical talent and worked very well together as a team, after some consideration he decided he would just work around the Christian "thing" and I, thinking he will eventually accept it for himself, proceeded with marriage plans.

Our marriage became a struggle because he embraced his Moslem belief, or at least was afraid to leave it because of a backlash from his Moslem family and the community. We were very visible in the community as we often performed in concerts together. Eventually, this worked against us.

Even though I went to great lengths to hide my relationship with the Lord, word that I was a Christian increasingly spread through the community, and my husband received very harsh criticism about being married to me. It escalated to the point where he was even receiving threats, so he slowly started distancing himself from me.

My Mother died in 1987 when I gave birth to my youngest son. My husband left us two months later. Two years later, we were divorced without any attempt at reconciliation.

In 1990, I decided that I would be baptized in water as our Lord was. I'm not sure how someone else learned about my decision, but a few days later I was fired from my job. As I was driving home from my job, I was involved in a very serious accident. I learned later that my car had been tampered with. It was only the Lord's hand on my life that prevented me from being killed.

Early in 1991, I was baptized in an Orthodox Church because no other churches officially existed in Baku. My life changed abruptly. Word spread very quickly about my baptism.

Since I had been a well-known jazz singer, and my ex-husband was not only a famous musician but a violinist and the conductor of the State Chamber Orchestra, the news that I had become a baptized Christian spread like wildfire. Within a few days I was approached by a journalist from a popular newspaper requesting an interview. I refused. To my knowledge, only two very close friends knew of my relationship with the Lord. I will never know how it became common knowledge so fast. Anyway, when taped concerts were broadcast on TV, scenes where I was singing were deleted. During my last concert in 1995, my microphone was switched off so I could not contribute.

In October, 1995, my oldest son was returning home from school when he was accosted and chased home by a group of other children. He was called many terrible words and told it was because he was a Christian. The same thing happened the following May.

I was a teacher's aide at the school where my children attended for four years. Toward the end, I was reprimanded for having the children in my class study Scripture verses and for singing psalms with them. I also celebrated Christian holidays with them. As a result, I was forced out of my job.

Class members would then prevent my own children from entering the classroom, and hassle them about being Christians. Eventually, they were coming home practically every day with injuries from being beaten up by older children or groups of kids. No teacher or administrator ventured to protect or help them.

During the fifth grade, my oldest son was taken out of the school, and I home schooled him because of the abuse. Even then, other children would visit him only to return to class the next day and contribute to classroom discussions about how we lived. Sometimes children would cry out, "Your mother is a Christian. You are a Christian family. You have no Father. You are beggars."

At one class discussion a teacher produced a newspaper for the pupils showing pictures of my ex-husband and exclaiming, "Here is your father's picture. He is a famous Azeri musician."

I eventually transferred them into a home school operated by a private family.

When visiting a government office for any reason, employees usually ignored me or spat out things like "Betrayer" to me.

In July, 1992, I got a private job to translate some materials for an International Conference on Science, which was to be held in Baku. In this position, I worked with a famous journalist who was also a poet and editor-in-chief of a very popular newspaper in Baku.

One evening, we had been working about three hours at my place when the doorbell rang. I asked from inside, "Who is it?" since I was not expecting anyone and whoever was ringing the doorbell was doing it forcefully.

"Police," was the response, and I could tell from the voices that there must be several.

I said that I would not open the door unless I first called my neighbor to my place as a witness to whatever might be said, or happen, and began to frantically dial my neighbor's number. Police then said they would break my door down and were preparing to do so as I realized that my neighbor was not answering the phone.

Then the Journalist who was with me said, "Don't be afraid," and opened the door himself. About eight or nine policemen entered my home. They were very harsh and rough mannered as they searched my entire home, even checking through the papers that I had been working on. They did find a big iron plaque of Jesus on the cross on my bedroom wall and became so upset that they frightened my children, who began crying.

The commander took my domestic passport and said, "Are you that popular Christian singer?" as he attempted to put my passport into his pocket. (In my Country, you can do nothing without a domestic passport. It is like a national identity card.)

The Journalist, who up to this moment had been listening in silence, now approached the commander and introduced himself and showed his credentials. He then produced a pen and paper and quickly suggested that he would like to do a story in his paper about this event so "Please give me some details starting with your name."

The commander grew red in the face and stammered, "Excuse us, there has been a mistake. We do not want to disturb you. Please continue your work. We are looking for a criminal who lives in this area."

He apologized several times and returned my passport before leaving. I can't imagine what would have happened had I been alone. I believe with all my heart that the Lord protected me. After that incident, it was difficult for me to answer the doorbell without some concern.

Many of my neighbors often suggested that I leave the country, saying, "Since you are a Christian, you must leave Azerbaijan and give your home to someone else. Don't you understand that you are not wanted here?"

Once, a neighbor who I was not acquainted with, came to me and offered a small amount of money to buy my apartment. He had a nephew who was about to marry and needed an apartment. Of course, I declined his offer. He was upset and said; "You had better consider my offer while I am offering money. Don't forget, I can come back and throw you out and there would be no money."

I didn't answer, just turned away.

The next day, his wife came to my apartment demanding that I vacate my place. Before I could respond, she proceeded to hit me on the head and back. I fell back into the room and she followed where she noticed my children. She grabbed the oldest by the head and rammed his head against the wall. She then turned to the youngest and hit him hard enough to knock him out of his chair.

With all my strength, I grabbed her by her dress and literally threw her into another room and slammed and locked the door leading into that room. Another neighbor woman, hearing all the commotion, came and removed the lady from my home and tried to calm her as they were leaving.

It was times like these when I could do nothing but rest in the assurance that the Lord loved me and would take care of me and my children.

In 1996, I obtained a job at the Western University in Baku. Eleven days later I lost it when staff members discovered that I was a Christian. Apparently, my students informed them. I didn't realize that the principal had been a former KGB employee when I took the job.

I was not even told that I had been dismissed. I came to class every day but could not locate my students because staff changed their classroom every day without informing me. I asked to talk with the principal but he refused. When I inquired of his secretary, "What is wrong?" She replied, "We have a lot of good literature books in English available. It's not necessary to use the Bible."

My name had been removed from the employee's list.

Another time, my children and I were on a trolley, going to visit my father in another part of town. Perhaps halfway there, a couple of ladies recognized me and began crying out loudly, "She is a friend of Armenians! She is a

Christian and she wants to spread Christianity all over Azerbaijan!"

Other passengers rushed to us and began beating us, when one man helped us escape from the trolley and we finished the trip by walking to our destination. Again, I believe it was the hand of the Lord as serious injury could have happened to us had not the man helped.

In 1997, while leaving my place of employment, I found I must pass through a group of mostly young people. I felt some apprehension but shrugged it off. As I passed these people, they began throwing stones at me while shouting derogatory remarks and chanting things about me being a Christian. I ran back to my place of work and waited for the thugs to leave before leaving for home again. I also changed my place of employment to evade this area.

On a warm Sunday morning, my children and I had made our way to a plaza located in the center of town. I was wearing a nice white suit, probably the best outfit that I owned at the time. There was an open fruit market nearby and employees and customers of this market started throwing tomatoes at me. Tomatoes would completely ruin my suit. They were yelling at me things like, "Shame on you! Converted!"

In February 1998, I was returning from work with a heavy bag full of items in each hand. Suddenly a man jumped up to me and yelled into my face, "Dammed Christian!"

He was in a rage. He beat me on the head several times. I couldn't run because of the heavy bags. He took one of the bags from me and hit me on the back with it then emptied its contents on the ground saying, "I could strangle you, you dammed Christian!" before leaving.

Because I could speak several languages fluently, including English, I usually obtained jobs at respectable educational establishments. In all cases, as soon as it was learned that I was a Christian, I lost those jobs.

I once worked at the Institute of Foreign Languages in

Baku. While there, a lab assistant was assigned to follow me everywhere, and she did, constantly. When providing lessons to students, she would stand behind a door to monitor class discussions while out of sight. They knew that, given an opportunity, I would share Scripture, including Psalms and Proverbs, with my students.

One evening, the chief of the English Lexis Chair called me into his office and announced that I was fired. My students rallied around me this time with petitions to the principal to let me continue until the semester finished. As soon as the students passed their exams, I was out of a job again.

Not long after, someone painted a large cross on my front door, which required that I repaint the whole door.

While I was with my children out for a walk in December of 1999, someone set my apartment on fire. The local fire brigade put it out before my place was extensively damaged, but the fire brigade leader told me that it obviously was set and was not accidental.

I was receiving threatening calls at all hours of the day by now. I was living in constant fear.

My relatives wanted nothing to do with the children and me. In fact, they had cut themselves off from us, so I never ask them for help. I think they probably don't even know that I am now in the United States.

Earlier, 1992, I began attending a local fellowship organized by Christians sent to Baku from Westminster Chapel in Seattle, Washington, for the purpose of helping Christians there. Their little work in Baku is known as Greater Grace. The last year or two that I lived in Baku, I opened my home to these wonderful Christian people for Bible study and fellowship. The Lord helped me compose music to many Scriptures, including some of the Psalms. I eventually became a composer of Christian music.

These folks from Seattle whom I had become acquainted with also knew of many of my problems and encouraged me to believe God for a safe passage to the

United States where I can worship the Lord and raise my children in freedom. I decided to flee to the United States with my children, where many of those Christian friends whom I knew in Baku have returned home, and we now see each other often.

Farida is now living in the Seattle area of Washington State. She is a valuable member of her church, assisting with Sunday school and teaching English to elderly and new immigrants attending her church. She leaps at any opportunity to share her faith as well as her music.

Eduard

I am an Armenian Christian, born in the City of Baku, Azerbaijan to ethnic Armenian parents who were also Christians.

Azerbaijan is a Country dominated by the Moslem religion and while there are a few in that religion who might tolerate other religions, the vast majority does not. This majority will sanction, if not participate in persecution of non-Moslems. Typically, this group is very hostel to Christians. Until the breakup of the former Soviet Union, harassment was generally at a minimum afterwards it came quick and was very severe.

In early 1989, Christians became the target of individuals as well as roving bands that beat, injured and killed Christians at will. An ultimatum was announced to all Christians living the Country to leave within three hours or they would be imprisoned and/or killed.

I, along with several hundred thousand other Christians left immediately with only the few belongings that we could get into a suitcase. Most fled to Russia including my wife and I where we lived as refugees for three years before being allowed to come to America to visit a daughter who also was one of those fleeing Baku but had been granted refugee status in the United States with her family.

While in Russia, we barely existed. The Russian

government's resources were inadequate to accommodate a large influx of refugees from another Country so we lived wherever we could find something to crawl into and managed to scrounge up a meager existence. Sometimes, we went days without adequate food. Locals resented our presence in their Communities since most folks were having a tough time making ends meet, and worried that we only burdened their ability to survive.

I had managed to develop one of the best restaurants in the City of Baku as well as had a very nice home and lived a prosperous life. There had never been any previous problems. I always tried to treat everyone equally and hospitality was extended to everyone who visited my place of business. I have since learned that my property was sized and my home was burned to the ground as well as the property of others who fled.

I did not doubt for one moment the original threat nor do I doubt at this time that if I returned to my Country, I would be immediately put in prison and or killed quickly. Refugees who did not leave immediately, bring out eyewitness accounts of the tens of thousands of ethnic Armenians (all are of the Christian faith, some more, some less) who were slaughtered openly on the streets, then piled, soaked with gasoline and burned, even while many were still alive. Authorities either chose to do nothing or could not do anything. It is my hope that in the future, the magnitude of this genocide becomes open knowledge to other people of the world that they might know of these atrocities. It is only by the grace of God that my wife and I, or for that matter, any one of Armenian descent, managed to escape without bodily harm.

The neighboring Country of Armenia will not accept those ethnic Armenians born in Azerbaijan either because they are not citizens. They are considered Azerbaijani and would consume too many of that Country's resources. Some did infiltrate into Armenian but to this day, they are considered foreigners and live a terrible life in refugee camps.

Zhanya

"Dear friends, brothers and sisters in the Lord! I, an unworthy sinner, would like to tell you about the great mercy of God which I experienced in my life," is the way Evgenia (Zhanya, for short) likes to start her testimony. She has shared God's mercy with many Church congregations, as well as individuals throughout the former Soviet Union.

As told by her, the story begins in the Country of the Ukraine, in 1941. Her Father had died and she, the oldest of the children, was expected to assume responsibility for helping her mother raise the other children. At first, this responsibility was limited to taking the cow to the pasture and most of the household chores. Later, she was pressed into a labor pool at the local kolkhoz or collective farm.

Here, she was assigned the task of taking care of 2½ hectares (6.2 acres) of sugar beets. Her duties included basic farm labor, planting, hoeing, pulling weeds, as well as participating in harvest activities. This was very strenuous work and especially for Zanya, since she was a small person anyway. She was often in the fields during summer storms as well as winter cold. Sometimes, the snows of autumn were falling as she harvested her share of sugar beets, yet she was expected to dig them out of the ground and get them to the shed by herself. These farms were not mechanized so most of the activity was strictly manual labor and very hard.

It was also here, working in the fields, that she became aware that something was wrong with her physically. At first, her hands and joints began to hurt as if she was arthritic. In no time, she was in almost constant pain.

Her superiors, aware of her difficulties in the fields, rearranged her farm duties so she now found herself milking cows. She was assigned the task of taking care of

15 cows and duties included milking them 3 times a day. If one of the other employees became sick, she was pressed into milking the cows for the ill employee as well. Again, it was all manual, no milking machines as modern American farms have.

Zanya endured this job for about a year before her pain increased to the point where she couldn't even sleep at nights. So, she was reassigned again. This time, it was feeding cattle, which required, lifting heavy bales of hay and sacks of grain. Her spine began to hurt and to deform, twisting her back into an unnatural position. Aggravated by the hard work, a hump began to form on her back. Her legs hurt so bad, it was impossible to walk without crutches, so for the next 2 years, she used crutches to walk to work and perform her duties.

After the two years with crutches, if was obvious to everybody that she was unable to perform even menial tasks. She was confined to her bed at her mother's home.

Not long after, she was admitted to the Regional Hospital where she lay, twisted and deformed. Her knees were pressed up against her breastbone until it became very difficult to even breathe.

To continue in Zhanya's own words; "I remained for almost the entire period of four years and seven months on one side, without any change in my position, unable to raise my hands and could only move my fingers slightly." She continues, "My ribs, on the side on which I always lay, began to be forced inwards and the hump on my back increased." Doctors indicated they believed the hump formed because hard work had damaged her spine.

"I lay a long time in the regional hospital." The doctors tried everything within their power to help, but her condition steadily deteriorated. The decision was made to send her to the Provincial Hospital at Rivne, the Ukraine, where she remained as a patient for approximately 1 year. Her condition seemed to continue to worsen.

Finally, these doctors concluded that Zhanya must go

to the Medical Research Institute at Kiev, where it was possible to receive Surgery to correct her spine. After a thorough examination by the chief medical specialist, it was determined that it was too late for surgery. The condition was not correctable. She was sent home.

There was no sense in returning to Kiev so her Mother thought the Hospital at L'viv might be able to do something? Inquiries were sent there, but, a few days later, word came back from L'viv, "There is nothing that we can do for her."

At this time, she was in the Provincial Hospital in Rivne, two weeks after the Kiev and L'viv rejection, the doctor came into her room and said, "Zhanya, we are going to send you back to the Regional Hospital. They will also discharge you. We want you to go home to recuperate from all the injections that you have received and afterwards, we will re-admit you here again."

"I didn't say anything" says Zhanya, "It was obvious to me that they had given up on me and were eager to be rid of me. Try to imagine, if you can, what it was like to lay motionless like a log. I remember clearly the thought that crossed my mind. Oh, my dear mother, how is she going to look after me? She's already too old and her own health is poor. She won't be able to lift me up or turn me over to change the linen or to care for me even though my weight had now dipped to about 55 lbs. I thought, "May the will of God come to pass, what will be, must be, I put my life in His hands."

Zanya was discharged from the provincial hospital with words "incurable" on her records. She was then taken back to the Regional hospital where she remained for several months. Even with a special diet, she lost her appetite and was fed intravenously. Her condition slowly deteriorated so it was apparent to the hospital staff that she would die. The decision was made to send her home to die with her family and friends.

She remembers whispered instructions to the

ambulance driver who delivered her home, "Drive her home quickly so that you can get her home alive." A doctor accompanied her in the ambulance, but with her body racked in pain and so thirsty, she felt her lips were parched and trying to cry out, yet she was largely ignored. Even though it was only a fifteen-mile trip home, it was a nightmare. Arriving home, Zhanya was barely alive.

"My mother, realizing I was dying, covered my body and then fell to her knees, weeping and praying, beside my bedside. Friends, hearing that I had come home, stopped by to check on me but, seeing my Mother on her knees praying, joined her," Says Zhanya. "Glory to God! I believe He heard their prayers because, I seem to feel strength entering my body." As word spread around the village, that she had come home to die, many people came to bid their respects and pray with her as well encourage her Mother since she had also suffered so much during these long years, feeling so helpless as she watched her daughter become crippled, twisted, hump-backed, and bald. "Now, I was home, so my life just became more complicated," Zhanya shares.

One particular day, while friends were visiting, one Christian brother, with head bowed, approached her bed and said, "Zhanya, don't be upset. We can see that the Lord will be soon taking you home. We're wondering if perhaps, you might have some last words for us."

She replied in a whisper, "We know that we are the temple of the living God and if the Holy Spirit lives in us and we are His temple, then we ought to feel Him within our hearts, because it is written, that signs shall follow them that believe!" Immediately, "I was filled with the Holy Spirit and began to sing very loudly in the Spirit. When all my friends saw this happen, feeling God's presence, they fell to their knees and began to praise and worship the Lord. As they were praying, the Holy Spirit began to speak to me and said," "You will not die until you see my glory, here upon the earth, with your own eyes."

After this experience, even though she was still paralyzed, Zhanya could sing and voice praises to God for his goodness and she did this often and as loud as she could.

Sometime later, while friends were visiting and praying with her, Zhanya says, the Lord spoke to my heart and said, "Don't you know why they released you from the hospital? The doctors believed you incurable. But, I am Christ, the One who suffered for you. I am He who asked the Father to leave you among the living. I am the One who has the power and authority to put new life in your body."

On many discussions, her mother, trying to encourage her, would say, "Maybe it will happen exactly as it was said. The Lord will heal you and people will run to see you as though they would run to see a miracle. You've heard of the great miracles the Lord is doing in America through Katherine Kuhlman. Maybe the Lord will have mercy on you and will do a great miracle for you." "I didn't realize it then, but looking back, I now understand that optimism was building in my heart as I began to believe that God was about to do something very special for me."

Approximately three years passed after she was released from the hospital. Doctors were visiting her at home one day when she asks, "Would you please take me back to the hospital so my Mother can be relieved of the burden of caring for me." One of the doctors replied, "Zanya, don't be angry with us but, you know very well that we are unable to cure you. There is no cure for you whatsoever. So, you may as well rest here until..."

Zanya interrupted, "No, I will not die! I believe the Lord is powerful and He will heal me and raise me up from this bed."

A few weeks later, she now exclaims, "Praise the Lord! It happened, He was merciful to me. Wednesday, the 19th of July 1978, the Lord did a great miracle for me. The Lord healed me. He raised me from my bed of affliction.

122

Glory to God! Hallelujah!"

She recalls, "On Tuesday evening, I awoke around midnight. I felt a deep joy welling up within my soul and I felt like praying. When morning dawned and the sunlight began to fill the house, my soul was suddenly overwhelmed with joy and beautiful emotions, which were impossible to describe. I had never experienced such emotions in all my life. It seemed like I was waiting for something unusual to happen, full of expectations. Finally, because I was unable to contain my joy any longer, I burst out singing with a loud voice. It seems to me at the time that God was about to bring me home."

Later, the same day, several Christian brothers were praying for her when one asked, "Do you believe that the Lord will heal you now and that you will be able to stand up from your bed?" Zanya shouted, "I believe! I believe! Please pray for me." He immediately laid his hand on her as they all prayed. Suddenly, "there were sounds of crackling coming from the bones in my arms and legs. Immediately, my arms straightened out and stretched upwards, my legs moved downward and straightened out. I jumped from my bed and began to cry out praises to the Lord, Glory to God! The Lord has healed me! Glory to God! Glory to God! Hallelujah!"

When her Mother saw her standing, she came to her on her knees and with her face still turned to the floor, worshiped God. A few moments later, she raised her self slightly and clasped Zhanya's legs to her breast with her arms and let her motherly tears flow. Later, she examined Zhanya for some evidence of the hump but couldn't even find a trace.

For days, there was only rejoicing in their home for God's goodness and mercy.

Word of what God had done for Zhanya spread quickly throughout the village since all knew about her condition and that she had been ill for years. Crowds pushed into their home as people came from far and near to see the miracle that God had performed. This news had such an effect on the village that no one went to work from that Wednesday till Monday at the local kolkhoz. Most were content to celebrate and acknowledge this miracle as though it were a great holy event. As always, Zhanya never tired of telling of the mercy and goodness of our Lord, Savior and Healer.

The doctors who had worked with Zhanya for many years summoned her to the hospital so they might examine her. At the exam, they were puzzled and mystified, but verified her complete healing and ask her to give a complete account at a staff meeting. She immediately accepted.

Zanya says, "My story began with Gethsemane and lasted for the next few hours. I feel the Lord Himself had ordered that opportunity because it was such a perfect one." After listening to her story, the doctors agreed that, "It is true. This has been done by some greater power and, truly, God is alive because this is certainly none of our work." As the interview concluded, Zhanya shares, "I wanted so much to fall on my knees there among the doctors and worship the Lord. I thank my Lord that He gave me the strength and wisdom to testify and be a witness for my beloved Jesus."

Returning home, Zhanya was surprised to find many people waiting for her. All were trying to see her healed body or touch or congratulate. Some had been waiting at her place for two days.

This soul-stirring revival among the people and the subsequent conversion of many to the Lord disturbed the KGB and they decided to change the Bus route so it no longer went near Zhanya's house. Still the people came. They would walk, ride bicycles or come by car, but they came to observe the miracle that the Lord had performed.

About two weeks later, she was forced to submit to a "health check" at the local medical clinic in the city of Ostrow by local communist authorities. "During the so-called health check, three men, dressed in white doctors robes approached my bed and made an attempt to seize me saying they were intending to kill me to shut up my testimony." Other patients in the room began to yell and cause a lot of excitement so the three men dropped her and ran away. As they ran, they threw a threat back at her, saying, "If you continue to tell people that God healed you, we will return and kill you."

In Kiev, the Ukraine, in October, 1979, "I was attending a gathering of Christians, (it was considered illegal to gather without a permit for religious reasons, so we were meeting in a wooded area) and had shared my testimony of how God had healed me when the police came. They surrounded the whole group and tried to catch me to arrest me but many of the other believers formed a tight crowd around me and managed to keep the police occupied while I slipped away with friends and escaped the area."

During 1980, I was summoned to the local KGB office several times. When I didn't appear voluntarily, agents would actually come and forcefully take me to their office. They tried everything to keep me from speaking about God healing me. In all cases I was questioned extensively, sometimes I was beaten. I was told that if I continued to talk about God, I would be arrested and put in prison where I would never see the light of day again. I told them, "I will not be quite about what God had done for me and will speak about it as long as God gives me breath."

May 1980, an ambulance with doctors, KGB agents, and a hypnotist arrived at my house and brought a stretcher into my home. They declared, "they wanted to hypnotize me and take me to the hospital on the stretcher." I fully believe they wanted to have me disappear because of what I was telling people about my healing. Neighbors saw the ambulance and came to my house to see what was wrong. During the time when communists controlled my country, they never liked to do things in the open. Their method was usually shrouded in secrecy so when neighbors became aware of what was happening they (the KGB) lost interest and left without me.

December, 1980: I was told by friends that the police, along with the KGB, were developing a plan to make me disappear so at their encouraging, I decided to go into hiding for the time being. It was a fearful time for me. I left all my family and close friends and with the help of caring Christian brothers and sisters, began a frightful trip that ended in Frunze, Kyrgyzstan, in the South of the former Soviet Union.

I had traveled about 2,000 miles away from the life that I had known in the Ukraine. However, I am convinced that God was in this move and had granted divine intervention because I later learned that the KGB had indeed come to my home looking for me. I remained in Frunze for the next two years but it was a fearful time. Kyrgyzstan is predominantly Moslem so I had to take additional precautions and trust in Him for opportunities to share, as I was aware that locals could delight in revealing my whereabouts to authorities. I contributed considerable effort to prevent the KGB from finding out that I was in that area.

January 1982, local believers learned that KGB had located me and were making plans to arrest me. I heard about it just minutes before they arrived at the place where I had been staying, barely enough time to grab a few things and flee town.

With the help of believers, I made my way to Nerva, Estonia, which was in the northwestern part of the former Soviet Union. This trip was again, over 2,000 miles and several hundred miles from my home in the Ukraine.

I lived here for about 5 years in semi seclusion, feeling checked by the Lord about sharing my testimony. I believed that He would again give an opportunity but for the time being, I was just to lay low.

In January of 1988, The Lord blessed me with a fine husband. I was married to Mykola K. and we moved back to Glinsk, (Mykola's hometown) in the Ukraine. For a couple of years, we were generally free of persecution. We traveled together, telling everyone about what God had done for me. After several years, in which I had not shared my testimony, it was such a relief and blessing to be able to do so again, and God opened the hearts of people anywhere we had the opportunity to share.

Even though the Soviet Union had essentially fell apart by the middle of 1993, persecution began again. There were many people who still had strong sympathies for the communist philosophies.

We were at an Evangelical services in Vinnitsa, Ukraine. I was sharing my testimony when a person who belonged to the communist party, came onto the platform and began shouting and threatening me. I tried to ignore him so he pulled the plug on the microphone. He then attempted to grab me but there were others on the platform so they formed a human shield for me. Police were nearby but when they were asked to help, they refused to get involved. After verbal threats against my life, he angrily left the service. There were threats again throughout the rest of 1993. We would hear that there were individuals that were unhappy about us sharing our testimony and the word of God and various times, we would receive word that we would be killed.

Understand that the freedom that exists in Eastern Europe today is a freedom that comes when no one is in charge. It's the freedom that occurs in chaos. You can do what you like as long as it doesn't offend someone else. If it does offend someone, they may cause bodily harm or even kill you and the authorities rarely show proper attention. In many cases, the authorities are participants in the incidence. Organized Criminals control large parts of the Country and they influence and/or, are local authorities. It can be difficult to find someone who you can trust.

In June of 1994, while visiting a family in Machaka, Ukraine, we were warned by them, the word on the street was that we would be killed. We were urged to leave the Ukraine and never return, as it was unsafe for our family to remain there. We were told the local MAFIA and ex-communist individuals were upset about our testimony and preaching God's word and that they intended to have us killed. In August and September, warning again came from different friends that authorities were developing plans to have us killed in a manner where there would be no trace of us left for anyone to ever know what happened.

1994 was a year of traveling and sharing our testimony, but we were always careful to keep a lot of people around us all the time. We avoided situations where we would be alone as well as isolated or deserted places and was especially careful about revealing the place where we were staying.

Threats were becoming common and we never failed to take them seriously. Even though anxiety was building within my family as well as with friends who worried about us, I never doubted that God would open a door and provide an avenue of escape for us.

Early 1995, God, in His providence, provided an opportunity for my husband, my son, and I, to travel to the Puget Sound region of Washington State, located in the Pacific Northwest of the United States. While visiting, we were introduced to an American, who assisted us with the submittal of applications for Religious Asylum and about two months later, (I'm told that this type application can take as long as 7 or 8 years and rarely under a year, but the Lord came through for us again) they were approved and we were granted permanent residence status, the first step in eventually becoming citizens of the United States.

Today, my family and I reside in Kent, Washington. We

THE GOD THAT DOES NOT FAIL

feel blessed by God and are grateful to the people and the government of the United States for extending hospitality and safety to us. Mykola is a Pastor of a local Ukrainian Pentecostal Church with about 500 people in attendance every week.

Looking back, I can only marvel at God's love and influence on my life as well as my family. What a great God we serve!

Looking forward, I am excited about what I know God has planned for our future. I don't know the details and don't need to know them. That's His call, but I know it will be exciting as He allows us to work in the local immigrant community.

I've come a long way from that farm setting in the Ukraine. During the long days of the illness, I didn't look beyond the next day. I could have never imagined that He would eventually heal me so completely and give me a fine husband and family. I know that He did because He knew me even before I was born and knows exactly how my life will play itself out.

Never in my wildest dreams did I ever imagine He would lead me all the way to America. I now know that had it not been for the persecution we suffered there, and because it acted as a catalyst to push us here, everything worked out as He willed. It's because of what He has done for us in the past, I look forward with anticipation to what I know He has planned for our future. Nothing in the world can be as exciting and fulfilling as loving and serving the Lord.

(Provided by Zhanya P.)

Vadim

I am a Pentecostal Christian from the country of the Ukraine, a former Republic of the Soviet Union.

I surrendered my heart to the Lord Jesus Christ in 1984 when I was sixteen years old. Shortly after, while attending a Bible study group of what was then called the underground Church, Police interrupted the meeting and questioned every one. Some were arrested and taken to the Police station. Since I was only sixteen, they checked my ID and gave me a warning that next time, I would be arrested. Interrogation and harassment of group meetings that I attended continued until the fall of the Communist government, then was continued by local organized crime officials.

In 1984, I attempted to register in the college at Alchevsk, Ukraine, but was denied admission because of a Police record indicating I was involved with activity associated with a local Christian group.

In 1985, In the City of Bryansk, I was arrested and charged with unlawful assembly as I attended a Christian service. I was fined and released with a reprimand. My employer was notified that I now have a criminal record and as a result, discrimination began on the job and continued until I was fired. Follow employees were assigned to watch me and report back to superiors my conduct indicating that I was a Christian.

In late 1985, I was drafted into the Soviet Army. There was no recourse, no alternative service for those opposed to carrying a weapon as I was, or anything. For two years, I was subjected to continuous harassment and deprivation of amenities afforded non-Christians.

On one occasion, an officer confiscated my Bible and destroyed it in view of fellow soldiers while they ridiculed me for being a Christian. Several times, in an attempt to get me to recant Christianity, I was subjected to several days at a time to isolation in unheated rooms and with no food.

In 1988, while attending as an observer, a water baptism for new converts, Communist or common thugs gathered at our service and started shoving people into the water. It was an obvious attempt to provoke trouble so the Police, who was also present, could get involved. I was trying to rescue people from the water when Police arrested me and falsely charged me with fighting.

Since the breakup of the Soviet Union, there appears to be a sense of freedom of religion but in the reality, those people who were in charge before the fall are still in charge and continue to control important positions in the community. They are in position to deny basic amenities to Christians (and do) that don't go along with their ideas or political ideologies. They have a strangle hold on jobs, housing and education.

I neglected to tell authorities that I was a Christian in 1990 when I applied for a job on a fishing boat. When the crew found out later, the political Officer on the boat insisted that I must spy on fellow crewmen and report back to him. I declined, so problems again plagued me. I was singled out and relegated to menial tasks or undesirable jobs like working in the hole or scrubbing the deck. I had no chance of achieving a promotion and because Christians were considered a security risk, they could not work on boats that would be entering another Countries territorial waters. When I was on a boat that was about to enter those waters, I was transferred back to Russia to await another boat to go out with.

In March of 1993 in Petropavlovsk, Kamchatka, Russia, local organized criminals, sometimes called MAFIA, burned cars belonging to Christians. They also wrote anti-Christian slogans on building and fences and generally threatened the Christians in this area. The authorities do not control these people and if the authorities aren't supporting them directly, they don't do anything to protect the Christians. Christians become targets, since they are philosophically opposed to their lawlessness and/or at least non- supportive.
(Provided by Vadim K.)

Mariya
I have been a member of a Pentecostal Church all my life. As long as I can remember, my family has been

discriminated against because we were Christians. Many times, our family had to hide in forests or secretly in homes unknown to would be intruders to worship God and when discovered, the Police would come resulting in fines for my Father followed by threats to send him to prison and take his children away if the activity continued. While in school, I was a diligent student, but I always received lower grades because I refused to join the young Pioneers or later, the Consomoles, both local communist youth organizations designed to focus and indoctrinate young people on the Communist Party mandate.

As a Christian I have accepted the fact that Jesus Christ died on the cross for the forgiveness of my sins and I have a duty to Him to share that information with others who might have an interest. It is to that end that I set my goal in life and exercise my considerable effort.

For three and a half years, I traveled with a group of youth, singing and expressing our faith in the Lord Jesus Christ. Increasingly, ex-communist and members of local criminals came against us to the point that weekly, members of our group including myself, were receiving direct threats of bodily harm and/or death. Toward the end, we never held a meeting without communist disrupting it. When Police were summoned, they either did not respond or would not get involved.

May 1992: While holding a meeting in the City of Kuznetsova, Ukraine. I was told by people disrupting the service that I would be killed after the service. Needless to say, I left immediately but secretly with a group of friends packed closely around me. I was very fearful at the time.

September: In a small Village near Armyansk, Ukraine, a group of communists disrupted the service and eventually created a fight involving a lot of people. They tried to size us to harm us, but people in the crowd prevented them. Police were called but they would not come. We carefully circumnavigated the scene to leave the area unharmed.

August 1994: In Feodosia, Ukraine, the authorities informed us that we had three days to leave the City or we could come into real legal trouble and/or other kinds of trouble as our religious philosophies were not wanted in the area. Two days later, a couple of the girls and the leader of our group were giving out Bibles when they were grabbed and beaten very badly. Again, Police were asked to help and provide protection. They informed us that they could not and would not. They said "it was not their job to protect Christians." We could not get the emergency medical technicians to respond with medical assistance either.

The ex-communist is convinced that their party will regain control of the former Soviet Union and then they can crush Christianity again. There is no democracy or freedom of Religion in Ukraine today. What is passed off as freedom is actuality chaos. Who has the power and/or position can do most anything he wants as long as he doesn't offend someone who has more power or position than himself. There are no constitutional rights and/or there is no attempt to protect your basic civil or human rights. It's sort of every man for himself. It's a very dangerous situation. People are killed and/or disappear often and the authorities make only a token effort to solve the cases. I don't know of any that has produced any arrest.

To return to the Ukraine today, I would have to live in constant fear as threats of bodily harm will resume as well as random acts of vandalism against my property. I cannot expect to get a job because they are controlled by people who are or were communist sympathizers or common criminals. They don't give jobs to Christians because of the philosophical differences.

Mariya K. (2-13-95)

Boris

Boris shared the following testimony with me in 1996. I have known Boris and members of his extended family since they arrived in the United States in the early Nineties, and have spent some time with him, attempting to assist him with getting other members of his family out of Moldova, a Country of the former Soviet Union. I have written numerous letters to various government officials for him, as well as his family.

I present his testimony in his own words, changes added only where clarification is required.

I, Nazarchuk G. was born and raised in a family of Baptist Christians. My parents as well as my grandparents on both my Mother and father's side were Christians. All their lives they believed in God and accepted His son, Jesus Christ as their personal Savior and the Savior of the world.

I would like to describe the problems my family encountered serving God in the former Soviet Union.

Starting with my grandparent's generation, continuing through my parents and even until now, Christians have been persecuted. They did not have possibilities to attend church services freely. They had to meet in secret places, and when authorities found out about the place of the meeting, they would come and scatter the people, take the Word of God from them, and in many cases, arrest them for illegal assembly.

My parents were arrested during services and retained by the police repeatedly. My father was a Minister and a choir director. Authorities frequently tried to force him to deny God, threatening to take the children from him. This was a prime concern since they often took Children from their parents as a means of preventing the children from being raised and taught about God. There were records and accounts of many children being taken from their parents and placed in orphanages. My father was very afraid of this.

They held their meetings in secret, in a narrow circle of homes. At school, we were taught that God does not exist. Our classmates teased us. The teachers despised us and did not trust us. In 1966, I married Eugenia P. My wife's father was a Christian, too. He was a member of Sabbath Pentecostal Church. My wife was attending the church also. This church has gone through a severe persecution. The authorities were coming to the meetings of the Sabbath Evangelical Pentecostal Christians, taking their identity papers, taking pictures, telling employers so that many were fired from their jobs. Some had to work at the lowest paying jobs, no one could profess his faith freely. Once they filmed the believers at the meeting and edited the videotape, adding some of their people instead and showed it on TV.

My wife and I have raised three children, and they have regularly attended church with us. We taught them to be hard working and honest, and always exhibit a Christian spirit. While our parents were alive, both my parents and my father-in-law prayed for us that God would touch our hearts, as we were not Christians at the time of our marriage. After the death of my parents, God touched my heart, and also the hearts of my wife and my children. When we repented we found a wonderful peace with God in our hearts and fellowship with God and His people. Our whole family received the baptism in the Holy Spirit, and the gifts of the Spirit. Then we made the covenant with the Lord through the water baptism and became the members of Sabbath Pentecostal Church.

After we had become members of the church, difficulties in our life increased. At that time, my youngest daughter, Inna, was in the 10th grade of high school. When the staff and her peers at school found out that she had made a covenant with the Lord and would not study on Saturdays (we believe Saturday is the Sabbath), classmates started to mock her without mercy while officials encouraged them. She was threatened with permanent expulsion, including denial of future education privileges, unless she agreed to attend classes on Saturday and denounce this religious practice. As her father, I had to write an explanation why she cannot attend school on Saturday. After long and many discussions with the principal of the school and her teacher, she barely graduated.

After graduating from the school in 1995-96 my daughter started to work in a kindergarten as a janitor, since she could not continue her education any higher then high school level, because of her faith. Later, the employer found out that she was a Christian and started to mistreat her and then fired her.

It seemed that after the collapse of the Soviet Union, legally, freedom to practice your belief came for Christians, but people minds don't change quickly.

Now this country is enduring tremendous ethnic conflicts. The People's Front was formed and the war in Transnistria began in 1990. (an area in the Country of Moldova with strong ethnic Russian ties) I think everyone in the world has heard about this little revolution in our country.

I also want to mention about my son. Soon after he got saved, in our city of Balti, Moldova, a group of missionaries was formed and my son joined this group. Under the leadership of a German representative the group went on an evangelistic trip to the Altai Region of Moldova. In one place, authorities prohibited them from preaching, confiscated their identity papers, agitated people against them and told them to leave for their own good health. They had to endure many of these difficult situations orchestrated by local authorities.

(Editor's note: In all the former Soviet Union Republic's even today, a national identity card (papers) are required for all citizens, usually called a domestic passport. It is required to be on your person at all times and you are often

stopped on the street by local authorities and asked to present it. If you cannot, you can be subject to immediate arrest. It is also used to track citizens when they travel internally around their own country, as they are required to check in and present it at passport registration offices located in all major cities. When traveling in Russia, hotel clerks usually register passports, if staying at one.)

I want to write a little bit about myself. Just as in childhood, up to the time I left for the United States, I was mocked and despised by authorities, neighbors and friends. I don't believe any dramatic changes have occurred over the years.

Since it is written in the word of God, and according to our faith, believed and accepted by my church, men are not supposed to shave, so, I also have a beard. People would often curse us with such words I am ashamed to mention. They have, at times, pulled me by the beard while saying "What have you done to yourself? If I were your wife, I would burn your beard at night while you sleep." I cannot describe everything that happened as these things happened almost every day.

Now the government and religious people are pushing to have the Orthodox Church approved as the only acceptable and legal religion in Moldova. That would mean the persecution of the Biblical or Evangelical Christians will start again.

Based on what my parents have told me, the situation now is similar to the conditions preceding the early fifties when Christians endured tremendous pressure. We do not know what will happen in Moldova in the future. Christians are afraid for what it might hold.

Boris N.

(Information confirmed by Bishop Petru B., Pentecostal Union of Moldova.)

Petr S.

My story starts in the summer of 1982. I was born and living in Moldova at the time and just turned 18. During the school break, I took a job in the Tyumen Region of Russia, which is located in Western Siberia. The job involved cutting trees and running them through a sawmill operation.

My first day on the job, I was assigned the task of feeding the saw. Being young and full of confidence and eager to show my new co-workers that I can do a good job, I remember the incidence as if it happened yesterday. I was pushing a small log into the saw when it hit a knot and the saw briefly went into a bind. The log quickly stopped moving but I was not careful and allowed my hands to continue to travel on the log.

There was a sickening sound as my little finger came into contact with the rotating blade. Once the little finger hit the blade, it fed my other three fingers into the blade also. For a few minutes, I didn't realize that my fingers had been removed at the top of my palm. I remember yanking my hand back and yelling for my friend to catch my fingers. He didn't realize what I was talking about for what seemed like a few minutes, then, he sprang into action, removing his outer garment and wrapping my hand before tearing my sleeve from my shirt to use as a tourniquet to reduce blood flow.

The trip to the hospital was a nightmare. We didn't have helicopters so had to depend on an old piece of motorized logging equipment and the roads in that area are terrible. After what seemed like an eternity, we arrived at a medical clinic in a nearby village. I had lost most of my blood and was in a very week condition. My condition stabilized in a couple days but the staff was concerned because I needed good food to return my body back to a healthy condition and about the entire clinic could offer was a watered-down soup and a small amount of milk.

I loved my Lord very much even as a young man and I

knew He could take care of me in any situation but it came as a surprise how He sent help to me at the time and who brought it.

After a couple days at the clinic, a nurse brought me a big box of food and informed me that my Mother had brought it to the clinic with instructions that it was for me only. My Mother was about 3,500 miles from me in the Country of Moldova and as far as I knew, had no idea that I had been hurt. Since being in this area only a short time, I knew no one.

I puzzled over the whole thing and ask to see the woman who had brought it. I was informed that the lady had already left. I enjoyed the food and even shared it with two others patients who were with me. Surprising, it contained cooked eggs, butter, fruit, and candy. These items were hard to get in that area and if you were lucky enough to find them, they were very expensive.

Three days later, the same thing happened. The nurse brought me even more food this time. I protested, "No, No, this is a mistake. The woman must intend this food for someone else." The nurse replied, "She exactly said, give this food to Petr, the man who had his fingers cut off in the accident the other day."

This was a small clinic with not many patients and surely, no other with my condition. I informed the nurse that if the woman returned again, I must meet her to learn why she was helping me. This time, it was enough for myself and three others for several days.

A few days later, I was told by the nurse, that the lady was in the entryway and would meet me if I came to her.

As she related her story, Petr was reminded of his own mother, so far away. She said that her son, who was near Petr's age had left home for the Army the same day that Petr had the accident. She felt that if she would help some other mother's son in the absence of her own, she was confident that should her son need help wherever he may be stationed, God would provide a Mother to help him. They both cried as they embraced.

Today, Petr says that throughout his convalesce, this lady continued to bring food and as time progressed, became like a second Mother to him. He learned that her name was Mary and his real mother's name was also Mary but he didn't share the news about the accident with his real mother. She was so far away he didn't want her to worry about him. He could always tell her about it after he was home and safe.

His first phone contact with his real Mother came in the fall as he was preparing to return to Moldova. Mother's first question came as a surprise to him when she asked, "Were you in some kind of danger or have some sort of problem on this certain day?" It was exactly the day of his injury so he asked, "Why?" Mother shared with him that on that particular day, she had heard his name called repeatedly from somewhere within her spirit and experienced a strong burden to pray for him and felt such strong feelings that he was in danger. She had spent considerable time praying fervently for God to protect him. Petr bowed in his spirit before God as he realized His goodness, and in appreciation for His love.

Moldova for many years had been one of the 15 Republics of the former Soviet Union. In the early 90's, the Soviet Union was breaking up and each of the Republics were given the option of deciding what form of government they wanted. Some of them were experiencing tremendous economic and political upheaval. Moldova was no exception. Sandwiched between the Ukraine on the East and Romania on the West, it had previously been an area located mostly in Romania with some of it extending over the border into the Ukraine. The Soviet Union extracted it from both countries and designated it the Republic of Moldova just before the second war.

In the spring of 1992, a sense of Nationalism was sweeping the country, polarizing around the capital city of Chisinau. (pronounced Kis shin nev) About 40 miles away was the city of Bendery and about 7 miles from there was the city of Tiraspol. These three cities formed a loose triangle with Chisinau on the top with Bendery to the southeast and Tiraspol to the southwest. The Dniester River separated Bendery and Tiraspol with a main highway bridge connecting the two cities. Chisinau was composed primarily of ethnic Moldovan people while Tiraspol and Bendery were an area of multi-nationals. It also included a complete division of Russian military left over from the breakup of the former Soviet Union.

The new president was making proclamations daily from the capital of Chisinau. One such edict required that all people of Moldovan descent married to someone who was not, was expected to get an immediate divorce, the non-Moldovan would leave the country and the children of such a union would be put into an orphanage.

The Moldovan Army controlled by the government in Chisinau was massed at the Bendery side of the bridge between Bendery and Tiraspol and was threatening to take Tiraspol and then deal with those considered non-Moldovan. After several days, they moved across the bridge and started shelling everything in sight of their guns. Those living there pressed the commanding general of the Russian division to release to them equipment to fight back. He did, and using the Russian equipment, they pushed the Moldovan Army back across the bridge and into Bendery.

Petr, now married, with two children and living in Bendery, recalls the terror that he and his family lived through for about two months. With shells bursting around them, buildings blown to pieces and people being riddled with bullets, he started out walking with his family. To escape the carnage, they would need to travel across the bridge, through Tiraspol and then cross the border into the Ukraine about 75 miles away. Most of that trip would be through heavy fighting and shelling. Because he had no access to a vehicle, they would have to walk. He knew the risk and recognized that their chance of making it was not too good, but he also knew that to remain in their home would mean sure death. He and the family had spent many agonizing moments in prayer seeking God's wisdom and protection. They did not make it very far before they found themselves huddled in a large collection of refugees who were also trying to find their way out of the country. They would wait there till a lull in fighting.

The morning they chosen to continue was influenced by word that a lull in fighting would occur to allow civilian refugees to clear the area. With much prayer and praying for God's protection on his life and that of his family, they resumed their journey. They, with the thousands of other people who were also fleeing for their lives, made it to the bridge, perhaps 10 miles before they were again stopped.

Petr was informed that since he was a male of fighting age, he must stay, however, his wife was allowed to take the children and continue. It was a painful departure, he tried to sound brave for his family's sake, but after prayer, tears and hugs, Nadya disappeared with the children into the crowd surging across the bridge. It wasn't till weeks later that he learned that they arrived at the Ukrainian border without mishap and that the Ukrainian military had set up a refugee camp just across the border where they were cared for, for two weeks, then, Nadiya located a relative who lived in Odessa, where she arranged to live with the children for four months.

Petr returned to his home but remained in grave danger. All buildings in the area where he lived had sustained heavy damage by the daily barrage of bombs and artillery shells.

A couple days after arriving at his home, he was accosted by the Moldovan Military who demanded he join them, including taking arms. He had been taught all his life that it was morally wrong to kill anyone, including Military action. He also knew that if he refused, he would probably be shot on the spot. With only a few minutes to make a decision, he prayed in his spirit for God to help him. Suddenly, he had an idea. He held up his left hand, which had no fingers on it and exclaimed, "I can't shoot a gun without fingers to pull the trigger." The soldiers reacted with anger and disgust. One hit him with his rifle butt and two others kicked him. He was on the ground but not seriously hurt as the soldiers moved off, leaving him with minor injuries.

After only a short distance, they quickly returned and said to Petr, "You may not be able to shoot a weapon, but you can use a shovel to bury the dead." A shovel was thrust into his hand. Again, he demonstrated how he could not even use a shovel because he couldn't grasp the handle without fingers. He was then asked, "What can you do?" Petr replied, "I can pray for you that God will guide you in your behavior" They responded with disgust and again kicked him a few times before leaving. He very quickly bowed his head and gave thanks to God for his caring protection.

He now understood that the accident years earlier had taken from him, yet because of it, he had escaped an unconscionable situation now and understood how God could take such misfortune and turn it into a victory.

Over the next two weeks, with dead bodies everywhere and the stench of death in the air, Petr saw the systematic destruction of his City. Apartment buildings several stories high, around his home were completely destroyed. Bombs and shells hit his home several times, yet he continued to sleep there. Every time it rained, he was soaked, but he was concerned that if he left, looters would move in and take anything of value, besides, he had no other place to go and the house provided limited protection.

After it was over and Petr surveyed the damage, it was a miracle of God that he had survived. The roof was badly damaged, all the windows were blown out and the front wall was blown down. It would require a complete rebuild. Even amid the destruction, Petr took the time to give thanks to God for his care. His home and possessions were gone, but he had his life and had not compromised his belief.

During the hostilities, his Mother had been admitted to a local hospital for a non-serious situation and was now about to be discharged. Petr wanted to go there to accompany her to her home. Upon his arrival at the hospital, he discovered his Mother had checked herself out already so he started back for his house on foot.

To get to his house required crossing a double railroad track. This day, he discovered an empty train parked on the tracks blocking the road. As he approached the train, he realized that opposing forces were using the train as a temporary shield. A group of Moldovan forces was on this side and he needed to get to the other. As he skirted their position and crawled under the train, they spotted him. He had cleared the train and was moving through some tall grass on the opposite side when the Moldovans opened fire with a rifle-propelled grenade. It tore a hole completely through the train and hit a concrete post as it passed near his head, throwing debris all over him.

He realized that he was on his face, on the ground, in the grass and was consumed by the feeling that he was about to die. He was searching his soul to determine if there was any sin between himself and God and praying with all his might, when he felt somebody grab him by his leg and started pulling him back toward the train. When he realized that he was being pulled, he rolled over where he could see and discovered what appeared to be an alcoholic, perhaps a homeless man pulling him. When they were very near the train, the guy told him to follow so they crawled some distance then raised and ran into some nearby brush.

There, the other man identified himself as a Russian Intelligence Officer who had been attempting to gain information about the Moldovan forces by pretending to be an alcoholic and homeless person.

Petr put his life and his future completely into the Lord's hands and again purposed in his heart to never fear again as he knew that God would not let anything happen to him unless it was His will. He would trust his life and future to God's will.

Nadiya had tried for some time, to interest Petr in leaving Moldova and immigrating to the United States where her Parents had already moved to, from the country of Georgia, but Petr was reluctant since he operated a business employing nearly a hundred employees and wasn't excited about walking off and leaving it.

After the incident at the railroad though, he was now looking at life through different eyes. He discovered that he had shifted all his values from material things to family and Spiritual things. It would be very easy to leave all he had and with only his faith in God, step out and see where He would lead. He initiated the process to immigrate.
*(*See Editor's note)*

In November of 1992, Petr, with his passport and permission to leave Moldova granted, said goodbye to his native country with all its problems and started the long journey to the United States. It would still be several months before Nadiya and the children could be processed through immigration to join him here.

Looking back to 1992, Petr laughs when talking about the war in his country. Moldova is a poor country so when all the bullets and shells were used up, and thousands of good people were killed, they couldn't afford to buy new military supplies, everyone just sort of lost interest in fighting. The Russian military has gone back to Russia and political unrest has settled even though there are still extreme economic problems. The country seems to have a quasi-peace. He's glad for that and continues to pray for Moldova, but the United States is now his Country and he's very grateful to those people here who embraced him and his family and helped with transition to a new country.

Petr has bought a home and now lives in the Puget Sound area of the State of Washington. The Lord has prospered him, but he will never forget those times in his life when God directly intervened to provide safety for himself or his family. It is with a heart full of joy and gratitude that he shares this experience today. He is quick to share at every opportunity.

He had worked at several jobs after arriving in the U.S. and thanks the Lord for everyone but he continued to look for one with better pay and was long term.

In 1996, he heard that a local shuttle bus company was looking for drivers so he applied. A few weeks later, he was called in for an interview and was hired. At that time, he explained to the personnel manager that he believed in his heart and his understanding of the Bible prohibited him from working on either Saturday or Sunday, nor could he work past 6:00 P.M. on Friday. Any other time, he could and would work whatever hours his supervisor requested.

He also assured the personnel manager that even though he felt compelled to share Jesus with everybody, he would refrain from preaching to his passengers but if they should inquire of anything about his belief, he must respond as the Holy Spirit directed him. He even had a statement prepared to that effect and had it placed in his personnel folder.

It was usual for him work 50 hours a week and everybody seemed happy. The company received numerous written letters of appreciation from his regular riders who were liberal with compliments about his friendliness and willing to assist those riders in need. This arrangement worked fine for both he and the company, until another company bought it out five years later.

A short time after, it was announced by his supervisor that he had been selected by management as the Employee of the Month for outstanding service There was cake for all drivers, banners and a special parking spot.

The next day, Petr was taken aside by the general manager, who asked him about putting his name on the schedule for weekend work. Petr tried to explain that his understanding of the Bible prevented him from working either Saturday or Sunday, that there were letters in his folders to that effect and that for over five years, it had not been a problem.

The manager was not happy by Petr's response, but let the matter drop for the moment.

Over the next three weeks, he again approached Petr about the same subject three times. Each time, Petr tried to explain in the nicest way possible that he would not consider it.

The third time the subject came up, the manager became very flustered and said, "Petr, today is Friday, I will give you the weekend to think it over. If you do not agree by 9:00 A.M. Monday, I will terminate your employment." Petr responded, "You don't have to give me a weekend, I will tell you right now, I will not work weekends. My Lord is very special and I will never risk offending Him for anything. He will provide for me." The day ended without further discussion about the matter.

Monday morning early, Petr appeared at work as any other day. He checked out his bus and proceeded to his assigned route. Just before nine, expecting a call on his cell phone from this manager, he began to feel some stress about the situation and in his heart called out to the Lord, "Jesus, If I lose this job, my family will suffer, I could lose my home with no money coming in." It was just ever so briefly, when the Holy Spirit came on him and he found praise to God swelling up from within and he knew that no matter what, the Lord was in control of his life. He would not fear anything.

Nine o'clock came and went. No phone calls. In fact, all day, there was no phone call. When Petr arrived at the bus barn to turn in his vehicle, he was prepared for an encounter with his supervisor and probably a termination. He parked his bus and went into the crew area, where to his surprise, there was a large cake and many drivers were milling around, drinking coffee and having cake.

Petr asked, "What are we celebrating?" an employee exclaimed, "Haven't you heard? That manager was fired today!" Petr felt like stealing away somewhere, alone with the Holy Spirit, where he could lift his heart to the Lord in adoration. He also felt bad about the guy losing his job because he probably had a family but understood that when a person stands against the Lord, anything can happen.

Today, a year later, Petr is still working as a driver, still witnesses whenever he has an opportunity and everyday growing in spiritual wisdom and understanding. On weekends you can find him at a state prison in a city nearby, conducting a Bible study for the prisoners. He is a real pleasure to know as he shares from the heart.
(Provided by Petr S.)

*Editor's note:

Today, the self-declared Republic of Trans-Dniester incorporates a narrow strip of land situated along the eastern bank of the Dniester (Nistru in Moldovan) river and bordered on its west by Ukraine, primarily populated by remnants of ethnic Russians (Romanian descendants settled the western side of the river). This region, one of the world's last surviving Soviet Communist bastions, has its own currency, police force and capital city (Tiraspol). For over a decade, Trans-Dniester has been trying to gain its independence from Moldova. Since the bloody civil war with Moldova in 1991, Russian peacekeeping troops have patrolled the border separating the two countries.

Albert

This is my personal testimony of some of the things that have happened to my family and I, before coming to the United States.

I was born in the former Union of Social Soviet Republics, also known as the USSR. I didn't know what freedom was compared to what the American people enjoy. The USSR treated people like machines, which might be hard to understand by people in America who have never experienced a loss of freedom.

I was born June 2, 1974, in the City of Batumi, Capital of the Republic of Georgia which was then, a Republic of the former USSR. My family was born into oppression because of their religious belief and their race. My Father was ethnic Armenian and my mother was ethnic Jewish.

In 1937, My Grandfather was killed because he was a Christian leader and spoke openly against Communism. KGB agents came to our home in the middle of the night and took him away. No one ever saw or heard of him again. I now have documents showing how my Grandfather, was killed by the KGB. Everywhere we moved, my family was persecuted and was marked, because of opposition to the Communist and the Community knew about it, and were encouraged by authorities to discriminate against us in whatever way possible.

This is one of the tactics the KGB used to isolate people who didn't accept Communism or were religious in any way. Family members were denied the right to work, or to participate in social events and all basic human rights.

In September of 1989, I began studies at a Maritime School to become a sailor. While a student, I had problems with the government, obtaining visa and permits required of the trade. The training required a visa or permission to leave the Country, allowing students to get hands on experience aboard ship. My family had never been permitted a visa, therefore, I was not allowed to apply for one. When I finished the training, minus the hands-on experience, passing the tests with excellent ratings, they eventually allowed me to open a visa.

In 1991, the situation in the Country changed rapidly. Independence movements gathered members almost overnight. When the fighting started, most wanted to expel all none Georgians, including ethnic Jewish people, ethnic Armenians and ethnic Russian. Keep in mind that these people were Georgian citizens, born there and lived there all their lives and in many cases, for generations.

As interest in this ethnic cleansing grew, everyone knew my mother was Jewish because of her name and my Father was Armenian for the same reason. Many times, our home was stoned, windows were broken and racial remarks written on our property. Hostilities were mostly confined to northern Georgia from 1991 to 1996.

All young men were required to join the military. I was no exception even if I was not ethnic Georgian.

I finished Maritime School in 1993 and in 1994, the Military Police called me in for an interview. Recognizing my family name, they sent me to an isolation Prison for 1 week and took all my documents. They had access to my family history so knew about our racial and religious background.

After a week in isolation, I remained in Prison until late 1994. Upon my release, I was expected to register and serve in the Military, since I didn't, a warrant was issued for my arrest. I ask for alternative service so I wouldn't have to carry a gun since my understanding of God's word wouldn't allow me to kill someone but they allowed no exception. I went into hiding by staying with different relatives, as I knew authorities were watching my family home. After a month or so, I escaped my country and entered Russia.

After entering Russia, the President of the United

Pentecostal Church, provided me a place to stay. In September 1996, on his recommendation, I was accepted at the Moscow Theological Institute that was operated by The Assemblies of God, an American Religious Organization.

Two months later, Military Police came to my family home back in Georgia and took my brother to prison following his baptism in water. Three weeks later, he was transported into the war zone with the military and was expected to fight. He refused to carry a weapon so he was beaten and tortured for the next seven months before he was able to escape from his tormenters and make his way into Russia where he joined me at the Institute in Moscow.

In May of 1999, upon finishing the Institute with a BA degree, The United Pentecostal Church organization sent me to St. Petersburg, Russia to Co-Pastor a Church called The Soul of the Land. There, I was appointed Director of their Social Service Program designed for street kids. This program was called the House of Mercy.

Historically, people from Georgia did not need a visa to move about in Russia, but in early 2001, that changed. About that time, I received an invitation from the Full Gospel Business Men International to come to America to speak at a Conference. I accepted the invitation with great joy.

As I was processing through the main International Airport at Moscow, Security Police advised that if I boarded the airplane I could not return to Russia without a VISA. They informed me that a recent law barred Georgians from entering Russia, who was not Russian citizens. That meant that I must return to Georgia to obtain a Georgian Passport and a VISA from the Russian government before I could return. (This law was a form of retaliation against the Country of Georgia for allegedly harboring terrorist from Chechnya)

By March 10, 2001, I had decided to board a plane

anyway, knowing that I would not be able to return and I also knew that I could not go back to Georgia because the Police were still looking for me and I could wind up in prison for the rest of my life, or tortured and perhaps, killed.

As of April 2001, the only religions recognized in Georgia are the Catholic and the Orthodox Church. A Bishop of the United Pentecostal Churches was attacked and seriously injured and the government has banned the assembly of people for religious purposes unless they are connected to one of the two Churches previously mentioned.

For Five years, the Police have come to my family in Georgia, harassing my family and looking for me. Now I am appealing to the American government for political and religious asylum on the basis that I cannot go back to either Russia or Georgia.

Ed. Note: Albert is currently ministering in various churches and conducting speaking engagements throughout the United States, primarily to Immigrant Congregations while residing in the Vancouver Washington area.

(Provided by Albert T.)

Aleksandr R.

Alek had worked for the KGB, the criminal investigation arm of the government of the former Soviet Union for many years. After the collapse of the Soviet Union, Russia assumed control of this agency and renamed it, the Federal Security Agency, or the FSA as it is called today.

Officially, Alek's job title had nothing to do with the KGB. He was officially known as a Senior Fisheries Department Inspector with an office at Magadan, capital city of the Magadan Region in Russia, Far East. His job required him to work out of this coastal city located on the Sea of Okhotsk, an expanse of water extending off the

152

THE GOD THAT DOES NOT FAIL

North Pacific. Because of his position, he enjoyed some of the finer things Russia had to offer, a life style not known to many Russian citizens at that time. His duties not only required him to fly over the Sea of Japan, the Sea of Okhotsk, and the North Pacific in a plane provided to him by the government but, carried him many times West, even occasionally, to Moscow. He knew many operatives and became known by many. He knew the FSA had become so tangled with organized crime that the so called, "Mafia" in most cases were also FSA people and vice versa. He understood the trail of the bribe money all the way to the top.

In April, 1989, He resigned from the communist party under sharp attack and harassment from its members because of increasing desire for freedom of expression of ideologies and the possibility of freedom to achieve an individual's potential. At his resignation, he was warned, "No one leaves the KGB, the only way out is to die." Even after his official resignation, he was still considered an informant, and was expected to collect information on friends and neighbors and report this to officials.

In October of 1990, Alek says, "I could not, with a clear conscious, continue to report to or collect information for the KGB. I had major philosophical differences with their tactics and the behavior of their members. I did not realize what was going on in my heart then, there was a stirring, a yearning for fulfillment that wasn't being satisfied nor could it until I surrendered my life to the Lord. I became increasing critical of the Communist Party and specifically the KGB and refused to spy on my friends and fellow workers. As a result, I was constantly intimidated and harassed not only on the job, but at times also at my home. My phones were tapped, conversations were recorded and later portions came back to me in the form of unsigned letters or would be passed to me when local KGB/FSA members were trying to induce me to go against my principals. From 1990 to

1996, my hours of employment were gradually reduced to nothing, obvious to me, it was subtle pressure to convince me to co-operate with authorities."

In spite of his internal conflicts, in the early nineties, Alek married a police officer from the Magadan Police Force and life seemed to be smiling on him, employment problems, notwithstanding. Life was very good to him compared to other citizens of the area. There was something that continued to bother him though. Knowing he had life pretty good, he was not happy. There was no peace in his heart.

Pavel R. immigrated to the United States as a refugee in the early 90's to escape religious persecution in his native country of the Ukraine. After living in the U.S. for 5 years or so, he had developed a burning desire to return to the former Soviet Union as an Evangelist and conduct missionary work. He eventually became director of a Slavic missionary group located in Federal Way, Washington. Since then, he has traveled to the former Soviet Union many times and conducted many services, seeing many people give their lives to the Lord.

On one such trip, while in the city of Magadan, Pavel and Alek lives crossed and Alek surrendered his life to the Lord. There was an immediate and profound change. That ache that he had held in his heart for so long had been transformed into joy and for the first time in his life, he felt at peace with his Savior. He lost interest in what he was doing for the government. He found himself sharing his faith with people on the job and in time, approached his superiors about quitting the security service even though he knew the fate of those who had tried to quit before him.

His superiors were very agitated about the direction he was going and warned him "you don't quit the service unless you die." Alek was very aware of the risk he was taking, never the less; he continued to try to disengage himself from his job.

About a year had passed since his conversion. He was sure his phone was tapped and sometimes he was followed and watched by people whom he recognized as agents. Concern was rising about his personal safety as well as that of his wife, Larissa, and son, Denise. Larissa had recently accepted the Lord in her life, so there was also a concern for her safety at the place where she worked.

One evening, there was a knock at his door. When he opened it, several men pushed in and began assaulting him. When it was over, he had several broken bones, many cuts and bruises and his throat was cut from one side to the other.

Larissa summoned friends from next-door and together, they got him quickly to a hospital where his condition was stabilized and his wounds were treated and broken bones set. It took about a year for Alek to recuperate from his wounds and injuries but the emotional drain on his family continued for several years. Alek was determined that he would not compromise his newfound faith for anyone but he also knew there was no longer safety for either he or his family in Russia. He knew that Larissa or his son could easily be next and he couldn't bear the thoughts of either going through what he did.

"I got the message. I tried to be more compromising but always looking for a way out or around those things that I felt were unconscionable, waiting for the right time to exit their control on my life." He was keenly aware that they could manipulate all aspects of his life including life or death. He started formulating a bold plan. He still had several passports because his job had required them. One was a seaman's passport that allowed him limited access to the United States. Larissa and Denise still retained a limited passport so he put his plan into action.

Larissa would continue to show up at her job as a Policewoman in Magadan to imply normalcy. He traveled to the United States and arrived in the Seattle area since he knew that Pavel lived in the area and may be able to assist him with the necessary paperwork to request asylum. In this area, he was directed to my office.

After contacting Pavel and verifying Alek story, I recommended that he contact his family in Magadan and have them fly immediately to the U.S., since I was afraid that once certain ranking individuals from his past knew of his plans, they might be persuaded to clamp tight controls on his family's movement. I further suggested that he not publish his intent to declare asylum until they arrived. I also ask that he let me put him in contact with the local FBI office just to make sure there was nothing that he knew, that they might want to know. After this contact was made, the FBI actually transferred him to Naval Intelligence and there were several things that he was able to reveal to them, which, this would not be the proper place for discussion.

Once the family was safely here, we proceeded to complete the application and quickly submitted it to Lincoln, NE. I have now known Alek and his family for several years and I continually marvel at their Spiritual growth, their deep desire to worship God, (sometimes, he and his family attend several different services in a single day) and the tenacity displayed by this family. If you look closely at the beard that Alek sports today, you can see clearly the scar across his throat that will forever serve as a reminder of darker days. Every day is embraced as a gift from the Lord and committed to Him. He and his family are keenly aware that if someone wants him killed, they could easily do it here by sending someone to take him out so they maintain a low profile. It seems to me that Alek may be a modern-day Paul. He had spent many years persecuting Christians as a part of his job function, but after meeting Jesus, he is now anxious to do what he can to help them.

Lyudmila

I was born in 1960 in Ufa, Republic of Bashkortostan, Russia.

Between 1984 and 1999, I worked as executive manager of a Republic owned Cultural Hall in Ufa, which is the Capital City of Bashkortostan.

Between 1990 and 1994, I served in an elected position on the State Professional Committee (Rai Prof Sozsh) and at the same time, I also served on the Local Executive Committee (Isopoll Com).

In the Cultural Hall, I organized three ethnic folk groups, the Bashkir, the Tartar and the Russians. Basically, these three ethnic groups represented the composition of our City.

After Murtaza Rakhimov, who was ethnic Bashkir, was elected President of Bashkortostan in 1993, the Bashkir folk group got all the possible government support, whereas, the other ethnic groups had to struggle to survive. I tried my best to be fair to all three groups. The new government felt that I was not trying to follow the government national ideology to bring the Bashkir national culture to the superior position because I believed that every nationality had a right to cherish its cultural background, and exercise ethnical diversity at the same time.

The new government also started a campaign to project the Bashkirs as a superior group even though they comprised only about 20% of the total population of Bashkortostan. The remaining 80% were comprised of Tatars, Russians, Mordovians, Chuvash, and Ukrainian, but these people were being forced to accept the Bashkir culture also. All government personnel were required to learn the Bashkir language even though Russian was the official language of the Republic. Russia, as the United States, is made up of 89 autonomous regions of which 15 are called Republics. Regions have governors and Republics have Presidents. In the U.S., they are called

States.

Bashkortostan is one of these Republics located in the southern Ural mountain region of Russia. All Republics are semi controlled by Moscow, the Capital of Russia, as the U.S. is by Washington D.C.

During 1996, non-Bashkir TV stations and newspapers were closed down due to limited government support and were replaced with Bashkir people with unlimited government support in what was an obvious move by the government to get their own people in the media and gain control of it.

During this time, Russia was increasing it tolerance for new Religious beliefs and allowing a greater freedom of Religion. With this in mind, I rented office space to any group who otherwise qualified without regard to their belief and included Pentecostals, Church of Christ, Jehovah's Witnesses and Mormon. It didn't take long before I received a notice from the Bashkir government to stop renting to these "cult" churches. I refused to follow the order and continued to allow them to have church functions and activities in the building. I was called to the Executive Committee to explain my actions. When I expressed my belief that government building should be open to all, regardless of Religious preference, I was dismissed from the position that I held on the Executive Committee and a short time later, dismissed from the Local Committee.

There was concern that I might "spread my antigovernment opinions" to others. The Groups using the Building were left alone, but my personal life became hell. My name appeared in the Republic newspaper very frequently where I was called "Satan's Helper." Someone set my apartment door on fire, my car was destroyed by vandalism and I received numerous phone threats.

All attempts to involve the police with my concerns proved to be worthless. Police at the police station laughed at me and when I went to the head department

158

officer, he said, "I better not open a case over the little fireworks by my door."

I started looking for support from other Cultural Hall managers throughout the area. Some chose the easy way by deciding to follow government orders. Those who refused were removed from their jobs and a few actually disappeared without anyone knowing what happened to them. Some I knew were dismissed under strange circumstances and others received unsupported charges against them. Many very talented managers simply quit. In all cases, Bashkir people, loyal to the new President's government, filled the positions. The cultural and ideological life of the State began to reflect the President's ideas and opinions.

In 1997, leaders of a large Bashkir folk group tried to convince me to eliminate any other National Cultural competition by limiting their promotional events, hence cutting off their source of income.

When I refused to do so, my Russian Nationality became an issue to them. They went to the upper levels of the Administration with the request to get me dismissed from my position since I "could not possibly realize the importance of the Nationalistic movement due to my Nationality." I retained my position, but since, my name is associated with the opposition against the government and I could not take a step without being watched by authorities loyal to the Administration. I began receiving threatening phone calls again. Police would not involve themselves.

In the Presidential election of 1998, the situation became almost unbearable. The Republic was readying itself for the election, which amounted to a re-election of the current President. I received a request from the opponent to rent the Hall for a political rally and agreed and the fees were paid. I was then informed that no building would be rented for any political rallies without the approval of the office of the existing President. I was pressured to promote the existing Presidential campaign and force others to do the same.

In May, I checked into a local hospital for health reasons and discovered that I was pregnant. After returning to work, one of my superiors phoned me and advised me to quit before I had the baby. When I asked how he knew about the pregnancy, since medical information was supposed to be confidential between myself and the hospital, he informed me that the government knew everything about me and that I, and the upcoming baby would be left alone if I quit my job.

Shortly after that call, my office was searched for any information about the Presidential opponents and I was again threatened unless I agreed to support the President and only him.

June 12, I was in charge of organizing the Independence Day celebration, and I opened it to all people of the City. About half way through the events, I was suspended for "not being devoted to the Bashkir Nationalistic Ideology." I had allowed the inclusion of Russian and Tatar people in the scheduled events. After returning home, I miss-carried and lost my baby. I am convinced that it was because of the stress that I had been enduring and specifically, that day.

The President's re-election came as no surprise to anyone. The Constitutional Court of the Russian Federation demanded new elections but Bashkortostan refused the court order so the situation became critical. Strikes and political protest occurred daily but were suppressed by Police. There seemed to be no hope that the political situation would improve. The Republic was on the verge of anarchy.

My daughter, who was attending the Bashkir State University, became targeted for discrimination. Administrators and Professors alike would direct racial slurs toward her like, "Russians don't deserve to live in this Republic" and "Russians must bribe teachers to allow them to graduate." This generated a hostile environment for her so I decided to send my daughter to the United States to finish school and protect her from personal attacks.

As Independence Day approached in 1999, I was relieved of my duties due to my "immature political self-awareness." I also found out that summer that I was pregnant again. I was concerned about the quality and safety of prenatal care available to me in Ufa, so I moved to Moscow where I had a son the following March. I lived in the Moscow area until moving to the United States.

Lyudmila's request to the Immigration Service for Political asylum has been approved and she currently resides in the Portland Oregon area where her daughter and son-in-law live near her.

(Provided by Lyudmila K.)

Sergey

I am from the country of Belarus. My family and I are of the Pentecostal faith and have been most of our lives. An important tenant of that faith is to witness and express that faith to others. In recent years, I have been involved with a music ministry where I performed on stage. My performance usually consists of several gospel songs and I usually have opportunity to share my faith in my God.

Within the last couple years, it has become increasingly difficult to perform because individuals from the local authorities, both uniformed and in civilian clothes, have threaten me personally or members of my family. I take these threats very seriously because of the frequency, severity and intensity. My family does not feel safe out of the house anymore because neighbors call them names and harass them because of their belief.

As American media reports have accurately portrayed my country's drift back toward the Communist philosophy, pressure is increasingly brought to bear against the fundamental Christians. I, and my family are increasingly mocked, hassled, accosted and performances at church meetings interrupted while subjected to interrogation by local officials or thugs. When protection is requested from local authorities, they fail to show interest in the matter or worse yet, will join in with the perpetrators. Today, officials in Belarus are increasingly finding it difficult to control protesters and on numerous occasions, have had near riot conditions in my home city of Minsk. As this pressure continues to mount, so does pressure against the fundamental Christians. Authorities are not interested in intervening to help us. The Fundamental Christians are labeled a sect, and as such, are not afforded any protection from authorities or local officials, rather, often suffer indignities at the hands of those who should be protecting them.

In my country, permits are required for all non-registered church services. Since many of the services in which I perform are in public places, I cannot obtain necessary permits to conduct this ministry of music.

The people who controlled the communities while my country was part of the Soviet Union are still in the offices they held previously and still control services such as goods, housing, education and jobs, without which, a person cannot obtain life's necessaries. There is a strong feeling in my country's leadership to return it to its former days when it was a part of the Soviet Union. This power hold is brought to bear against Fundamental Christians to force them to succumb and conform to the wishes of those who hold that power. Because of my participation and involvement with this Fundamental Christian group, I am denied these services and cannot provide for my family.

My wife was denied access to a higher education because she was associated with my ministry and was told exactly that by the College officials.

I solicit the prayers of all believers that God will bless

this ministry to expand His kingdom by reaching young people who are the Church leaders of tomorrow.

Sergey currently lives with his family in the Portland, Oregon area and has a successful ministry as a popular singer with several CD's. He has ministered to thousands of young people in immigrant communities across the United States, while concentrating on the West Coast and the Pacific Northwest.

(Provided by Sergey B.)

Aliaksandr

I am from the country of Belarus, which is a former Soviet Union Republic.

The Byelorussia government is a staunch supporter of the Socialist mentality and even speaks openly about the return of communist control of the country. Their official perception of any group other than the Orthodox Church mimics the old Soviet view. We also have a group known as skinheads who bully many people on the streets, especially Christian people. They appear to feel threatened by just hearing a Christian share his faith.

In my country, the government will support and recognize the Orthodox Church but any other group of believers is considered illegitimate. Request for support or protection is rejected outright or ignored. I am a born again Christian and subscribe to the Baptist faith. I regularly attend a local Baptist church.

I believe that it is a commandment of the Lord to share my faith with others as the opportunity arises. I equate it as about the same as having a medical cure for a dying world and to withhold that cure, would be criminal. I have shared my faith within the church as well as on the street. As a result, many locals know, some who are known as skinheads, are not very pleased and given an opportunity, they not only accost me but any Christian that they can. It happens often and local authorities treat it as just a religious problem and recommend we settle things ourselves.

In September 2001, about 10:00 P.M., I received a phone call at home, someone on the line told me that I should stop this religious "stuff" or I would be sorry. The tone of his voice was very frightening. I had been previously taunted and heckled before, but never such a direct threat. Several days later, while sharing my faith with a person on the street, I was accosted by 3 people who appeared to be skinheads. They indicated that they had previously warned me by phone to stop this religious stuff then proceeded to attack me. I was on the ground and they were kicking me and hitting me with their fist and yelling at me. I managed to escape and make my way home with only bumps and bruises.

I notified police but as usual, they were not interested, because, "it was a religious thing and they weren't interested in getting involved. I have to work it out myself."

October of 2001, returning home one evening, I was confronted by a gang of young street thugs who beat me with various items, including sticks or tree limbs, before leaving me on the sidewalk. Police were nearby but didn't seem to notice so when I approached them and ask for help, they only laughed and suggested that my problem would go away if I got away from religion.

January of 2002, while posting flyers on a public posting board, advertising an upcoming Christian event, two policemen began tearing the posters down then arrested me, handcuffed me and took me to the police station where they berated me for about 3 hours, (having fun, they called it) before letting me go. The arrest was not for posting the notices, but when the Police tore them down, they threw the paper on the ground, which they blamed on me. My arrest was officially for littering.

The evening of May 5, 2002, my friend and I were sitting in the city park, reading our Bibles and discussing our faith, when about 6 skinheads approached us. After

164

about 5 minutes of taking verbal abuse about being Christian or religious, they jumped on us and beat us with sticks and their fists for several minutes before being scared off by other people who came into the park. We tried to report it to police but the station was not occupied. We were not able to find a policeman till the next day, and by then, they weren't interested.

My soul yawns for a place where I can worship my God without concern for my safety all the time.

Aliaksandr is currently living in the Denver, Colorado area and enjoying the blessings of the Lord. At last word, he was working three jobs and he said that he had one day in the week where he figured he could get that fourth job because on that day he had four hours open so he was trying to find a short part time job for those four hours. He still finds time to share his faith.

(Provided by Aliaksandr L.)

Valentyn L.

I would like to share something that happened yesterday. (3/7/11) A young man came into my office and it was clear that he was using prosthetic legs and quickly began to tell us a story about a recent event in his life.

Flashback to December of last year. A Ukrainian lady came to us for help. Her son, who was 25, had disappeared and she was in tears. No one had any idea what had happened to him. She had left him at home while she was doing some errands and when she returned, he was gone. No evidence of foul play so authorities would not help her look for him, in fact, she could not enlist anyone to help her. She was in terrible agony. There was very little we could do to help but show moral support and assure her that we would pray with her for the safe return of her son and reassured her that the Lord can do anything. We continued to monitor her situation and over the next few weeks, we learned that her son had been found but he was deathly sick and his legs had been frozen to the extent that they were amputated.

The young man yesterday identified himself as the same young man as he shared his side of the story.

It seems that he has no idea what came over him, only that he had such strong compulsion to remove himself from other people the day he disappeared so basically, hid himself from others in a forested area near the local airport and as near as he can recall, simply bedded down there in the forest, exposed to the weather including cold and rain. He was there for three weeks before being found nearly frozen. He says that during the time in the forest he remembers very little, in fact, knew very little about what was going on around him; it's as if he was numb to everything including the cold and apparently had drank polluted water from a nearby stream which developed a severe stomach infection. Medical professionals believed he was very close to death when found.

He was hospitalized where a large portion of his stomach was removed leaving probably one of the largest stomach scars I have ever seen. His legs were removed and today he has prostatic.

But the best part of the story comes next. He said after being admitted to the hospital, he was aware of the Lord standing beside him and through all the pain, he felt only the joy of the Lord as His presence permeated throughout his whole body. While there, he had another brush with death as medical staff administered the wrong medicine and he experienced a severe reaction but he is still amazed at the peace and a sense of completeness the Lord brought him as He remained nearby. He says it appeared he was in a garden that even contained animals and might be characterized as paradise, but nothing was more meaningful than the presence of the Lord nearby.

Today, He is basking in the change the Lord brought in his life. He says he lost his legs but gained his life. Before his life was empty, like most folks, just reacting to whatever came his way. Today, he is embracing life and enjoying every minute of it, full of expectations, he has become very fiscal by working out every day, swimming, gym work, trying to use his experience to influence other young people by sharing and establishing himself as a role model. "Hey, look at what I went through, you can go through yours too" "I lost my legs but I gained my life" The Lord will be there with you all the way.

Why did he "get lost"? Says he suspects demon influence or even domination. He has no clue what else could have happened. He said before it "came over him" He had never experimented with drugs, alcohol or even smoking. There was a girl, a rejection and some depression but he considered himself, just a "normal" young person.

Darkness came from, he thinks, the Devil and overcame him and he was numb for several weeks. Now he is free and amazed that the Lord came to him when he would have otherwise been going through such pain and anesthetized him with joy and a sense of completeness that is unexplainable yet full of joy.

He stopped by again the other day and was sharing that some organization was going to provide him with some prosthetics designed for running and he planned on leaving in a few days for a special marathon in California. He's still amazed at what God has brought him from and where he is today Spiritually. He shared that up to the time of the accident, if someone had suggested that he would take an interest in running or any sports for that matter, he would have thought the idea crazy.

(Valentyn L.)

A Godly Woman

Viktor recently visited my office and while there, shared an important part of his childhood with the following excerpt.

As a child in the Ukraine, his father was an ungodly person, a hard person who thought nothing of abusing his family. His Mother would often display bruises and the children walked softly to avoid arousing his anger.

A particular incidence stands out in his memory. His mother, a Godly person who loved the Lord very much, had tried for a long time to obtain a copy of the Bible and after years without one, she finally got a copy from somewhere. She loved it and would spend long periods of time reading it. Father absolutely hated it. There was an incidence when he raged at her about it and actually took it from her and threw it into a burning stove. As she tried to retrieve it, Father was raging about how he was stronger than God and didn't need Him or the Bible, etc., etc. Viktor remembers that even though he was just a child, he challenged his Father that "If you really believe you are stronger then God, let me see you put your hand into the fire and retrieve the Bible without getting burned since God could easily do it" Clearly Father didn't take the challenge but mother was able to retrieve charred pieces of it which she cherished for years after.

Mother, even in dire circumstances, held her peace and spent considerable time fasting and praying that Father would give his life to God knowing that if he did, the Holy Spirit would change his life including his personality and instill peace in the home. The harder life got with him, the more she prayed and fasted for him.

At 32 years old and after terrorizing his family for several years and producing 5 children, Father was diagnosed with cancer. For the next 4 years, he would go through considerable pain and suffering as his health deteriorated.

A couple years after the diagnosis, Viktor remembers his Father sitting on the side of the bed and for the first time in his 13-year lifetime, his Father puts his arm around his shoulder and tells him, "you know Viktor, your mother has been right all these years".

Toward the end, as Father was close to death, he aroused and was considerably animated with excitement as he was telling family members and others in the room that Jesus was there in the room. No one could see Him and Father couldn't understand that no one else was seeing Jesus as he could clearly see Him. This scenario formed a lasting and vivid memory in Viktor's mind up to even today and confirmed that Father had made full repentance for his sinful life but is quick to give the credit to his Mother who had the fortitude and resolve to dedicate her own life to petitioning Jesus for her husband's soul.

Of course, this incidence creates considerable conversation concerning a comparison with a typical situation today when most likely, a spouse would have very quickly vacated the premises because there appears to be very few today who would share the perspective or have the commitment or resolve to take the time to deny themselves for their spouse expecting there is a good chance that they will not reap any benefits this side of heaven.

Who Was He?

Yesterday a man visited my office who, even though I was told that he could speak 4 languages, he could speak no English so he brought along someone who could translate for him.

After two hours in my office and seemingly discussing everything with his interpreter and his interpreter trying to relate everything to me, I understood that he had been a Scientist associated with the University of Moscow, Russia and more recently, a scientist with a National Institute in Bulgaria but still had no idea why he had come. I did learn that because of a divorce, he was estranged from his family who lived in the area and desperately wanted to reconnect with his elderly mother. I asked the interpreter several times to just please ask him why he came? What was it he thought I might be able to help him with? But with no success.

The interpreter was becoming exhausted and I was tired of trying to get anything from him that I thought I could work with so I begin to wonder what was going on, why had he come, what is the meaning of him even being in my office? He was very intense in trying and/or wanting to share with me and I could see it was very important to him, but... I had no idea.

As I thought about this, I realized that I have always thought that no person comes to my office by accident. Everyone who comes through the door is someone whom the Lord has sent. Realizing that, I begin to meditate on what the Lord might be doing with this situation and as I did, I had the strongest feeling to simply pray for him and that God would remedy his situation directly to and for him.

I then asked about his background and discovered he was Jewish so I told him that I served the same God that the Jewish people believed in and that I feel I should pray for him, that I would and that I expected him to contact me in a few days and let me know how the Lord had worked his problem out. I shared with him through the interpreter several incidents where we had prayed for individuals and the Lord had met their needs and it was clear that He was involved.

He consented to allow us to pray for him which we did. After his initial surprise from the sudden change in tone and context of the conversation, his countenance changed immediately. He stood up (It seemed he was much taller than when he came in) smiling, thanking me and assuring me that he also believed in prayer.

Afterwards, Lena and I prayed specifically for him and even though we never understood what he was hoping for, we know the Lord does.

I never saw him again, have no idea who he was, where he came from or where he went. Wherever he is today, he is in God's Hand.

Typically, I can have 2,500 to 3,000 people through my office a year and in recent years, from over a 140 Countries, many with very limited ability to speak English but this occurrence remains the most mysterious in my memory throughout the 30 years that I have assisted the immigrant community, assisting an estimated 14,000 families.

God's Goodness

Lidiya entered my office with a somewhat unusual request for help on October 10, 2014.

A couple years ago she had been awarded guardianship of her mentally/physically challenged son and now the court was requiring her to file an expense report detailing and breaking down amounts she spends annually of his behalf.

I've help with many things in the Immigrant Community but this was something that I did not have any experience with so looked for the first place to start. On the court request, it provided information for requesting a court facilitator to assist with completing the required forms but after calling the number provided, a message machine indicated that it could be 48 hours before they returned my call and more importantly, seemed to be suggesting that it would be necessary to travel to downtown Seattle to get any help which appeared unlikely that Lidiya could or would be able to get there.

By the next day, I still had no response from the Facilitator's office and had another appointment with another lady for a different reason. In the process of discussing this lady's problem, she revealed to me that she worked on a side job as a court facilitator and not just any court facilitator but one that worked specifically with guardianship forms. Imagine my surprise! I have assisted the Community for 25 years and never had a court facilitator in my office nor have I ever met one personally.

Esther, Elena and I took a few minutes to get

acquainted and learned that Esther loved our Lord and attempt to maintain a close walk with Him at all times. The Spirit of our Lord revealed her great love for Him and we rejoiced together.

I'm beginning to get the feeling that our Lord was setting up the situation where He will be doing something for Lydiya. I briefly shared with this lady Lydiya's issue and she very quickly agreed to meet with Lydiya and help her complete the required forms and indicated she was an expert with this as she worked with these forms all the time, at no charge, of course. She indicated that she loved the Lord and always looked for ways to serve Him and that He had always assisted her throughout her life.

I quickly called to Lydiya and had her come over to meet Esther. They hit it off very quickly and agreed to meet again in my office a couple days later. Esther would drop by the court house and pickup information on the case that would be required to complete the forms and have that ready for the next meeting.

By now, Elena and I had just become observers and started experiencing a meltdown as we could see what the Lord was doing for Lydiya and how it was coming together.

I might add that Lydiya is originally from the Ukraine and Esther is originally from Romania. They had never met before. Esther had originally scheduled a meeting with me a day earlier but had to cancel and reschedule. Without knowing it, had she come for the first appointment, the timing would have meant she could have missed being made aware of Lydiya's issues and/or need.

Out of the Fire, 30 Years Later

As these people mastered the English language, obtained employment and adjusted to the local culture, they have assumed responsibility for most of their needs. Today, my help consists of assisting with immigration problems, which can require writing letters, I frequently write business letters for various reasons, assist with various applications, compose job resumes, assist them with filing tax applications, and/or make phone calls when it is essential to understand English. Increasingly, people are coming about marital problems including divorce and child support concerns. This often includes prayer with them and can include attorney referrals. Before starting a new business, some may come for advice. The types of situations that come to me are as varied as each individual who enters my office. I always try to help and I pray daily that the Lord will allow me to mirror Him to these folks. He has given me a love for these people and they are very dear to my heart. Each passing year has seen immigrants from new Countries visit my office pushing the total Countries to approximately 140. Many, of course, are not of the Christian faith, but I always strive to allow the love and compassion of the Lord Jesus Christ to extend through me to them. It has been exciting to share/discuss our Lord with people born into any of the other religions from around the world and some have shown strong interest. I've concluded that young children growing up in a religion accepted by the culture they are born into will generally embrace that religion without question and by the time that child is grown can find it difficult to respond to another religion but we have had some who do.

Today, if I receive information about a donation of household items, I relay it to individuals in the immigrant Community who arrange for pickup and delivery to a family in need.

I have traveled to Russia four times, visiting Moscow every time and twice traveling on to Izhevsk in the Ural region, and once to Novosibirsk, deep in the heart of Russia, a little northwest of Mongolia. I remember bowing my heart before God, as I understood what He has done for me the past 23 years. Standing on the streets of Izhevsk, (Izhevsk had been a secret or closed City during Soviet Union Times because of nearby military and Industrial complexes.) A place where those of us who grew up in the cold war years had assumed would be an impossibility of ever visiting, gave me an eerie feeling, yet, looking at the streets full of people, knowing the majority are without a personal knowledge of Jesus Christ, tears swelled my eyes as compassion filled my heart. Elena, whom I had just met and was with me at the time, seeing the tears, asked, "What is wrong?" I responded, "So many people and so few have a personal knowledge of God." She then asked, "Doesn't God love the Russian people also?" I choked back my emotions and tried to take a few minutes to explain that, "God loves all people, if only they knew about it and turned to Him, He would forgive them and put joy in their hearts." I was keenly aware of the greatness of God and what He is capable of doing.

I marveled that so many of the people, whom I met, were without much knowledge of God, yet were basically good people, and had a strong knowledge of right and wrong. I also sensed a hunger for God that I believe is not matched in the United States. It seemed that many had put their faith and security in the Soviet system and now felt betrayed after its collapse. Their heart is open and hungry as they look for something to stabilize their personal lives. One young person confided in me that she believes that the Russian young people cannot commit to a future because they don't have a sense of future. As a result, they turn to drugs and alcohol.

I understand that some Regional Ministers of Education have asked American Church denominations for quantities of the Holy Bible and New Testaments so they can pass them out in the schools to offset the void in the young people's lives that is causing them to embrace drugs and enhance moral decline.

I hope the Lord will allow me some personal time after I go home to Him. I would like to ask Him, "Why the wall around the Soviet people?" In effect, they were imprisoned for about 70 years and understanding that He often used or allowed 7 or 70-year periods in dealing with His people. I also believe there is some significance to the 70-year imprisonment of the Soviet people. Every time man threatened to breach the wall, militaries bristled, but when God broke it down, man could do nothing but watch. It seems to me that the Lord is making final overtures to the people of the former Soviet Union prior to His return. Almost daily, I hear reports of large numbers of people giving their lives to God and new Church Congregations forming in most large cities and enjoying rapid growth.

Some of the immigrant children who arrived here with the first immigrants, now grown and educated, are returning to their country of origin as American Citizens to preach and teach the Gospel and open new churches in towns and villages across the former Soviet Union. They speak the native language and fit into local customs better than those who were not born there.

I recently assisted a local Ukrainian Minister develop papers and complete applications for U.S. tax exempt status for his organization. This will allow him to solicit funds from local Slavic churches to be used to open Bible Schools and Churches in those countries of the former Soviet Union. Today, there are several Slavic organizations in the area that are training young people to send as missionaries, both short and long term, to these countries. Some share reports of Spiritual breakthrough and Revival where before there was little knowledge of God.

One such young person was about 13 when I met him. After high school, he attended and graduated from Oral Roberts Bible College in Oklahoma and today is a Pastor for a new and rapidly expanding Church in the area that God is using to reach many of the young people in the Slavic Community as well as many non-Slavik for that matter. I praise God for what He has performed, not only in this person's life but the others in the Community who are also reaching the next generation for Him.

I have visited some of these new churches as well as various concerts put on by the Slavic Community and cannot express to you the amazement that I have when I witness the musical/acting talent displayed by these young people. It's incredible!

I don't mean to imply that everything has been rosy for them here. There are some families breaking up and young people visit my office on occasion while under the influence (for unrelated help) while some are getting into trouble with the authorities, but generally speaking, that applies to a small portion of the community. Every day, I give thanks to God for his sustaining power.

I also know that this generation will face incredibly monumental attempts by the devil to destroy them as our culture and even our world melts down around them and sin will be thrown into their face constantly, as the impure is glossed to look like the pure and the depraved and/or the asinine are made to look like the normal. My heart cries out for them and my prayers are for them that the Lord will walk with them and they will not forget their God.

I have met hundreds of immigrants with stories worthy of someone capturing and sharing. My greatest disappointment is that I have not been able to share all of them here. I commit those to the Lord knowing that He knows all, and He will someday read from the great book and call them by name as he says, "enter in my servant."

The Lord has put a love in my heart for all these people. I have heard that there are some of them that are not good people, but I haven't met any that I don't like. I feel a kinship with them as if they were my own people and can develop righteous indignation when I feel or learn that someone may be taking advantage of them are using them.

God is prospering them as they open new businesses and services. Within a recent week, three families have visited me asking for help in getting information on starting an Ambulance Service, opening an East European restaurant and opening a Carpet/floor covering store. One Trucking business generated in excess of 6 million dollars a few years ago and employed 53 truck drivers. I was recently informed that one of those families opened a business locally perhaps 20 years ago and grossed over 35 million dollars last year. There may be as many as 50 new immigrant Churches in the area, ranging up to 2,500 attendees. I've had recent contact with a young person whom I met when he was an early teen, who opened a new Church in the Ft. Walton Beach area of Northern Florida in September, 2017, and by Christmas of that year, was consistently running over a 100 people a Sunday service.

Having said that, I don't want to imply that there have not been some struggles;

The thirty years after the first immigrants from the former Soviet Union arrived in the area, the effect of this culture on their families and church structure has been dramatic. During that 30 years, having had an opportunity to assist perhaps 14,000 families in one form or another with several thousand coming through my office annually, today we see many who are first generation Americans, having arrived here when they were very small or was born here, the under 30 group. This group is the most vulnerable to the social pollution that America offers and we see too many who have been impacted by the influence of exposure to, and acceptance of this culture's standards.

My heart aches as I witnessed the breakup of some families and the effect of that on many young people given the fact that I have invested a significant part of my life within their Community. I was there when they arrived and saw such Spiritual strength in their parents as well as a strong Community spirit. Today, I see little of either. Some have agreed with me that many would have been better off Spiritually if they had not come to the United States.

Persecution, the prevailing reason so many were allowed to come here, historically has only made the Lord's Church stronger no matter how unpleasant it might be. The Devil ploys persecution in many Countries against His Church, but in America he uses a much more sinister method to demoralize Christians. He uses temptation as he did with Eve in the Garden with promises of prosperity, happiness and prestige appealing to each of the three types of sin identified in the Bible as the Lust of the eye, the lust of the flesh and the pride of life. (1 John 2:16 KJV) Those tried and perfected by persecution were not prepared for the subtleness but magnitude of temptations experienced here. Their senses have been bombarded constantly and the change in their lives so gradual, it is not obvious as it occurs. It even has had an anesthetic effect causing priority change and life style change. I have heard that if you put a frog into hot water, it will immediately jump out but if you put it into cold water then slowly increase the heat, you can boil it without it jumping. It's the same affect.

Some today don't claim to be anything and many others claim to be Christian but appear only religious.

They may find the biggest Bible they can and try to look so religious on Sunday but make no attempt to appear religious the rest of the week. To be sure, there are many who really love the Lord and you can see Christ in their lives but too many are running around like chickens trying to get whatever they can at any cost. Often, there is someone in my office, upset because a member of the Community has taken advantage of them in some way, often with a real estate or mortgage transaction or having worked for someone else in the community and now that person refuses to pay them their due salary, or? I frequently hear, "I trusted them, they are supposed to be so Christian, they are at Church every time the door opens, yet they cheated me so easily."

There must be many reasons for this break up, but the foremost in my mind would be the accessibility of "things." Most have become so materialistic that all energy is expended trying to obtain the biggest or the best of whatever. Where they came from, things were not within their reach no matter how much they wanted them so most were resigned to never having a lot of anything. In the United States, you can have just about anything you want if you are creative and are willing to work for them. Usually, the real price paid for them can be measured in terms of "loss" rather than gain.

To their credit, they see opportunity just about everywhere. For example, soon after arrival, passing junkyards, they would see automobiles that they could repair economically with their own hands or perhaps, with the hands of a friend or relative and these cars were cheap. Americans passing the same junkyards saw only junk cars.

Within 2 years, it was common to see families driving new, sometimes expensive cars while neighbors in their low-income apartment units where they lived were driving old beaters fostering jealousy and comments about the "Russian speaking" immigrants must be receiving more welfare then their American counterparts.

Today, many are making hundreds of thousands of dollars a year, usually working 12 to 14 hours a day and often 6 days a week. Husband and wife are often working, leaving children home alone or if they are lucky, with Grandparents. Sergey was sharing with me that he was working in such manner. I advised him that he may do that for a short time, maybe 2 years on a need to basis, but he should plan on being able to cut back within 2 years so he could have more time with his family. I advised that he should take the time to go boating, mountain climbing, hiking, or whatever the family enjoys. If he does not, he could very easily loose them. He responded, he cannot stop working such hours or he would have to take some of his toys back and I think he nailed the biggest problem in the Community today. He was driving a very expensive car, living in a very expensive home, etc.

Let me state at this time. If you love the Lord with all your heart, soul, mind and body, He will give you a full life including things as long as you walk in his will and put Him before everything else. I absolutely do not believe there is anything inherently wrong in having "things" but it must be balanced with common sense, real time with the Lord and family. If you lose those, you've lost everything no matter how much things you've accumulated and keep in mind the Bible tells us, "We came into the world naked and we shall leave the same way." The only thing we will be able to take with us are the lives we touched and encouraged while in this life. We should always remember that those "things" that God allows us to enjoy, including our lives, was given to us by Him and may be taken away at any time by Him. We should be always looking and listening for the shout so that when He comes, we can separate from everything quickly and completely. Jesus said in Luke 17:31 (NIV) "On that day no one who is on the roof of his house, with his goods inside, should go down to get them, Likewise, no one in the field should go back for anything." Then He makes an interesting statement. He says "Remember Lot's wife!"

So many who struggle so hard and put such effort into getting their share of things, have very little time or insight to be watching for Him, but even if they do, I suspect they may look back wistfully when He comes and could lose their place with Him.

Another problem that may be contributing to the overall Spiritual decline or misdirection of many of our people, especially the young, is a lack of Spiritual perception and/or improper teaching from our churches. Many Spiritual leaders seem anesthetized to what is going on in the Community. I'm reminded of an incident a few years ago when some young people told me that there was some checking out porno movies to watch while parents were at Church. I approached the Pastor of that Church to inform him of what was going on thinking he might develop some sermons or teaching indicating there are many activities here in this new Country that can destroy you or at least, take an interest in what his young people were getting involved in. He wasn't interested in even listening and quickly informed me that his young people did not do such. His attitude was such that I dropped the subject. There are considerable examples of lack of interest or refusal to accept reality of the many activities harmful to the Spiritual welfare of our people.

There are a number of our youth in Bible Schools across the Country and a few already doing missionary work in other Countries. I think the Lord for every one of these and am proud of each, but there are too many being lost. A few years ago, an acquaintance who works in the County Court system was telling me, at that time, that as many as 80% of the young people coming through the Court were from the immigrant Community. A gynecologist, also immigrant with a large immigrant clientele shares that many of the immigrant young girls coming to her have some form of Sexually Transmitted Disease but the law prohibits her from telling parents. My concern is that there has been no Community or Church safety net to try to reach these young people.

I don't want to come across as just a negative report, I can say that there are so many of our young people that I am soooooo..... proud of, so many that I have accepted in my heart as my own. Those addressed in this section would clearly be a minority, but it's still too many and troubling. I am aware of possibly, 2 groups in the area who have developed programs and are trying to reach out to troubled youth. Both groups are not sponsored by any one church but as far as I know, are independent.

Several years ago, a young person was brought to me with family problems. Her family had been church folks but was quickly becoming dysfunctional. I tried to pray and counsel with her as much as I could but there was so many, I was spreading myself pretty thin. I approached a Pastor whom I was very familiar with and ask if there was someone in the church who would take an interest in her, and her family, perhaps a youth Pastor? He was up front with me, and quite frank. He explained that the immigrant Churches didn't want problem people, at least, at that time, as churches struggled to legitimize themselves in the eyes of the community. If he showed an interest in such a person, his Church may remove him as Pastor. The young person that generated the discussion went on to become involved in drugs and worked for a few years as an exotic dancer in Seattle. I am convinced that if a Church leader or group, had taken an interest in her at the time she needed someone, she would not have gone through what she did. Thank the Lord, she was in my office several months ago, about 12 years older, wiser, had just gotten married and was telling me that she is now trying to get her life back together. She is attending a non-immigrant Church. She is the second such person that I know of who got involved with exotic or strip dancing.

Young people have visited my office under the influence of both alcohol and drugs. Some in the Community have died from such. Others influenced by homosexuality. An adult with small children was recently telling me that he is switching Churches because drugs and sex were being sold in his Church's parking lot and he didn't want his children to be influenced by them. I was told by another who attends this Church also, that the Pastor has made an attempt to stop the parking lot problem but had the tires on his car cut in the same parking lot.

A member of a youth group was telling me that a young person in another local Church was sharing with him that he has been sexually involved with an animal. This youth leader tried to share that same story with the Pastor of that young person but was threaten with disbarment from the Church if he didn't shut up immediately. It's as if the Pastor plugged his ears from hearing anything. Today, the person with the problem is deeper than ever in the sinful stranglehold but still attending the same Church. Not a pretty picture but its reality.

Lack of role models in the Community including Church Leaders, Teachers and the Business Community are misleading or confusing many young folks as well. The young are being pulled everywhere by unscrupulous people from both within and outside the immigrant Community.

Sexual deviants have historically viewed the immigrant young as open territory to find naive subjects unprotected by sense of Community and immigrants, no matter where they are from, and having an aversion to getting involved with authorities. Often these deviants present themselves as persons of success and/or good guys whom the young person can look up to, but in the end, wind up being abused and taken advantage of, as was the case a few years ago when authorities discovered such deviant had sexually abused as many as 30 immigrant boys in the local area.

Many who could be role models are wasting the opportunity by exhibiting themselves as people without integrity, driven by desire to get more things and suggesting by their behavior that the only important people in the world are those who have the most things and that those things should be the most expensive. This attitude is quite pervasive throughout the immigrant Community, yet without realization that if you win in the rat race, at best, you are only number one rat. This attitude is destroying many of our young people as they become blinded by a sense of competition to see who gets the most things. Others feel they cannot compete so they wash out and wind up in Spiritual trouble then in trouble with authorities.

I'm reminded of an incident that happened recently. I assist about 2500 families (90% immigrants) with their Federal tax preparation every year in addition to hundreds of others problems or concerns. During the year, those folks who are self-employed often need a letter from their Tax person to get a mortgage, indicating their length of employment and I always do this for my folks. I don't charge anything, I'm glad to be able to help. A lady loan officer within the immigrant community, seemingly successful, well known within the Community as a religious person, very involved in her church, called me about a person whom I have assisted, asking for such letter. I informed her that this person was not self-employed so would not qualify nor need a letter. I forgot about it.

Recently, a Mortgage Company called me to verify whether I had written a letter. I ask them to fax me a copy and I would gladly verify whether it was mine. Upon receipt of the letter, it was obviously not mine but someone had signed my name to it.

I called the loan officer lady whom I had the previous conversation with and asked how it is possible that such a letter was written and who had forged my name to it. She quickly became upset and begged me to not report it to proper authorities. I promised her that I would not report it if she would tell me who had written it for her. She told me that she had paid some college young people to make and sign it for her. I was aghast. I told her, "But you are a very religious Church person, what kind of message are you sending those young people? You're saying that it is OK to cheat and steal as long as you can get money for it, what kind of a role model are you to these young people?" I think it was her own kids as she has a couple in College. This situation has happened frequently with several immigrant loan officers over the last few years (I have several copies on file) with one loan broker currently in court charged by authorities for repeatedly making and signing false letters, among other things.

I was recently contacted by an immigrant Pastor and ask to help him get a mortgage by telling his Mortgage Company that he had a business besides being a Pastor. (He didn't) I informed him that I couldn't lie for him; The Lord would not be pleased with that. He says, oh don't lie about it, when they call you, just say some words" I told him that when they call me, I will tell them that you do not have a business on the side" and when they called, I told them that he did not have a business. I don't know if he ever got a mortgage but he doesn't come around anymore either.

Recently, a young person visited my office and was telling me a Pastor had damaged his car in the church parking lot, then had the audacity to ask him to tell his insurance Company that someone else had did the damage. He, understandably, found it incredible and was in a lot of turmoil as to how a Pastor could suggest such a thing.

At this time, I am not aware of many within the Community who would qualify as role models. They may be more that I am not aware of. By this statement I mean, of all the young people that I know and/or have come through my office, I've heard very few indicate that there is a leader or even a non-leader in the Community whom they look up too or respect or admire. One of whom I did hear such admiration from all who knew him and even those who only knew him by name, died a couple years ago in an aircraft accident in Alaska. It is my opinion that all looked up and admired him. He had the ability to identify with them and a strong interest in them. He stood a head taller than others in their eyes.

Young people everywhere need role models and young people are very intuitive. God seems to give youth a special sensitivity to adults who are disingenuous and can spot them very quickly, often even without anything being said and without involving the cognitive thought process. Adults who have been successful in their Spiritual and Business or Professional Careers are those whom these young ones can look up too with respect and admiration and use as people they can model their lives after. In the absence of such, young ones will follow after those offering alternatives and can wind up destroying themselves. It seems that with each life destroyed, we don't lose just one but the impact of that destroyed life can dramatically affect many others.

There are numerous other stories that I could share but it is not my desire to just expose all here for the sake of expose or to sound critical or cynical but rather share some of those things happening in the Community and hope that it might challenge our people to rise to the need. I know God is on the throne and He can burden the hearts of people of vision to pray for revival in the Community and especially our young people, others as workers and others as teachers, all with a burden for our young people. Perhaps the most critical to such ministry are folks who walk and communicate daily with the Lord and who can touch Him with their prayers.

I pray that those individuals in the Community with a burden for our young people will organize to fight the enemy and in prayer and by prayer, wrestle our young people from his clutches. I pray that those who do not see the need will have their eyes opened and that they will pray for such burden. We are losing too many.

My Travail, My Success

Toward the end of the summer in 1996, my first wife of 32 years was going through some terrible struggles.

I might offer some of my own opinions as to why, but since, at best, they would just be my opinions, I will leave all the reasoning up to the Lord. He understands and knows everything and He does that even before they actually happen. I am not recording this to assess blame but to show how the Devil can come into the best of situations and destroy.

Also, I want to show how God can take some of the most hopeless situations and turn them, around and show His love and goodness through it all.

Around the first of August, there was a knock at my door. When I opened it, there stood an old Ukrainian man with a boy who appeared to be 10 years old. I did not know either, but I assumed they were there to ask for help of some sort. I invited them in and they followed me downstairs to my office. Before I could ask them to be seated, the boy announced to me that the old man was visiting this country from the Ukraine for two weeks but felt the Lord had impressed him to come to pray for my wife. She was home at the time, but upstairs, and as far as I know, he had not seen her. I was puzzled and inquired why he thought my wife needed him to pray for her. As far as I knew, she was not ill. Through the boy, he said that he had come to pray for her salvation. As far as I knew, she was not ill, had no known problems and had been a Christian for as long as I had known her, but when someone wants to pray for me or mine, I never treat it lightly. I informed him that, "She has been saved for a long time, but if you feel you should pray for her, please do!" He prayed for some time, then left. Since he was praying in Ukrainian I had no idea what he was praying for, and I never did learn who he was or who he was visiting, as I never saw him again. I tried to forget about it but the whole scenario would come back to me months later.

Late August, things spiraled downhill and I seemed to have less control on my life and things that were happening to the ones that I loved. Life seemed very dark.

Over the next year, sparing details, she and I literally went through "hell" as our marriage came apart. In November of 1997, we were divorced. It seemed that I was caught up in a storm where situations and events were happening around me but I could not interact with them, much less control them. It's like I was on a rollercoaster. There were tremendous ups and downs, but all I could do was hold tight till the ride was finished.

I was numb. Divorce had never been an option to us. Our marriage had been so solid. Through the worst period, probably that first year, I experienced a full range of emotions. I was aware that God was with me and I often heard His voice coming from deep within, encouraging me, and counseling me. I picked up a copy of John Starnes' CD with a song whose lyrics included, The God of the day is also the God of the night; the God on the mountain is also the God of the valley." I played this tape for hours. It always lifted my spirit and encouraged me. People would remind me that I had certain scriptural rights. This often-generated seeds of anger or rebellion in my heart, but the Lord would remind me that my rights were not important; what is important is to do what was right by what I knew would please Him.

With this knowledge came the assurance that when it was all over, God would take the broken pieces and make something good out of them. The Lord reminded me that He knew, even when I stood up in my wedding ceremony years earlier, exactly how and when it would end. He didn't ordain it or sanction it, but because He knows all, He knew that it would happen. Therefore, He was not surprised.

Part of my grief, was due to the unexpected happening; I wasn't prepared for it. It seems some of the most challenging situations in life are the ones that come suddenly and catch us by surprise. We never expected it!

Later, as I began to pick up the pieces, I looked back and reflected on how God had placed certain individuals in my life. Even though I was perfectly capable of taking care of myself, many of the immigrant wives, fearing I would go hungry because I didn't have a wife to cook for me, sent prepared food to my home, often by the young adults in their family. Other families were there to pray with me and uplift me. Still others just wanted to befriend me and would drop by to encourage me or to just visit. All made me feel supported.

By late 1998, there were some who even thought I should start looking for another wife, and even tried to help arrange it. I consistently expressed my feelings that when the Lord felt I was ready, He would put everything together. I felt I was made a very special person by Him and there must also be a very special lady out there somewhere. He knew her already and could bring us together. In my wildest imagination I could not have pictured what would eventually happen.

In early 1999, an acquaintance showed me a picture of a lady who lived in a place called Izhevsk, Russia. (Izhevsk is the Capital of the Republic of Udmurtia, a republic within the Russian Confederation.) My initial reaction was startling. Not only did I see that she was very attractive, but something happened inside my heart, that to this day, I can't explain. It's as if I knew that I must meet this person. Yelena was her name. At first, I wrote her a letter, but discovered it can take 28 days or more for her to get it, and then that many days to receive an answer back. It's pretty hard to express feelings when you don't get a response till days later.

By May, my curiosity got the best of me, so I made my first call to her. I had no idea of the time difference, it was about 5:00 pm. my time but 4:00 am. her time, so the phone woke her. She spoke very little English and I didn't know much Russian, so our conversation didn't express much. But the one thing that impressed me very much was that, although I had awakened her, she was so incredibly sweet about it. She had no idea that I would call. It was a complete surprise, yet in spirit she was almost angelic. I knew even more so that I must meet this person. Yelena later shared with me the impact that phone call had on her life. She said that she can't explain it, but she knew that I would be coming for her. Sometimes, her friends would caution her that she should be open to dates with other men, but she would reply, "No, I will wait for Jim to come."

I located an organization on the Internet who could deliver her a dozen roses, and proceeded to do so. Things escalated quickly after that.

Yelena started taking private English lessons there in Izhevsk. Her teacher was on the staff at the University of Udmurtia, also located in Izhevsk, and had a computer at work. So, I started sending e-mails to Yelena at her teacher's computer. The teacher would print them off and take them to her when she had her lesson, and even translate them for her. Using this method, we made plans for me to come to Izhevsk in October, 1999. We would meet in Moscow for a few days and if we were both comfortable, we would then go to her city, which was about 1,200 miles east of Moscow. She had a 22-year-old daughter who would accompany her.

Excitement built during the month of September. I graduated to calling her every day. (I bought a special rate phone card.) Even with the excitement, I remember dealing with a lot of soul searching. It just didn't make sense for me to go halfway around the world to meet a lady that I didn't really know, but then I would argue with myself, "Even if it doesn't work out, I will have a fine trip and see places that I never would have otherwise."

I thought about it being cold, but I didn't want to buy warm clothing because I wouldn't need them after I returned home.

Eventually, an immigrant friend, worried that I could get cold over there, took me shopping and purchased a goose down coat for a $100. I later learned that it is usually below freezing in her area of Russia at that time of year. It's important to remember that, all along, I felt very strongly that God was in this and would put it all together. I just needed to go.

I dealt with fears about going alone to the former Soviet Union. After all, I had grown up during the Cold War years. All kinds of things would come to my mind, but deep down there was a voice that kept saying, "Just go." I didn't know at the time just how well God had planned it.

There was a family living in Moscow who had relatives living here that I had helped. As soon as they heard I was coming they insisted that they wanted to take care of everything for Yelena and me.

I visited with my brother about a week before I left for Russia and remarked about how nice the shoes he was wearing looked. A few days later he was in town again and presented me with an exact pair. They were not expensive, but I just liked the style. I could not imagine wearing them around Russia because they were new, stiff, and just not for walking. Besides, they hurt my feet some. I had been told that in Russia most people walked, and that I should expect to do so also. With this in mind, I went to a local department store and bought the best walking shoes I could find. They cost a little over $200. As a Type 2 diabetic, I did not want my feet to start giving me problems. Anyway, I decided to wear the cheap shoes but change to the expensive ones when it appeared that I might have to walk very far.

I left Seattle for Moscow on the October 18, 1999, and Yelena left Izhevsk for Moscow the same day with a 20-hour train trip ahead of her. She arrived in Moscow early on the morning of the 20th and our Moscow friend, Irina, as promised, was there to pick her up. She brought her to their home and prepared a meal for her. I arrived at the Moscow airport in the early evening of the same day, and Irina brought Yelena there to meet me and then took us back to their house. I learned that Irina had booked reservations for me at the Moscow Hotel which is on Red Square. She made the booking in her name to take advantage of the Russian discount. I cannot thank the Lord too much for Irina, she was just an incredible help for Yelena and me. She thought of everything and took care of all our needs while we were in Moscow.

After a week in Moscow, taking in the sights, Yelena and I were getting to know each other (she was even more wonderful than I had imagined, and she said the same about me). We decided to go to her hometown of Izhevsk, which was about a three-hour flight.

One thing that I puzzled about was the beautiful weather. I had been told to expect it to be very cold by late October. In fact, many people living both in Moscow and Izhevsk, told me that it was usually very cold at that time. I would remark, "Don't worry about it. The Lord gave me this weather just for my trip. The day I leave, it will become normal."

That's exactly what happened. After two weeks of gorgeous shirtsleeve weather in Izhevsk, the day I left Izhevsk by train for the return trip to Moscow, it was raining very heavily, and before we got to Moscow, it had turned to snow. Before leaving the Moscow airport for my trip home, the plane had to be de-iced before takeoff, it was so cold. But while in Izhevsk I ran around in short sleeve shirts only.

Remember the goose down coat? I never used it, not

even once. When I left Izhevsk, I gave it to Yelena to give to her Father. I walked just about everywhere.

Remember the $200 shoes? I didn't even unpack them. The cheap shoes were very comfortable. After returning to Seattle I took the $200 shoes back for a refund from where I had purchased them.

One day, Yelena and I may have walked 20 miles which included walking to her dacha (summer home) that she told me was about ten miles out of town. There was no road, it was all by trail. With the increase in exercise, I lost about ten pounds and went completely off my diabetes's medicine. My sugar level was very normal.

I was two weeks in Izhevsk before returning to Moscow. During this time, I fell completely in love with this little Russian lady. I became convinced that I could search the whole world over and never find another who was better suited for me. She was such a gentle, kind and soft person. Our first day at her place, she told me that all her life she had known there was a God, but did not know him personally, so we prayed together and she accepted the Lord into her heart.

Returning to Moscow, our train arrived at 6:00 A.M., Irina was there to pick us up at the train station. She again took us to her house and prepared a meal for us. Afterward, she took us to the airport where she and Yelena saw me off. She then took Yelena to the train station for her trip back to Izhevsk. Irina was just fantastic! We nicknamed her "Our Moscow Angel."

At the airport, it was crazy. Pushing and shoving. Before 9/11, at every airport I had been, friends could accompany you into the boarding area after checking your luggage. Not so at Moscow's airport. I checked my luggage and was then pushed with the surge of people past the ticket taker. I looked back for Yelena and Irina, but they were nowhere to be seen. I didn't get to say a proper "Good-bye" to Yelena and would not see her till several months later. I knew though, that if possible, I would be seeing a great deal more of her for the rest of my life.

After a painful 29-hour flight back to Seattle (with a 16-hour layover in Copenhagen, Denmark), I immediately sat down and composed Yelena the following letter. It had to be done quickly to capture all the feelings of the moment.

My Dear Yelena;

I remember the trip to the airport at Moscow. I had rehearsed in my mind how our departure might go. I had thought I would check my luggage and then you and I would have an hour or so to say a proper farewell, time to share with you how much you had come to mean to me and how much I had enjoyed this time with you. The trip to the airport went much, much too quickly. Before I knew it, we were there and it was hectic. Lots of people, pushing and shoving, we were moving quickly, trying to get all the paperwork taken care of and getting luggage checked. At the baggage check, there was only a quick hug from you, no talk, and then you were gone. This beautiful lady who had been by my side constantly for the last three weeks and had totally captured my heart was gone and I felt very alone. I remember moving toward the boarding area after the security check and feeling a very important part of me was missing. I looked back toward where I had last seen you, but you had disappeared into the sea of faces. My heart was torn and I resisted the impulse to turn and run back to look for you. Somehow, I maintained control as I moved into the boarding area, all the time searching the faces of the crowd where I had last seen you, hoping for a glimpse, a wave, one of those beautiful smiles. In a daze, I managed to find my way onto the plane where I pressed my face against the window, watching the windows of the terminal, hoping to see you one last time. I was numb all the way to Copenhagen.

At Copenhagen, I was still torn with many emotions. I just wanted to get away from everybody so I rented a room downstairs at the airport and went quickly to bed. My sleep was restless. All I could think about was my Yelena, and was tortured by the thoughts of not seeing you again for several months and knowing that you were on the train, going to your house all by yourself and probably every bit as miserable as I. I ached to return to you, to comfort you, to reassure you.

After boarding the plane at Copenhagen, the next morning, I still could find no rest. On the plane, I would try to shut my eyes and hope sleep would come, but every time I shut my eyes, there was my Yelena, right in front of me with those beautiful gray/green eyes, smiling sweetly, teasing me and I remember hearing you saying so sweetly, "Come to me," and "hold me tight," but when I reached for you, my arms came back empty. Tears were now coming to my eyes and I was afraid that people around me might see and not understand why a grown man might cry. I opened my eyes and turned my attention to a movie being shown on the plane. There seemed to be no escape. My mind always returned to my Yelena and those smiling, teasing eyes.

The tears come again and I no longer care if people see me. A stewardess passes me and hands me a napkin without saying a word. I am no longer functional. My emotional side tells me to turn the plane around and go back to you; my logical side tells me that I must move beyond this stage if I am to make it through to the time when we will be together again. In the end, logic wins.

Today, I am home again, but it's not the same place that I left. I suspect my life will never be the same again. I spent three weeks with a beautiful little Russian Lady halfway around the world, and her love changed the way I will look at life forever. I know you will come to me. We have to survive until I can get the paperwork approved, but for now, I've left my heart in Izhevsk and I will not be a complete person until you and I are together again.

I know the pain will not stop quickly. I must encourage you lest you worry that we might never see each other again. I will do that often while I wait for you to come to me...

In retrospect, I can see how the Lord was with me all the way: the weather, Irina to help Yelena and me in Moscow. Without Irina's help it would have cost considerably more for me to go, and I think I would have felt lost trying to find my way around and trying to coordinate everything with Yelena's arrival. Even the way it worked out about the shoes. If I believed in luck at all, I believe all that I would have, would be bad luck. When something good happens to me, I always give the credit to the Lord.

Soon after returning home, I submitted an application to the US Immigration Service for a fiancé visa for Yelena. It took some agonizing three months to process, including her interview at the US Embassy in Moscow. Irina again assisted her and was just marvelous. She arranged for Yelena to stay with them and provided transportation to the interview and moral support.

Yelena received her visa on the March 9, 2000, and my youngest son (who took a week's leave from the US Army) and I flew into Moscow on the 10th. We had to stay a week to get our return flight, so that gave my son time to see most of Moscow, and he enjoyed every moment. Irina and her family hosted us, and their hospitality was a wonderful blessing.

We returned to Seattle on the 17th and Yelena and I were married a few days later. Upon our arrival at Seattle, Karen, (pronounced Kareen) one of the refugees, had started a limousine/town car service, wanting to give us a proper ride home, met us at the airport with a town car and brought us home without charge. The whole trip was just incredible.

As I reflect back on my life, I am amazed. Every time the Devil takes something from me (and I know he can't, unless the Lord allows it), the Lord always provides something better. That has happened many times throughout my life. It sometimes seems that the Lord must love me more than anyone (probably seems that way to every Christian), because He has allowed me so much opportunity and has been so good to me. He has been with me through everything.

Yelena is the same angelic lady I met in middle Russia. Since meeting her I have never heard her raise her voice, and she seems to feel that God created her just to take care of me. I view her as a present from God.

She is an incredible lady as well as wife who loves the Lord and daily learns from Him. I am convinced that I could search the world over and would not have found a person better suited for me. She assists me in ministering to the community and is invaluable in assisting with translation and interpretation of the Russian language, which would be the native tongue for most of our folks.

I give God the glory and thanks from the bottom of my heart, and marvel that He can take such a tragedy in our lives and rebuild it into something so meaningful.

Today, after almost thirteen years of being married to that lady from Izhevsk, I can only continue to marvel at how God can put broken pieces back together. We have others coming into my office that are going through a divorce, and I share with them that if they will strive to do the right thing and maintain a right relationship with Him, He can and will restore them to an even better situation.

I do not believe it pleases the Lord for His children to divorce, but I'm also a realist. It clearly happens. Rather than let it destroy us, we need to put all our effort into maintaining our relationship with Him even though it may be the toughest thing we ever do.

We have now been married 18 years and every day I

think the Lord for Elena continue to believe that I married an Angel!

Trials than Praise!

June 25, 2009

While sitting in my office contemplating an upcoming open-heart surgery, realizing this would be the fourth major surgery and the eighth one total in my lifetime, I considered calling someone to prearrange for the possibility that I might need some help from sources outside my family. I work with the community of immigrants living in the local area. They have come from different places around the world, and I know at this time, perhaps 12,500 families from over 78 Countries, most of whom, if they thought I might need help, would come quickly to assist.

But in my lifetime, I don't recall ever asking anyone for help. If I needed help, I asked only the Lord and He has always provided for me. As I thought about this, the Lord spoke to me that if I needed help, He would send it, giving me the assurance that He will do the same now. So, I put the idea out of my mind. I sent out an e-mail to a few people stating that I would be in the hospital for a few days while receiving open-heart surgery. But I neglected to even mention which hospital I was going to. I just asked those folks to remember me in prayer, and then I shut down my computer.

June 26, 2009

In a phone discussion with Elena, an Armenian family from Azerbaijan, Garik and Karena, learned that I would check myself into the hospital, so they volunteered to drive us the eighteen miles. Upon my admittance, and after further tests, my surgery was set for 8:00 A.M. on the 28th, a Sunday. I can honestly say that at no time did I feel fear or dread, as I know that my life is in the Lord's hands and nothing can or will happen to me without His knowledge. I joked with the surgeon that we've got to get this done as quickly as possible because I have a yard that I needed to get home to mow.

Before it was over, I received six bypasses.

July 2, 2009

The surgeon was pleased with my progress. On the second and third days after surgery, nurses came to take me for a walk. Instead, I actually took them for a walk. I was released from the hospital on the 2nd, four days after surgery. During my stay, a family from Iran, Dariush and Maryam, responded very quickly by visiting us and bringing a pot of cooked chicken with rice. (She didn't like the hospital food.) The first three days at home were very tough because of all the medicine that I was taking, and before I returned to my feet, this family was just like angels to us. We know the Lord brought them into our lives at this time. They also brought us home from the hospital and Maryam spent a day with my wife as she was exhausted from taking care of me. While there, she made lamb and rice. I didn't know, but they told us that in their country, everyone having surgery is expected to eat this dish afterwards because of its healing properties. I've since heard others say the same thing. She was just a jewel.

Hamid and Nasrin, from Iran, also came. They brought a visiting relative—an orthopedic surgeon from Canada—who advised me about the surgical cut of my breastbone (for free, of course).

Dennis, a friend, came and helped my wife locate and rent a hospital bed for me so I would not have to manipulate the stairs. It arrived quickly, and Phil, a neighbor, helped Dennis rearrange the family room furniture to fit it in. Dennis's wife Natasha, a pharmacy technician who is from Russia, was with my wife often, helping her understand and sort the various medicines. There also came to help, Branislav from Serbia, and Paola, his wife who is from Italy, and a couple from Ukraine, Andrii and Larisa. Another lady from Ukraine, Lyuba, came to spend a day with my wife just to be with her. It was such encouragement having someone with whom she could share her concerns. This lady did not know that I had been in the hospital, but called and said that for some reason, the Lord had been nudging her to contact us. When she learned what was going on, she hurried over.

Phil came over and watered the lawn and mowed the grass for several weeks, and he and his wife, Lynn, checked up on me for a couple months after. Another neighbor, Sergey, came and edged the lawn. Several weeks later, a Ukrainian fellow, Yaroslav, stopped by and mowed the grass for us again.

At the time my chest was opened during surgery, it put a lot of stress on my back, which resulted in some back pain a week or so later. A neighbor, Oleg, a massage therapist, gave me a back massage and the pain never returned.

As word leaked into the community, still others phoned and/or stopped by to let us know that they were praying for us and pulling for me and inquiring if there was something they could do for us. Two weeks after my discharge from the hospital, I returned to see the surgeon for a final release but was still not able to drive the eighteen or so miles. Hamid and his wife, Nasrin, called and insisted on taking me there, and returning me home afterwards.

During the night of the third day after arriving home, Elena, came to me in the night crying, feeling overwhelmed by the stress of caring for me 24/7, and concerned about all the medicine she was giving me, not being sure she understood well when to give it and when not. Some interacted with others, etc. I felt completely helpless to do anything for her, so all I could do was pray that the Lord would do something very special for her. I couldn't have imagined what He would do.

She likes to have a pedicure periodically, but had not had one for a couple of months. While noticing this on the afternoon of the third day after my arrival home, she resigned herself to the fact that it would have to wait as she could not leave me at this time.

After asking the Lord to do something very special for her, the next day we received a call from a Russian lady we knew very little, Nataliya, who lived about eighteen miles away. We had seen her perhaps only twice before. She informed my wife that she was a pedicurist and wanted to come the next day and give her a treatment. And she did exactly that, plus she even gave her a foot massage. The personal attention was exactly what my wife needed at the time. It did so much for her. She now weeps as she understands that the Lord cares for even those little things in our lives.

An incident right after the surgery stands out in my mind even today. As I was being taken upstairs from the operating room to the recovery area, the sedative was wearing off and I was returning to a normal state. One of the hospital staff asked me if I was talented. I told her I didn't think so, why? She replied that while I was under sedation she heard me singing. I've thought about that and often wished I had asked her what I was singing. It seems unlikely that I was actually singing, however, since my throat had been paralyzed with an injection and there were two breathing tubes down my throat. I was aware that from somewhere deep within, I was humming the chorus;

Praise the Lord; Praise the Lord, Let the Angels rejoice.
Praise the Lord, Praise the Lord, Let the earth hear his voice.

Praise the Father through Jesus the Son and give them the glory for great things they have done.

Maybe she had heard me humming it? I could not shut it off, even five or six weeks later, night and day; it was going around and around from somewhere within, and for several days after returning home I could feel the nearness of the Holy Spirit as if He hovered over and filled me, and my soul rejoiced. I shouldn't be, but I'm amazed that every time the Lord does something for us He does it so well. As I've said, I could have called and lots of folks would have come, but it's so beautiful when the Lord puts it together; it is spontaneous, as the Lord lays it on a person's heart.

It also amazes me that so many people from such diverse backgrounds came to us. Some were Christian and some were not. I believe that after the Lord assured me at the beginning that He would bring the help that I needed when I needed it, had these folks not responded, He could have commanded the trees or the rocks or anything and they would have rose up and assisted us.

It is now eight-and-a-half years after returning home from the hospital. I was instructed by the medical staff that I would most likely be taking a number of pills the rest of my life. I had already taken medication for type 2 diabetes for about seventeen years. About six months after the surgery I felt inspired to just stop taking any medications, and promptly did so. It has now been two-and-a-half years since I've taken medication of any sort other than the common aspirin. My doctor became concerned right after and lectured me about how he was trying so hard to keep me healthy and I wasn't cooperating. I told him if he wants someone to take pills, he can take them himself. After reviewing lab results, he agreed that my statistics looked fine. Through extra diligence and support on Elena's part, and through diet and exercise, my physician consistently gives me an excellent mark as glucose levels and blood pressure readings are normal.

I'm usually not an emotional person, but I can get emotional when I dwell on the goodness of the Lord toward me and my loved ones. This was one of those times.

THE GOD THAT DOES NOT FAIL

"The Vegetable Garden"

Every year, my wife raise's a vegetable garden in our back yard. She plants her plants in an area specially set aside for this purpose but before she ever plants anything, she purchase's several bags of special soil from the local market, but not just any soil. It has to have just the right ingredients by her standard to produce the best plants.

I selected timbers (natural, no treated ones) from the hardware store to frame a raised area to backfill with organic soil. After hours of laborious preparation, she is ready to select just the right plants for her tomatoes and took time to select the right seed for her other vegetables.

Through late Spring and early Summer, had you noticed her doting over her plants, you might conclude that she really loved those plants considering that she inspected them daily for disease, insects, decay or dying plants. And wild plants? Weeds etc., they were yanked and disposed of in the compost pile quickly. She could easily recognize which were her plants and those that were not.

She hoes and waters her plants regularly as they need it. She knows what is best for them.

But you know what? Her concern for those plants only extends until they produce fruit. She doesn't plant then labor over them just to produce beautiful plants. It is the fruit of the plant that she anticipates. You should see her pride in them at harvest time. It had been well worth the labor put into them.

After the Tomato plants had produced their last tomatoes and/or the Green Bean plants have produced their last beans, she tears those plants up and dumps them on the compost pile. You say Cruel! But it's her call. Her caring and feelings for those plants are conditional on the probability that they would produce fruit for her. There was no inherent value in the plants themselves. Their value was in their potential. It was to that end that she had been directing her effort. If she noticed any that had become diseased, she knew exactly what to provide to heal them, however, if any embraced a disease that there was no known cure, recognizing that they would never overcome, she quickly destroyed them. Cruel? It's her call.

As I recently enjoyed one of her tomatoes, I admired its taste as it was very delicious, its color was a perfect red and it appeared that a more perfect tomato would be hard to find anywhere when the thought hit me that it was nothing more than dirt and I marveled that God could create a process where He can turn common dirt into such a perfect fruit. I was aware that this perfection came from the dirt and will go back to dirt and that our human bodies follow the same process. Only our spirit, fruit of the body, will be lifted to Him if it is deemed perfect by Him through the redemption of His son.

Something very interesting happened to one of her cucumber plants. She had planted it in a large container and placed a 6-foot vertical rod for it to climb on as it grew. It succeeded in reaching the top of the rod but if you were to see it, you would quickly surmise that it must be one of the ugliest plants you've ever seen. It appeared to be alive only in the upper foot or so of the plant. There were no branches and leaves on the lower part as they would quickly turn brown and fall off as it grew. Life for this plant was clearly a struggle but you know what? It produced about 15 large beautiful cucumbers on it and undoubtedly became the most productive plant in her garden, demonstrating that no matter what the odds you face in life, you can overcome and still produce fruit pleasing to the Master, even an abundance.

By mid-September her sweet Banana Pepper plant had produced about 17 nice long red peppers and to look at it, dressed out with all those red peppers, it was beautiful and added so much color to her garden. I thought it was a great plant and with its bountiful harvest, she must be extremely pleased with it but she came to me and ask me to remove it for her and cast it onto the compost. My immediate question was why? How could she do this to such beautiful plant? What about its fruit?

She replied; I have tasted the fruit and it has no flavor and is a bit woody in texture. Not what I was expecting therefore I have no desire for it and this late in the season, it has no time left to produce fruit that I might find tasty. It was her call.

I removed it for her and unceremoniously tossed it into the compost to destroy itself.

Matt 3:8-10 John the Baptist, Speaking to the Pharisees and the Sadducees, both Jewish religious sects, stated; Produce fruit in keeping with repentance (9) and do not think you can say to yourselves, "We have Abraham as our father" I tell you that out of these stones God can raise up children for Abraham (10) The ax is already at the root of the trees, and every tree that does not produce good fruit will be cut down and thrown into the fire. (or compost)

I believe there is a lesson here for life. God will bless, guide and care for us as He see's value in our potential to bear fruit pleasing to Him. If on the other hand, we do not or cannot bear Spiritual fruit pleasing to Him, He will cut us off or pluck us out of His garden.

You ask; what is fruit pleasing to Him? I think it would always involve and result from obedience to His Holy Spirit and a desire to allow Him to model our life. Our goal in life should be, to be like Him and as we allow the Holy Spirit to nurture our spirit, we can develop our relationship with him thereby pleasing Him.

Jesus, in John 15:1-8 uses this allegory about Himself to illustrate His desire for each of us to produce fruit and declares that the Father is our gardener and explains how we can/should produce fruit pleasing to the Father. Paul, in Colossians 1:6-10, also alludes to producing fruit as Spiritual growth including Spiritual knowledge and wisdom mixed with love for each other.

An interesting thought; Man was created to fellowship with God and was assigned (planted?) in a garden. Was it the creator's intention to raise a crop of new spirits that would inhabit the bodies of man for development? That flesh of humans was not intended to be anything more than a human robot created expressly for allowing the spirit to interact with the physical world having the effect of maturing it but at some point the body became infected with a disease (sin) that required it to be put outside the garden? At death, as a result of that disease, those who have accepted redemption, the spirit will leave that human body (robot) and return to the state it was originally intended with the Master Gardener, those who don't qualify for redemption, will be thrown on the compost pile.

The word garden usually refers to a place where things are grown but other words can also be used to refer to such places, such as Paradise. Jesus told the repentant thief on the cross in Luke 23:43, "This day, you shall be with me in Paradise." Has the Garden referred to in Genesis and called Eden always existed and does even today but somewhere, perhaps in a different (Spiritual) realm, where we cannot access it because of the disease we carry in our genes? And we would carry that disease there and contaminate it as well if allowed to interact with it without first cleansing from that disease called sin? Thereby being provided with a new body as Jesus was provided upon His resurrection. Cleansing comes only from the blood of Jesus as shed on the cross for our atonement.

Pondering these thoughts, the idea came to me that even today, when people become infected by a non-treatable disease such as e-bola, what does society do? They quarantined the infected people, that is, set them apart from the rest of society. How is that done? They are put into an area where they cannot come into contact with other people who are not infected. There was a time in my life when I had contacted an infection in my chest (incident related earlier in this book) and was quarantined for over 7 weeks. I lived in my own little world. While I knew there was another world on the outside of the curtains that defined my quarantine area (my world) and people from the other side could come to me, I could not go to them. Also; nothing from my world could be taken to the other side, it had to be bundled and destroyed, same with the spiritual application. This seems a fitting allegory indicating similarity with the Spiritual dilemma humans find themselves in.

Lesson of the Fig Trees

A few years ago, I was given 4 small fig trees as my wife likes figs and I planted each on the four sides of our property with the one thing in common, I expected each to bear fruit. Each tree varied in height from about eight inches to maybe 6 feet and none looked alike. That is, some were slim with few branches and others were bushy with a number of branches.

I selected a place for the smallest thinking it will need extra protection from the elements and what I thought was good soil for it to grow rapidly and to achieve a great height with abundant fruit.

The second one was about the same height and I planted it in what I considered a special place for it. Since the soil didn't appear real good at this place, I built the soil up and even put 4x6 timbers to help prevent the built-up mound from eroding.

The third one was located in an area that seemed just right for it to grow and spread it branches. It was about 6 feet tall, was lush and leafy and appeared the best candidate of the four to produce an abundance of fruit quickly.

The fourth tree was possibly the ugliest tree you have ever seen. It was about 6 feet tall, skinny with few branches and no leaves. It might have been dead from its appearance. I planted it in my garden.

An interesting picture formed the following year.

Tree number one; it has showed no growth let along having any fruit on it. It had a large group of leaves on it but has constantly struggled just to maintain itself and it appears at the time that it will never achieve its potential.

Tree number two; it has done quite well in the mound that I created for it. It was about two and a half feet in height, branchy and leafy but as of yet, has shown no inclination to bear fruit.

Tree number three; it is a gorgeous tree. Maybe eight feet tall, leafy and lofty with lots of

Branches, it's a beauty to the eye. Any owner would be proud of it, but... it has no fruit.

Tree Number four; is still probably the ugliest tree you've ever seen. Tall and skinny, few branches, looks unhealthy, no leaves except just on the very tips of the branches; but...

It had ten figs on it the first year and by the 3rd year, had too many to count. My wife has also verified that they are very tasty.

I had a decision to make. You see, I didn't plant these trees just to have more trees around my place. They were never intended to be just ornamental trees nor would their size and shape lend toward consideration as an ornamental tree. I planted them to bear fruit. The next season, I will watch them and those which do not bear fruit or appear to be able to achieve that potential; I will cut down and throw into the compost. You might say, "But that's cruel!" I would say, "But that's my call." I would emphasize that I planted them for a specific purpose and that purpose exceeds just being alive and/or have a lofty lifestyle, while it might mean something to the tree, would have no value to me. But you say, "You love those plants!" I say, "My love for them is conditioned on expectation!" They did not live up to my expectations of them so they will be destroyed."

As I contemplate this situation, I am reminded that this metaphor mirror's God's expectation of the human life. After "planting" the original human in the garden He placed certain expectations on that human and those expectations extend to all humans since. Those who do not embrace His expectations, never raise to the level of achieving value to Him, so, at the end, will be cut down and thrown into the garbage (fire). Again, it is His call since humans were and are His creations so they belong to Him giving Him the authority to save or destroy. There is no value inherent in life itself but its value is in its potential.

I'm reminded of the parable of the Farmer sowing the seed that Jesus told us about in Luke 8:4.

Now, several years later, I have only one fig tree. You guessed it! I have the ugly one. This year it is still ugly but it is showing signs of becoming beautiful as it matures and assumes a loftiness and it's... loaded with figs. My wife loves them as they are very tasty.

The Vine

4:20 AM; July 24, 2011

As I lay in bed, having awakened from a sound sleep of several hours. My mind turns to several incidents that I had recently read in the Bible while studying the book of Genesis. For several days, I had puzzled over what appeared to indicate that the Lord often involved Himself personally and directly in the lives of humans considerably more in the Old Testament then we see today. Now, in these early morning hours, the idea comes to mind again.

Incidents include Jacob wrestling with the Lord in the vision about the ladder to heaven, (Gen 32:22 - 30) Judah's sons, Er and Onan, (Gen. 38:6 –10) whom the Lord considered bad people so "the Lord put them to death", even Moses, the great lawgiver whom most of the Judeo-Christian values written into our laws today are attributed to, barely escaped death by God and only when his wife intervened (Exodus 4:24-26), to name a few. There are numerous accounts throughout the early books of the bible where He intervened or sent Angel's to pronounce blessings or carry out retribution as the recorded incident with Abraham prior to the destruction of Sodom and Gomorrah. Today, the world we live in has become so ungodly, many of the early incidents seem trivial in comparison yet we benefit from His sense of tolerance. In particular, the account of Er and Onan; would seem pretty drastic by today's standard and the question arises, does He still put bad people to death? Does He allow hurt and pain to befall His own? Why seemingly tolerance now but not then?

215

Lack of tolerance would not be consistent with the modern concept of our God. The perception of God by many today is that He is a kindly old grandfather that winks at the sin or transgressions of man and is so full of love that ultimately, He won't hurt anyone. Some internet religious philosophers' even state that when it's all over, it won't matter how you have lived or what you may have done while in this Life, God is soooooooo... much love! He will give everybody a second chance since He loves everybody so much, He doesn't have the resolve to destroy anybody. Emphasis is exclusive to the aspect of His love without consideration to the aspect of His sense of expectations and justice which dictates retribution. I don't know of any situation in my life's experience that I would consider death to anyone as direct intervention by Him, but then I don't know for sure, it may have happened. After all, it is His call. As I pondered this...

Memory of just yesterday came quickly to me; I had spent considerable time pruning my yard and garden plants including my grape vine that I have labored with to get it right. I realized the idea of the vine is often used to illustrate a family tree or the linage of an individual or group and as I realized this vine was mine. It belonged to me. I planted this vine and as a young vine, I have an image in my mind of what I want it to become complete with bountiful fruit, not just this season but for future seasons even if it means sacrificing branches or new growth now. It's not just a today thing, it is meant to stretch into the future when I expect to reap something from it.

To get it to conform to the image or the vision that I have of its future, I need to prune it. Similarly, vines in every vineyard around the world go through extensive pruning. To see a vineyard after pruning, you get the impression that the vines have been extremely abused. Pruning includes cutting off those branches that are diseased or that would be either nonproductive or

216

counterproductive. It can also include cutting off perfectly good branches that I might determine would create a burden for the vine and or interfere with it producing fruit. If the plant had the ability to speak, I'm sure it would put up an argument against cutting when the blades of my pruning shears cut into its fiber. This could also pose an argument by some that I am being selective and/or unfair, but.........It belongs to me. Ultimately, whether in the face of argument or evidence, it's my call. These pruned branches are always destroyed. What! The branch protest, but you are a person of love; you love me and all my branches. You would never destroy me, Why, you love me so much that no matter what I might do or become, you will just overlook it no matter what negative influence, or rot, or disease, or decay which could ultimately destroy me or render me useless, having no value or burden me. How is it possible that you can destroy my branches when you are just so much love...? That just doesn't fit my understanding/perception or concept of you.

My response to the pruned branch might be, "Maybe you should review your concept of me." It's of dire importance that you get it right.

When it comes to understanding God's expectations of man, it's critically important that we get it right. Our life in the physical world is a one-shot deal; if we don't really understand Him and His expectations until after death and we've got it wrong, we can't start over again.

Jesus vicariously identified with the vine when He said in John 15:1 – 2, "I am the true vine, and my Father is the gardener. He cuts off every branch in me that bears no fruit, while every branch that does bear fruit He prunes so that it will be even more fruitful." Verses 3 through 16 continue the idea that he is the true vine and the Father is the Gardener and the reasons branches are/must be trimmed.

Additionally; I have tied branches of my vine to

supports. I want to train the vine to climb in a manner that creates the idea that it belongs to someone who cares. It's not just a wild vine, growing wherever chance may take it. Again, if it could talk, it might be crying out or whining about the discipline but I know what's best for it, to bring forth good fruit. After all, it is becoming my creation as it conforms to my preconceived image of it.

The simplicity of this truth seemed to reach throughout the essence of my being. It's His call, we are His creation and it is like the vine, stretching from the beginning of time to the end and He would know everybody all along the way. He knows everything from the beginning of time to the end and even beyond. He knew me even before I was born; He knows the how and when I will see Him face to face. He has a concern about what I (and others) become and every time I feel the pains of life, it's the process of pruning away the parts of me which prohibit my spiritual growth. He has allowed it for my benefit, to bear fruit of the Spirit.

Does He directly involve Himself in the matters of humanity today as He did in the beginning? Yes, even if we don't seem to notice. Could it be that as we pursue the cares of life, our careers, our need to exceed and gain material possessions and its sense of power or associate with power figures in the Community; we have become anesthetized to His presence or the influence of the Spiritual world on our lives? Have we become so dependent on ourselves today that we find it easier to look to or depend on our own perceived ability or on some gadget that might be available to us from the technological explosion of recent years? or some medical professional? to avoid critical pruning.

Fruit (of the Spirit) that is pleasing to God, Love, joy, patience, kindness, goodness, faithfulness, gentleness and self-control (Gal. 5:22 – 23), is today considered weaknesses by our culture and as members of our humanity strive to move to the top of the rat race, they shrug off or shy away from the perception these fruits of the Spirit, (attributes) might project to others. It's all about image and our need to protect or reflect it in front of others, oh, the limits we go to disguise these weaknesses. Even if the Lord came and sat beside many of us, we might not recognize Him as our Spiritual eyes are blinded by our distorted perception of reality or might not want to acknowledge Him because it might affect our image of ourselves. Yes, I believe He is involved with the thread of humanity today even if we don't often acknowledge it. After all, we're His creation. It's His show. He's not only interested in individuals producing fruit but humanity as a whole to produce a select fruit and only those select fruit are, or will be called His own. Ultimately, the fruit diseased by sin will be cut off and destroyed. He knows where His creation is going and will prune or nudge it to affect its growth, which will not be finished until His return.

From our Lord Jesus' statement in John 15:1-2 NIV; "I am the true vine, and my Father is the gardener, He cuts off every branch in me that bears no fruit, while every branch that does bear fruit he prunes so that it will be even more fruitful". It should be clear that if we are followers of Him, we can expect the same process to occur within our lives as His Holy Spirit shapes and molds our lives to make us more pleasing to Him. "This is my Father's glory, that you bear much fruit; showing yourselves to be my disciples" (v:8) Notice the word disciple is also a major component of the word discipline. The two cannot be separated.

It is also important to remember that He sent His Holy Spirit right after the Lord's ascension, to minister to the needs of His people and teach them all things. While He might not choose to send Angels when we need help or communicate with us, we do have access to Him today through the Holy Spirit. He is still concerned but His method of interacting directly with humanity has changed. I know from experience that His Holy Spirit is always very close and will assist in our spiritual growth even if it might not be pleasant to us at the time.

Looking back across my time here, during the most difficult periods, not realizing it at the time because of stress of the moment, I now see His handiwork on my life and signs of His footprints in the sands of time, right beside mine. He has been with me every step of the way and especially during the toughest times. I tell many young people, "You must look forward and believe by faith that God will be there with you" where I have the benefit of being able to look back and see and know that He was there. During any pruning, you are allowed to say "ouch" but no matter what, always know that the Lord will be with you and afterwards, you will have grown; or you may have to go through the pruning again... And maybe again... until you get it. Perhaps some never get it consequently their ability to deal with life deteriorates and they go into ruin. Some spend their whole life as a pinball in a pinball game, just bouncing off one situation to another, never learning to allow His Holy Spirit to stabilize their life.

Hebrews 12:6 NIV; likens this pruning process to discipline, "because the Lord disciplines those HE loves and He punishes everyone He accepts as a son" (v7) Endure hardships (pruning) as discipline; God is treating you as sons. (v:11) No discipline seems pleasant at the time, but painful. Later on, however, it produces a harvest of righteousness and peace for those who have been trained by it.

My vine? By the second year after its initial pruning, you should have seen it. It has exceeded my best expectations! The weight from the abundance of fruit was so heavy, it started pulling the support post over so I had to put guide wires on the post to prevent it from being damaged. I have done seasonal pruning on it each year that it has been mine.

Vertigo Problem

May 21st, 2013; my wife has asked me to pick up a clothing item from an alteration shop about 7 miles from home.

I had just paid for the item when I was struck by very strong vertigo and everything was spinning so bad that I could barely stand. The owner of the shop could clearly see that I was in trouble so asked if I would like to lie for a while on a small bed she had in a back room. I declined saying that I must get on home. She ask how I thought I would do that in the condition that I was in. I replied that the "Lord would get me home." She didn't seem to buy that and I left her in a state of shock and disbelief, but I knew He would. She still had her doubts.

After struggling to stand and exit the shop and into my car, I, from deep within, told the Lord, "Jesus, it's now just you and I and I need you desperately, so please get me home" I cannot explain the feeling that come over me. It's as if some force blocked the nausea and spinning sensation. It's like I assumed an altered state of consciousness that continued all the way home. I was conscious of actually driving and at the same time, conscious of somewhere from deep within my soul a gentle voice cautioning me to slow here, careful of this curve, approach this intersection carefully, constantly coaching me. I placed my left elbow on the car window frame and using my left hand, propped my head with it to restrict movement of my head, driving pretty much with my right hand, arrived home without incident.

However; As soon as I parked the car in the garage and exited the vehicle, the nausea/spinning surged again as a

221

normal state of consciousness returned so entering our home, I grabbed a large pan as I struggled for the sofa where I quickly started heaving. I had asked the Lord to get me home and believed absolutely that He would. He did exactly that!

I had been bothered by vertigo for several years. Despite several medical test including hearing, brain scan for tumor and various test/x-rays of my neck area, nothing came back conclusive. Physicians were perplexed leaving me with nothing to expect but more vertigo with no proposed remedy.

Acting on a hunch from a Prosthodontist, I proceeded to have the metal from dental fillings and crowns inserted in my teeth over the years, removed in June of 2013 and after completing that task, it has now been two and a half years since and I have not even had a slight indication of vertigo since.

It appears it was caused by something called "metal toxicity" which occurs when enamel is worn away on teeth and the metal underneath is exposed, allowing the chewing process to grind away at the metal and traces of it is ingested into the stomach. Once in the body, it compromised the immune system creating neurological problems. It's like an allergic effect and seems to create a problem for only a small percentage of people.

About the little drive? Wouldn't recommend it to anyone unless that person had the absolute assurance that our Lord would be there for him. At that moment, had someone tried to tell me, "Don't do it!" would have about the same effect as trying to tell young David, "Don't go after the giant," Only He could have brought me home in the condition I was in and I remember a supernatural assurance that he would do it. That He might not just wasn't in the plan. Had He not got me home and rode with me and took charge of me and the vehicle, I most likely would have wound up hurting myself or others. It's with adoration and amazement that I look to Him for His dependability, ability, and resourcefulness when we need Him. You say, "But someone who knows Him should never be amazed?" I have to admit, I am still human and He amazes me all the time! And my heart is filled with "Praise and adoration for Him" He is an awesome God! I'm reminded of Nahum 1:5; "The mountains quake before Him and the hills melt away, the earth trembles at His presence, the world and all who live in it."

He could have removed that metal Himself and even given me new metal free teeth had He wanted to. I respect that it's His call.

Maybe it takes situations in life for us to come to where we have to totally depend on Him. Maybe that is why He allows us testing situations? Not that he has to know what we will do or how we will react, He knows everything so would know already how we will react but we need it as it develops our spirit and increases our value to Him and enhances our trust in Him.

Dream

May 15, 2009

Early this morning, as I lay sleeping in my bed, I had a strange dream.

There was an arm stretched before me. It gave the idea that it was attached to a body but I didn't see a body, only the arm stretching from the shoulder to the fingers. I was writing some kind of symbols on it with what appeared to be a marking pencil. The symbols were large, maybe 2 inches tall and I had marked the arm from the top to the wrist and was about to make the last mark.

I pondered the meaning of the symbols as I simply was making them but didn't know what they meant. As I wondered about what they could mean, the understanding came to me and I realized each symbol stood for a year. I than wondered what the total of the symbols amounted to and it came to me that they would total 16 and as I continued to wonder, the word came to me that it meant 16 years and a strong feeling that something significant would happen in 16 years.

I awoke, still wondering what it meant. Would the Lord come in 16 years? Would the world end in 16 years? Would it be the death of a loved one? My death? Or ???

Throughout the day, I continue to puzzle over it and continue to be puzzled about it to this day.

An event did happen shortly afterwards that might tie into it but I have not been able to make a direct connection yet. Maybe our Lord will tie everything together for me later but within 6 weeks, I went to a Doctor because my left arm was hurting and he immediately informed me that every time your left arms is hurting, it means you have heart blockages and pushed me in for test which were inconclusive but still he insisted that he knew what he was talking about and suggested that if I died before I left his office, it would not be his fault so I made tentative plans to take the recommended angiogram, afterward, I was told that the results were positive either way and recommended to continue with follow on surgery which resulted in 6 bypasses being performed when finished.

It gets more interesting though. After the surgery was over, the Surgeon informed me that everybody has blockages in their arteries but don't require removal until or unless their blockage exceeds 85%. He indicated that none of mine was that bad but since he already had my chest open, he went ahead and performed the bypasses whether I needed it or not.

Additionally, when admitted to the hospital, my concern level wasn't any higher than if I had just dropped by to say "Hi" to everybody. The Surgeon told me that he could cut on me either on Sunday or Monday? I told him to cut me on Sunday as I didn't have much time to mess around with them, that I had a yard at home that I need to get back to, to take care of. And; within a day after the surgery, the nurse came and got me out of bed to walk me but I walked faster than she did, creating some surprise for her as well as for the Doctor when she informed him. Four days after the surgery, I checked out and went home while others were staying for at least, a couple weeks. In retrospect, I puzzle over a lack of any real concern that I had and the rapid turnaround while conceding a high level of confidence that our Lord was with me at all times and my life was in His hands no matter what happened.

Oh Yes, the Doctor who made the initial analysis, he immediately retired and disappeared.

The diagnosis was related to a problem with my arm, is there a connection with the dream?

Since the heart surgery, I have experienced a heightened understanding of many "things." This includes time, space, our physical world as well as Spiritual things. Sometimes it comes to me slowly over a few days, other times it is as if understanding burst somewhere within me and floods throughout my innermost self. It's not just a mental understanding but comes from deep within my soul. It fits perfectly with my own sense of logic or expands it and I find myself exclaiming inwardly, WOW!

The Glory of Heaven

Early morning on August 23, 1993, while at sleep in our bedroom, I experienced something pretty dramatic. I couldn't say for sure if it was a dream, vision or an out of body experience. I have since come to believe it was an out of body experience because of the reality of it and its content and the after effect.

As if in a dream, my wife and I were eating at a table with some folks on a porch or deck, I don't know where we were or who the other folks were but there were flowers near us and all of a sudden, the flowers started waving as if to someone, not like they would if blown by the wind, it was a distinctive wave as a greeting. The folks with us became very alarmed but we knew somehow that the Lord was coming and these flowers were waving to Him and even without verbalizing it, were singing praises to Him. We didn't hear them with our ears but we heard them from within.

Within seconds we were wrapped in the Holy Spirit and I cannot find words to describe the feeling of euphoria that burst within us. It was absolutely incredibly astounding. We were immediately caught away to a place where we could observe the physical world through what appeared to be a glass wall. Our side of the wall was bathed in a bright but very comfortable light which we recognized to be His presence while the opposite side from us was total darkness. There were people crowding the wall from the other side trying to compete for the dim light that spilled through the glass. It seemed that I was peering into the physical world from heaven and the wall was as if a veil that separated the two dimensions. Those

227

near the wall were Christians within the physical world that had experienced or had knowledge of the Lord and was pressing toward the light who was the Lord. I remember realizing that I did not recognize any of them. Further away from the wall, into the darkness, I could see what appeared to be some sort of vehicles moving rapidly in the darkness and in their headlights, were people trying to escape them. Some vehicles appeared to be trying to run over people while other vehicles seemed to be trying to rescue people.

I did recognize one of the people in the headlights as one of our sons. My wife mentioned "He's trying to get himself killed so he can join us." I had no knowledge of any other people while there. I was aware that none of the people on the other side of the veil was aware that we were observing them.

During this time, I experienced a sense of movement but no sense of effort as if weightless. It was the most blissful feeling I've ever felt. I cannot find words to describe it. I recall thinking, "I must be dreaming so I will pinch myself." I did and I wasn't dreaming because I felt it even though I appeared to be without physical form. There were other "Beings" with and around me and they were also without physical form, yet clearly discernible. I knew them as Spirits and could communicate with them but there was no audible sound such as voices. It might be characterized as telepathy. I absolutely knew and understood their communications with me.

Other than my wife and the son, I do not recall knowing anyone else yet was comfortable with all as if family.

The scene changed and I was no longer with my wife but with 2 or 3 other people in a sort of machine like an automobile and we were moving through the darkness on the opposite side of the wall as if to rescue someone. I remember I felt no compulsion or desire to help anybody in particular and we passed several people and made no attempt to stop them or engage them in conversation. I distinctly remember passing a woman with a baby who seemed traumatized as if having escaped a war zone yet felt no compassion or anything for her. It's as if we had another reason for being there. As we traveled through the darkness I was aware that at some distance to our right was the area where the Light was and that it was expanding and would, in time take away the darkness from the area that I was in. I also had the feeling that my wife was awaiting my return to the lit side of the wall.

I became aware that my wife in the real world had entered the bedroom where my body was asleep and as I concentrated on her presence, I struggled ever so hard to return as if from a very deep sleep. After I managed to do so, I swung my legs over the side of the bed to get up and immediately experienced the most dreadful sensation that I have felt in my lifetime. I was keenly aware of being in a body again and the effort of just moving my limbs and feeling aches and pains. I looked at my arms fully expecting them to look different and checked my body to see if it still had surgical scars on it, then the overwhelming realization that I was in the body that I had occupied since birth. It took a minute or so to orientate myself to being housed in a body again and realizing that it was the same old body that had housed me before. In my mind, I was expecting to find myself in a new one. I was briefly swept by depression as if I had been put back into a prison after experiencing freedom for the first time and knowing that for the first time in my life, I had experienced a feeling of being fully complete, in the state that I was created to be.

I might be inclined to dismiss everything as just a very vivid dream except I am now sure that I had been out of my body and the things I had witnessed had been real. It was no dream. I continually search for words to express the feeling, the sensations and images that I had seen but after attempting to express them, always feel somewhat frustrated that I have not done so adequately. Only those who have had such an experience seem to grasp what I'm sharing and I can sense it as I share with them.

I am reminded of the account the Apostle Paul shared in 2 Cor, 12:2 (KJV) when describing the experience of a man who was caught up to the third heaven, even to Paradise, "and that he heard inexpressible things, things that man is not permitted to tell" and in 1 Cor.2:9 where Paul is quoting from Isaiah 64:4; ..."No eye has seen, no ear has heard, no mind has conceived what God has prepared for those who love Him".

I do know that for days, even years after, every time I think of that feeling of bliss, that sense of comfort, euphoria again swells within me and a song springs from my heart and even though I don't sing very well, within, I hear the most beautiful song in the world and Hallelujah exclamations as I feel the Holy Spirit well up within me. I would not continue to experience these feelings had it been just a dream.

I had a visitor to my office a couple years ago from India who belonged to the Hindu religion whom I had an opportunity to share the above with. He immediately began to share with me an incident he had experienced while a very small child in his home Country. He said that he had fallen into a river and drown when he was immediately ushered into the presence of God and as he related the story to me, he described almost exactly scenes that I had experienced in my story and I had the witness of the Spirit that his was true, as I feel when other Christians share with me Heavenly experiences they have had. As I puzzled over the fact that this guy admittedly was a Hindu. I believe the Lord spoke to me and shared that all small children upon death, no matter what religion their folks are, go directly to heaven as they are innocent, they just exist in time and space and have no religious leaning. As they age, at some point, they establish and build a religious belief system, even if an atheist one, which could exclude them from entering heaven unless their belief included the Lord as their Savior.

At his age today and belonging to the Hindu religion, it is my belief that should he die today, he would not enter heaven as his accepted religion does not acknowledge the Lord and our Bible states that there is only one name by which we may be saved, that is the name of Jesus.

Also; A Ukrainian friend shares with me about a time when he experienced an out of body experience while having been gravely ill for some time and details match mine pretty close to include the sense of depression after re-entering his body and the sense of euphoria experienced while in the presence of the Lord and the positive change he has encountered in his own life since.

- *Jim Pemberton*

Florida Angel

November 2, 2016

Early morning, I'm still lying in bed, my mind seems to be awake but my body seems still asleep. Vivid images began displaying in my mind, not like a dream but yet involving the thought process. In my mind, Lena and I are discussing going away someplace on a trip but no specific place was mentioned. We had previously made plans to go on vacation to Florida and even though Florida wasn't mentioned, I knew that was the place we were discussing.

Suddenly, a voice spoke to me from somewhere deep within my soul saying "in 5 weeks, you will walk alone" and I knew they were connected with the Florida trip. The words startled me and propelled me into deep thought wondering what possibly it could mean, leaving disturbing thoughts about maybe something happening to Lena or? Later, in the morning, I was careful to note on the Calendar a reminder to me about five weeks from the date. Because of the onerous tone of the words, I did mention it to Lena but kept it low key as I didn't want to set off alarm bells for anyone.

Four weeks later Lena and I boarded a flight to Florida and enjoyed out time there tremendously with the thoughts of the voice lingering somewhere out of or in the back of our minds.

December the 8th, Lena and I was walking together on the beach. She was picking up shells and had accumulated enough in her hands that it was apparent that she needed something to unload them into. I suggested to her that I would return to our resort unit to get a plastic bag and will meet her back in a few minutes.

While in our unit, I noticed some bread and remembered that I had seen some birds on the beach that would probably love it if I brought them some. With the bread in the bag, I returned to the beach but didn't go directly to Lena but the opposite direction to feed the birds. Upon finishing giving the bread to the birds, I looked down the beach in the direction of Lena and noticed some guy chatting with her. They were some distance down from me but could quickly determine that I didn't know him and if I didn't know him, she probably didn't either.

I started walking toward them as they were walking toward me so we came together fairly quickly. I could see that the guy appeared to be around 70 years old but was pleasant looking and I had no clue who he was.

He immediatcly bcgan to tell me that he had walked pass Lena as she picked up shells and his attention was arrested by what appeared to be an aura around her that suggested to him that she was an Angel. He asked her if she was an Angel which she simply smiled but didn't respond. I joked that I have known for a long time, that she was indeed an Angel, suspecting at first that he might be just developing a line to get acquainted.

He proceeded to say that he had suggested to her that she needed something to put the shells that she had collected into, as it was clear that her hands were full. She informed him that her husband was getting her a plastic bag, was on his way to her and in fact, was just a short way up the beach as they slowly began to move in my direction.

He inquired about whether we believed in Angels and we assured him that we did, then he stated that he walked with Angels every day. We discussed their roles in the Bible and how they sometimes interject themselves into some people's lives as well as are instrumental in human activity. I shared with him a report that Lena and I had seen on TV about a woman who was convinced she had briefly died during surgery and shared that as she left her body, she drifted up toward the hospital room ceiling, looking down, she could see Angels or Spirit beings standing behind and among the medical professionals and it was her feelings at the time that the Angels were coaxing the medical professionals but they were not aware of it. He assured me that the woman was quite correct.

I asked him how old he was and he chided me in a pleasant voice that it is never appropriate to ask a guy his age. I smiled it off and informed him of my age and that it didn't bother me to reveal my age. He did say that his name was Thomas. We mentioned Chicago, he said he had been there, we mentioned Georgia, he said he had been there but most of our conversation centered on the reality of Angels. He stated that if Russia and America could work together, they could take out ISIS in three days. Information about us that we tried to volunteer such as where we were from, get acquainted type of stuff, produced a lack of reaction other than a smile, which conveyed the idea to us that he already knew.

We may have chatted for 15 minutes when he announced that he must be going. He asked Lena, "Would it be OK if I just give you a little kiss on the cheek?" She assured him it would be OK and she actually gave him a hug in exchange. He then stated that he would like to leave her a present while running his hand into his pocket. Producing a small coin or medallion he presented it to her. Closer examination reflected that it had the word HOPE imprinted on one side but on the other, was the raised print of an Angel with its wings open.

He turned to the direction behind us and we started back toward our Resort area, going in opposite directions. We had walked for a minute or two when I looked back to see where he was heading and he had already disappeared. Maybe he ran? Or walked very fast but the beach was several hundred yards across at that point. No way!

Throughout out our brief visit, there was something both Lena and I experienced that we do not understand nor can we fully describe. There was a warmth emanating from the guy that was very warm, very pleasant and very comforting, it made us feel as if we had known him for a long time. I have never known Lena to give any man a hug that she doesn't know but this guy, it was if he was a longtime friend or maybe a close relative.

As we returned to our Resort unit, we puzzled over several things as we realized that it was exactly 5 weeks from the early morning incident in November, that I was walking alone when the encounter occurred confirming the voice, the warmth and extremely pleasant feeling that we both experienced emanating from him. His seemingly knowlcdgc and interest in Angels and his attempt to convince and/or substantiate our idea about them. We begin to wonder if he had been an Angel. Also: An Angel might not want to tell anyone his age as it could be eternal and he wouldn't want to shock or confuse us.

Also, interesting and not well explained; while talking with him, we hadn't noticed that he was fully clothed and Lena recalls that the quality/style of dress suggested affluence, with only above the neckline and hands exposed to include a long sleeve garment, not typically beach clothes. He at one point was moving his hands up and as he did, his sleeves moved down and exposed skin area around his wrist. While the flesh on his head/facial areas and hands, appeared normal for his estimated age, the skin around his wrist areas did not look like human flesh. He noticed that we had noticed and quickly lowering his hands, in an apologetic tone of voice, tried to explain that he must have damaged his skin there while engaged in an earlier job.

We know that the Bible states that "flesh and blood (physical) will not (does not) enter the kingdom of heaven" so when Angels visit mankind and they have the appearance of man, what do their bodies consist of during their visits?

Today, I tease Lena about being kissed by an Angel and we continue to wonder about the whole incident as we both feel like we were touched by it. We continue to feel, even though we don't understand all the ramifications', that we experienced a profound encounter. Was he an Angel? He wasn't dressed in dazzling white garments, He didn't have wings, but...?

We were left with the feeling that we'd had a very unusual and significant encounter mystified by the earlier 5-week pronouncement about walking alone.

During the following 3 weeks, two other unexplained events occurred in our lives that might be connected to this one as explained in separate scripts below.

December 13th, 2016

Lena and I were driving north on 84th Street from downtown Kent, WA, when we were stopped because of a red light. 84th at this intersection is a 5-lane street, 2 lanes going north and two lanes going south with a center left turn lane both directions.

After stopping at the light, there was a large truck stopped along the left side of my vehicle as I was in the curb lane. While waiting, I noticed a large Semi Truck approaching southbound from the other side of the intersection in the left turn lane indicating it intended to execute a turn across in front of me assuming his left turn light remained green. This assumption also assumed that if his green light turned red, he would stop, allowing northbound traffic to proceed through the intersection. Pretty standard logic.

Northbound traffic got the green light so I accelerated my vehicle to move through the intersection. I had the green light so the truck would abort his turn in front of me. Right? I had gotten about a full car length into the intersection when I was startled by realizing the Semi approaching from the north was not stopping, in fact it had accelerated its speed, apparently hoping to complete his left turn before his light turned red. He clearly didn't make it as he was executing his left turn across in front of me and my light was green. He was going way too fast and I was expecting to see the freight tied down on his flatbed trailer break loose and tumble into the intersection at any moment.

I braked my vehicle as quick as I could, mindful that vehicles behind me could ram my vehicle because of the quick stop and because they were right behind me, I couldn't quickly reverse my vehicle. The Semi was coming directly at my vehicle as the driver struggled to manipulate his big rig around my vehicle without losing his trailer or losing control of his truck to complete his left turn across in front of my vehicle.

The image is still fresh in my mind. This huge truck coming straight toward us with its huge front bumper moving within inches across the front of my vehicle. How he managed to avoid colliding with my vehicle and/or spilling his cargo will remain a mystery to me forever. With the speed he was traveling, there would probably have been a complete wipe out to my vehicle and both Lena and I would have likely sustained severe injuries. In retrospect, it was almost as if a giant indivisible cushion was placed between my vehicle and the truck allowing the truck to glance off the cushion without actually touching my vehicle and leaving no sense of impact.

In my heart, I rejoiced in knowing that our Lord had extended His protection to us once again and give Him glory for it.

December 28, 2016

Lena and I had decided to go for a walk at Redondo Beach, WA so had driven there.

When we arrived, there is a 3 way stop on the one main street. I was driving south and had stopped at the stop sign controlling southbound traffic. The street is a 2-way tight street, one lane north and one lane south and there are no shoulders, only curbs and sidewalks. My intention was to execute a left turn through the intersection to seek a parking spot that was available on the side street. Another vehicle heading north had stopped across the intersection but having stopped just seconds before him, I had the right to go first. I hesitated for a few seconds then decided to let the northbound vehicle move through the intersection first. I didn't realize till later that the few second hesitation probably avoided what could have been a very serious accident to us.

The vehicle across from me moved through the intersection and when it was just about to clear the intersection, approximately beside my vehicle, another vehicle south bound, in the northbound lane appeared coming at the other vehicle very fast. The northbound vehicle, coming through the intersection took the sidewalk to avoid a head on accident at a point across from my vehicle. The speeding southbound vehicle in the wrong lane, nearly sideswiping my vehicle, passing through the intersection without stopping, continued south forcing all northbound traffic to drive onto the sidewalk to get out of his way and avoid colliding with him as he was exceeding the speed limit considerably. I did notice his rear window was broken as if it had been shot out by a gun.

It became obvious why he was in such a hurry as we became aware that there were several Police cars pursuing him. We later heard police and news reports that he was fleeing a robbery and that he had exceeded a hundred miles an hour in his attempt to escape and that further down the road, he has crashed his vehicle then escaped on foot.

Later; as I reflected on the events, I realized that if I had made a normal left turn based on arriving at the stop sign first as I had intended to do, it would have put my vehicle directly, in the process of making a left turn, blocking the northbound lane in the intersection at the approximate moment that the speeding vehicle would have arrived at the intersection and certainly would have been a broadside accident as his vehicle would have plowed into the left side of mine.

Today, reflecting on these events, I rejoice in knowing in my heart that Jesus is with me every step of my life. I can't help but wonder how often we, in pursuit of and absorbed by our daily activities, become anesthetized by them so that after such occurrences, simply minimize it by whispering whew! Or writing it off as a "close call" or "near miss" subsequently trivializing them. Maybe under our breath, manage to mutter some unpleasant words or give a dirty look but fail to contemplate the mercy of our Lord and His protective influence on our lives to include directly involving Himself into those dangerous situations with potential for bodily harm.

It is with a humble heart and one full of thanksgiving that I bow myself before Him and give thanks for His involvement in and concern for my life to include events as those described above.

Interestingly enough, a couple months later, a person was in my office relating to me his own experience with what he believed was an Angel in Florida where he had been on a ministry trip. He was at the Jacksonville airport waiting to board his flight to return to Seattle with a few hours to go., he hadn't eaten since early morning, had no money but was getting pretty hungry. He began to pray that somehow God would provide and/or sustain him until he arrived home in Seattle.

Within a few minutes, a person approached him as he waited in line and asked if he would like a coupon that the person would not be using. He wasn't excited about a coupon but took it and began to examine it and discovered that it was for $15. off on food purchase at a fast food place near him there in the airport.

He quickly surmised that the Lord had sent it to him

and turned to thank the person who had given it to him but could not find that person anywhere. She had just disappeared! She was nowhere in sight and at the moment, he was in position to see a large area and it's just no way the person could have gotten out of sight so quick.

He purchased his food from the fast food place and was surprised that the total amount was $15. Exactly the amount of the coupon so the food cost him nothing in terms of money. He experienced a momentary Spiritual meltdown when he realized that the Lord was so good to him and his heart was filled with praise. As he shared with me, he is convinced that the Lord had sent the coupon in the amount he needed by an angel.

The Lord's Protection and Sustenance

October 26, 2015 @ 7:10 am. Renton, WA

While caught up in dense traffic, I found myself in the right lane of a 4-lane street. I was approaching a freeway on ramp so immediately in front of me, my lane split and an additional lane began which led to the freeway ramp for traffic intending to get on the freeway.

It was still very dark, raining very hard and visibility was poor, even at the next vehicle level.

The vehicle next to me on my left, decided to move into my lane. There's was one slight problem, I was sitting right next to him and as he moved toward me, his vehicle pushed against mine. I could hear metal crunching, tinkling noises, popping sounds like glass breaking and metal groaning and it sounded like my vehicle was being crushed on that side. The driver of that vehicle realized he had made a bad move so quickly cut his front wheels away from me and moved back into his lane, again making crunching noises as if he was tearing metal on my car, there were popping sounds like glass breaking and a noise like a side mirror breaking loose. When he had hit my vehicle, I felt him push me to the right and when he backed off, my vehicle tipped back to a normal position.

Traffic in his lane opened and he sped away. I quickly took mental notes of the description of his vehicle and the license plate number until I could move into a position about a block away where I could stop out of traffic and write the information down. It was still very dark, raining, traffic was tight so I made a mental note to wait until I reached my destination as I had a concern that my all-day seminar might not by an all-day one if I arrived too late and I still had about 10 miles to drive in atrocious traffic. I could see very quickly that my side mirror was still intact.

As I continued on my way, from the noise that I had heard and the impact to my vehicle, even though from the inside where I sat, I could see nothing, I was convinced there would be significant damage and was making plans to contact the Police to file a hit and run report and contact my insurance after arriving at my destination and generally not feeling very good about the whole thing.

I arrived at my Bellevue destination and by then, it had become much lighter. I parked my vehicle and stepped out to survey the damage to my car. Looking quickly, I was shocked. I saw no damage! I got very close to it and even ran my hands over the exterior panels and there wasn't even as much as a faint scratch in the paint, anywhere! I couldn't believe what I was not seeing! I had felt the push on my car from the other one. I had heard and still remember vividly those sounds and the pull and tugging on my vehicle as the other one pulled away from mine. The popping sound of metal tearing loose. I saw his vehicle just inches away from my face! He opened his right window and said to me that "he was only trying to change lanes" before he sped off.

How is this possible? Only God could do something like this. I can't explain how but understood it's His call and I believe 100% that somehow, He repaired the damage or He prevented damage from occurring. Based on my perception and what I was hearing and experiencing, it is easier for me to believe He restored my vehicle to its original state and I have no words to convey the feeling of excitement that I experience as I embrace this knowledge. It causes Praise and Adoration to spring from my innermost being! A song burst forth from deep within,

"Praise the Lord, O my soul, and all that is within me, Praise His Holy Name." I find myself becoming emotional as I feel His love envelope me. He is an awesome God!

You might think it was just my imagination, that I just imagined the whole thing, Impossible! I never had an experience so real in all my life. You ask, can God do such things today? Does He still do things like this for His people? In Habakkuk 3:6 states "He stood, and shook the earth; He looked, and made the nations tremble. The ancient mountains crumbled and the age-old hills collapsed. His ways are eternal." Verse 9-10; "You split the earth with rivers; the mountains saw you and withered; torrents of water swept by; the deep roared and lifted its waves on high."

For such a God, taking care of my vehicle would have been nothing for Him. I Praise Him! And I know from other experiences in my life and others that I have known, that He has a strong and ongoing interest in those who know Him.

The other vehicle info:

White Chevrolet Pickup Truck, maybe 2 to 3 years old, could have been ¾ ton as it sat pretty high. Washington License #62355B, driven by dark featured male, possibly Hispanic descent, maybe 35 years old. He lowered his right side window and yelled to me that he had been trying to move into my lane, which of course, was obvious. I told him that he first has to make sure a lane is empty before trying to move into it.

Missed Opportunity?

In early October of 2017, while driving through a local shopping plaza parking lot, I noticed a rather large, middle-aged lady, using a walker, laboriously approaching me as my vehicle moved toward her. It appeared that she had just come off the side street.

As I neared her, it became clear to me that she was distressed and was attempting to get my attention. I stopped my vehicle within a few feet of her and rolled my car window down. I quickly noticed that she was crying as she rested on the walker that she had been using as she moved about.

She began to confide in me that she was ill, lived nearby and was trying to get to the drug store located in the shopping plaza to pick up medicine prescribed for her but had not enough money as it was expensive and she needed $175.00. She asked if I had that amount on me and whether I would be willing to give it to her to purchase her medicine.

I informed her that I did not have the money on me but inquired if she had taken time to ask the Lord for it, and suggested that He was generous, that He loved her and could assist her with any and/or all problems she might have. She only wept more profusely and stated that she had talked to God about it but He had not provided at this time. I took a few moments and shared with her about a time in my life when I desperately needed healing and how He reached down and touched me and instantly healed me and assured her that I believe He could and would do the same for her.

After encouraging her to trust the Lord about it and

244

commit her life to Him, we broke off and I returned home. Even though I had driven through this parking lot many times, I had never seen this lady before nor have I seen her since. After arriving home, I became troubled about the incidence and quickly became almost overwhelmed by the strength of the conviction that if I had just stepped out of the car, taken her by the hand and stated something like Peter had stated to the cripple beggar in Acts 3:6, "Silver or Gold, I do not have, but what I have, I give you. In the name of Jesus Christ of Nazareth, Walk"!

I could never be more convinced that Jesus would have healed her of all her problems right on the spot. I continued to be troubled in my soul for the next two days that I had let the Lord down and I repented to Him that I had not been sensitive to His Spirit and made a promise that if I had another opportunity, I would not be shy.

Two days later, after visiting a friend in Renton, before coming home, I decided to stop by a family there close by his place and as the husband let me into their home, I became aware of his wife sitting at the kitchen table crying and applying a bandage to most of her face. I inquired about what had happened? She told me that she had been in the back yard and encountered a wasp nest and for whatever reason, they had become agitated. She wound up being stung 11 times on her face, mostly in the cheek's areas.

I immediately felt that compulsion again to pray for her so her husband joined me as I did just that. After praying for a few minutes, I simply declared her healed in Jesus name and was convinced that our Lord had healed her. I ask her if she would remove the bandage but she didn't want to as she said that her face had looked so ugly and swollen. I told her that she didn't have to, it was her choice but I was convinced the Lord had healed her and if she will remove the bandage, we will see what the Lord has done. She consented and her husband and I looked as she removed the bandage, we marveled that there was no swelling or anything. In fact, there was nothing that we saw that would suggest that she had been stung? We told her there was nothing there and she got up and went to a mirror and for a while, couldn't believe what she was not seeing.

We took a moment to join hands and praise our Lord for His mercy and kindness and reflected on how life would be so different if we did not have him in our hearts. I also believe the Lord put me there just at the right time as a follow up on the incident a couple days earlier, not that He had to test me but knew that I would need to test myself as a part of my lifelong Spiritual growth pattern. I also shared with them the previous experience when I felt so strong that I had failed our Lord and we rejoiced that our Lord had brought us together at just the right time.

Reflecting on this incident has given me considerable insight on how as Christians, we can become anesthetized by the world around us and our daily routines to the point that we miss opportunities to allow our Lord to use us to reach out to the hurting world, to be His hand extended and minister to others. I'm not suggesting that He needs us to accomplish His will, He has everything at His disposal. He could have simply appeared to her as He did to Saul (Paul) on the road to Damascus (Acts 9:4) and met all her needs by Himself but He knows that we need it and He allows us to become involved in His service as He knows that it will grow us Spiritually, sharpen our sensitivity to the needs of others and our relationship with Him as we utilize the power of the Holy Spirit resident in us.

On the other hand, if we are not given such opportunities, we can wither Spiritually. It's like if we are not going forward Spiritually, we are going backward. If we don't use it, we lose it, and His concern is that we go forward.

We have seen a noticeable increase in opportunities to pray with individuals who come into our office since this incident, both where prayer was requested and as a result of our suggesting it, with such incidents reaching about 6 in one week from about one a week or so before and even a neighbor wanting us to come to their home and pray for their Grandchildren as well as a Grandfather. A few days ago, a young lady on Facebook messaged me asking that Elena and I pray for her as she was in considerable pain from an illness. We give Him praise for what He is doing for both us and the ones being prayed for.

The following is an excerpt from the December 18, 2017, World Challenge Newsletter and statements are made by Gary Wilkerson.

I heard the Lord's voice speaking to me; "Gary, do you bring me with you everywhere you go?"

"His Spirit reminded me, "Your life in Christ doesn't happen when you gather with pastors. Your ministry is with everyone you meet." Suddenly, I felt a deep conviction, and it wasn't a negative feeling. It was just the opposite: I felt excitement." The remainder of his article shares how he now views personal encounters as personal opportunities and how that idea has led to praying for so many more individuals, from all walks of life, with positive results where before the Lord spoke to him, he more often than not, could/would encounter a person without even noticing them.

Worship

A recent Face Book post critical of a God who would expect His adherents to worship him piqued my mind to thinking about "what exactly do we perceive as worship and what might God consider as worship and why? What exactly is Godly worship? Is it merely a strong display of emotion? If so, how or what differentiates it from what we see at sports events, rock concerts or even at parties, dances and festivals all around the world at any given time.

Do strong displays of emotion during a Church service indicate powerful worship? During a recent church service where loud music (so called Christian rock) was blaring and considerable emotion was apparent, a young boy who was visiting for the first time and was not participating in the display, inquired of his mother, "when is the rock concert going to be over." To be sure, Humans are emotional beings and under proper circumstances, can and will display emotion, some events can trigger strong positive emotions, particularly when we encounter personalities (or teams) whom we adore and look up to. That is not to be criticized except perhaps when it is attributed to the move of the Holy Spirit but may be nothing more than the person's emotion displayed. If the presence of the Holy Spirit moves on a group of people, it's most likely they will become emotional also as it touches their personality but the emotional display is the human spirit's response to the touch of His Spirit, the emotional responses from the human spirit may be triggered by other stimuli as well. This examination is not to sound critical of the influence of the Holy Spirit and I want to be careful to state it. I merely want to suggest that we often equate emotion with the presence of the Holy Spirit and may even call it worship.

I have a picture of fans cheering at a LA Lakers basketball game while the Lakers are performing. It reflects just about everyone with their hands raised toward the ceiling, shouting and displaying considerable emotion, but a caption across the top clearly states it's a Lakers game. I often show this picture to young people who are in my office and ask them what church they think this picture shows. They quickly point out that it is actually a basketball game. I cover the Lakers sign with my hand and ask again what church this is. They are contemplative as I point out that the picture could be any church where you see the same kind of emotional display and they nod agreement.

That raises the question; what is real worship of our God? If you see the same behavior at so many other places that you see in the Church, but the Church calls it worship God, how do we know? While not to the Lord, isn't what we see at the Lakers game also a form of worship? But in Church, we feel so good afterwards, it must be true worship. But those who left the game will display signs of having had their spirit lifted as a result of the game and exhibit signs of pleasure.

On the other hand, we've all seen Church services where high states of emotion have been displayed service after service, afterwards, you might hear comments like, The Lord surely blessed me tonight" yet over a period of time, the respondents have shown very little progress in their relationship with the Lord. If you run into them on the job or somewhere else on a different day, they come across just like those who never attend a Church service, even using coarse language, etc. I mean their lives appear to remain unchanged. Is it just the square dance effect? Is it just a conditioning that occurs in humans as a result of exposure to a given environment? Is it possible that we can be manipulated by the environment we are submersed in at a given moment and/or by those around us? Or succumb to what we are exposed to at a given time?

50 years ago, it was common to see an audience of believers display a strong sense of humility accompanied by weeping, usually on their knees, displaying signs of a broken spirit as they knelt in church and afterward testifying of the move of the Spirit on their lives. Today, they are usually standing, often with arms lifted and shouting with a loud voice. Which behavior might have the greatest effect on the life afterwards? Is it possible to be contemplative, letting the Holy Spirit search your heart while participating in noisy behavior or when you are of a quiet, broken spirit?

As a young person, I remember times when I worked of the farm all day. I would be dead tired and only wanted to go home to relax. Friends would stop by and encourage me to go with them to the local square dance. I was tired but they were persuasive so I went. After 2 or 3 hours of exposure to the music, hand clapping, back-slapping and stomping around, I would feel fantastic. But I have to tell you, it had nothing to do with the Lord nor was the Holy Spirit involved, and no Spiritual growth.

In those early years, I would think about it. If the fantastic feeling derived from that environment mimicked what I would feel after a Church service, how do I know which is real? Is it possible that other environments would produce the same feelings after emotional displays as the Church service had?

I could see that certain primitive people groups could work themselves into a frenzy, displaying tremendous emotions in false religious services yet I never thought of them as worshiping the God of my choice but appearing to work themselves into a feel-good state.

So, is displaying emotion a true barometer of the move of the Spirit? If the Spirit moves on you, you will become emotional but I have concluded emotion may not always be trusted. Human emotion can be triggered by a number of things and the music and environment encountered in a "worship" service as well as many other events would be conducive to triggering human emotions. I once heard," I don't care how high you jump; I want to see how straight you walk when you are on the ground."

The need to worship is inherent in all humans and is an extension of the need to reconnect relationship/fellowship with our Creator. He created us to fellowship with Him and that was broken when man sinned which separated us. This need is apparent when we look up to and/or find ourselves devoting special attention to some person whom we consider has successfully succeeded in achieving some socially favorable position. It need not involve a deity as we see with North Korea, where constituents of that Country exhibit the same behavior toward their leader. I've seen documentaries where people will lift their hands in praise to him, other times bowing with hands folded to his picture simultaneously weeping profusely and exhibiting profound emotion. If humans are not connected to their Creator in a divine relationship, they will find a substitute to produce a false feeling of connection and they have labeled the activity producing that feelings with the word 'Worship'.

Last year, there was a man visiting my office from the Country of Iraq, who gave a good example of humans just satisfying their human need to worship, who indicated that while the United States hated Saddam Hussein, the Iraqi people for the most part liked him or at least accepted him in a subtle form of worship or adoration and that he had maintained control over their Country. He indicated that he had shared a staff position on a University there and as such, considered himself a learned man who could think for himself. When I inquired how it was possible to like or adore any person like

251

OUT OF THE FIRE

Saddam Hussein based on what I had heard about him. He stated that to "understand the answer to that question, you have to understand the nature of humans." He went on, "it is inherent in the nature or heart of man to seek three things in life, a desire to connect to and worship their creator, to have a sense of feeling that someone is in charge of their life and a sense of feeling secure."

He then provided an example, "If you put several hundred humans on a deserted island in the middle of the ocean, cut off from all contact with other humans, at least two things would happen. The majority would quickly elect an individual from the group to be their leader and the group would also quickly select something to worship, satisfying the need to connect to their creator. Could be a rock, maybe an animal or bird or whatever but selecting these two items would provide the sense of security. He was making sense to me.

He said Saddam Hussein, to most Iraqi people, satisfied the sense of feeling like someone was in charge, the Muslim religion satisfied the need to worship a deity and those needs satisfied, the people had no need to feel like they had to think on their psychological needs anymore, leaving them freedom to move through time and space in pursuit of an existence. I think there are religious situations that I have witnessed where I came away with the feeling that some of the participants were just satisfying their psychological needs, leaving them with a sort of a "gassed up" feeling.

There are many Scripture verses exhorting man to praise God but these verses including the one stating "God inhabits the praise of His people" does not suggest that praise is all He inhabits. We know that God is omnipresent meaning He is everywhere present, not just in a single expression of an emotion. Does He get a charge out of humans exercising an emotional "worship service" directed toward Him? That's His call, He is also omniscience meaning He knows all and would understand the motive causing the expression of adoration and it could be that anything expressed by the creation toward the Creator could please Him. It's our motive that we need to analyze. What parent isn't pleased when children show an interest in them and/or children express love or intimacy toward them. We didn't create our cat but we are very pleased when she displays an emotion toward us such as purring or even a simple act of obedience when we call to her, try to teach her or when she acts like she wants to be near us.

This conclusion raises the question; what is true worship, pleasing to the Lord? I believe a greater source of pleasure for Him is how you live your daily life, the maintenance of your relationship with Him and surrender of your body to the will of His Holy Spirit to enhance the regeneration of your soul. There is something about a thankful heart that moves God and brings great pleasure to Him and results in Spiritual growth for His created. When we live like Christ, our whole life becomes a worship song to God. He loves it, and He lets us enjoy it. Live like Christ, because our identity is in Him. Have a worship-filled day.

Am I suggesting that a display of emotion when we get with others who are collectively praising God wrong? No! If you love the Lord, you will respond that way but I've concluded that emotions by themselves cannot be trusted as an accurate barometer of Spirituality. It's the daily activity and behavior that truly pleases God and is a true mark of Spiritual level.

I recently had an older person in my office who proudly exclaimed that he had attended Church all his life. He didn't verbalize it but the message that I got was that he was so "Christian" as a result. I suggested that I could go the McDonnell's all my life and never become a hamburger. Going to Church all one's life might create a fine Christian who walks daily with the Lord. On the other hand, it might just make a person "religious" and if religion is enough, he could actually pick any religion. Wouldn't matter since all seem to have a security blanket effect on its adherents. It is extremely important to build that relationship personally with Him which may not have anything to do with going to Church as I believe there are many people whom the Lord has chosen who may not get the opportunity to attend Church regularly.

Jesus said, "By this all men will know that you are my disciples, if you love one another." (John 13:35) Additionally; expressing love for other believers as well as expressing love for Him clearly pleases Him so could be in line with worshiping Him.

Below is a poem written by my son that captures much of what we might expect in our relationship with Him after submitting our life to him.

When God called me...

I didn't know what to expect!
The words he spoke to my heart. I won't forget!

What God said to me...I remember so vividly.
It awakens me in the night so unexpectedly!

When God spoke to me... I "jumped out of bed."
I wanted to hear what his spirit said.

What God wanted for me...Was to follow him!
I wanted to obey and trust him as my friend!

What God desired was to have a faithful heart!
He was there for me... Right from the start!

My worldly possessions... I left behind!
A new treasure in Christ... I did find!

Many of my "past habits" begin to leave me...
As I felt God's awesome love all around me!

My thoughts and attentions were decided.
Everything I needed... My God provided!

I've chosen to follow him 100 percent!
Fellowship with my creator Is time well spent!

He is my beloved and I am his!
For he is with each day that I live!

Won't you too beckon his mercy and call?
Living for Jesus makes it worth it all!

By Jim Pemberton   05/25/12

The Anniversary Cake

April 4th, 2018, Elena and I was very busy as the office filled with clients and new ones were coming every hour when Elena looked at me and asked "Do you know what today is? I put my hand to my head as I was thinking then it occurred to me. I replied, "Today is our anniversary" She nodded and said, I had hopes that I would have time to go and at least buy a cake, some little something to celebrate but as you know, there is just no time to do it because of our full schedule. I assured her that as long as we knew, we could have our silent private celebration in our hearts.

Within a few minutes later, there was a knock on our office door as another client arrived for their appointment and when Elena opened the door for her, to our surprise, she had brought with her a gorgeous chocolate cake and presented it to Elena. We knew very little about her but had heard that she baked cakes for Weddings and special social events in the community.

Elena, of course, made a special effort to thank her and commented on her handiwork. She also enquired of her, "How did you know today was our anniversary? And of course, she did not but had just felt like she should bring us the cake.

Elena took the cake to the kitchen and placed it on the table then returned to the office to the lady to accommodate her appointment.

Within a few minutes, I finished with my client and sauntered into the kitchen where, immediately noticing the cake, I leaned over it, savoring it's smell when the Lord spoke clearly in my heart and said "you forgot but I didn't" referring to the cake. Elena entered the area a few minutes later and quickly noticed that I was emotional and inquiring why?

As I choked back tears, I explained that I had just heard the voice of the Lord and shared His words with her and we both rejoiced. For those who have had Him speak clearly to them, will quickly understand that it is different from a revelation or understanding that His Spirit impresses on you and you just know something that you didn't before. When he speaks to you, you hear verbiage from inside your heart. There is something about His voice that no human could duplicate. It's strong, firm and reassuring but at the same time, has a softness and gentleness to it, containing a feeling of understanding. For me, in most cases, it triggers a sense of humility that is overcoming and It doesn't seem possible, but my love for Him and His closeness abounds prompting an emotional reaction.

In God's word, there were many situations where people wept before the Lord although I don't believe I have seen it even once in recent years. As a child, it was common to see weeping in Church as people praised the Lord or while praying to Him, today, it would seem that the individuals worshiping Him during a Church service has moved away from that. I think most church attendees would look at you as if you had a problem if you were observed weeping as His Spirit moved on you in today's church.

Faith

It seems today we hear so little about faith yet it was given such importance by the Bible. (Heb 11:6) states "But without faith it is impossible to please Him: for he that cometh to God must believe that He is and that He rewards them that diligently seek Him". It further defines faith as "being sure of what we hope for and certain of what we do not see." (Heb 11:1 NEV) and in Heb 10:38 it states, "but my righteous one will live by faith" The 11th Chapter of Hebrews, often called the faith Chapter, lists numerous individuals who by faith, conquered all kinds of situations and it was counted to them as righteousness. Their righteousness was not determined by what they did but the faith they held in their heart which resulted in their actions affecting the situations favorably.

Our culture places great value and emphasis on works or a sense of charity and today, rather than the Church influence the culture we see the position reversed where more often than not, it's culture influencing and conditioning the Church and as the Church has embraced the culture, believers often equate works with pleasing God or earning righteousness yet it may be only stroking our sense of goodness and enhancing our perceived perception by others but deluding us by giving us the feeling that we are doing God a favor therefore He must be pleased with us. To truly attain righteousness, we have to know what it is and what it isn't. Is it just right behavior? No, you can do the right thing while having the wrong motive. Many churches proclaim "Christ died for you. What have you done for Him?" This mentality has become pervasive throughout the church and can elicit right behavior for wrong motives.

I want to clarify that if we believe God daily for answered prayer and maintain a relationship with Him that allows an exercise of faith, we can go through anything unwavering, knowing He is with us constantly and in charge of our lives, there will absolutely be works. Works should be the result of righteousness rather than to gain righteousness. (Righteousness=Right standing with God) The point is, works apart from faith will not necessarily please God nor will it substantiate a relationship with Him. It may be just noise, not rising above the level of rattling brass or tinkling symbols. Keep in mind that the Pharisees of Jesus' day were experts at compelling/completing works, if they showed up in our churches today; we would give them leadership positions. We would see them as the most holy people in the church. We would ask them to pray for us, and to teach classes. Paul said, (Rom 10:2) "They have a zeal for God but their zeal is not based on knowledge" and Jesus even chastised them by stating (Matt 23:27) "You are like white washed tombs, which look beautiful on the outside but on the inside, are full of dead men's bones".

People often share with me that they are going to or have just returned from some exotic place on a missionary trip where they were able to meet some wonderful people and were able to accomplish such wonderful things in helping the locals and how these people so appreciated them coming and the interest shown to them by the missionaries. The thing I usually don't hear is what the Lord accomplished through their efforts or evidence of the work of the Holy Spirit. I don't believe I have recently heard anyone indicate lives were saved, set free, changed or even that the Holy Spirit moved on them and compelled them to go in the first place. In the absence of such testimony, it suggests just a pleasure trip. Anyone would enjoy such a trip with members of their peers but by calling it a missionary trip sounds so holy and suggests they accomplished something impressive for the Lord, and even backed up by photos of themselves interacting with or hugging natives of a different culture they suitable for them to post on Facebook, increasing the strokes from their peers.

I like to hear what the Lord has done through the work of His Holy Spirit. God will not bless anyone's effort to establish their own righteousness. He blesses only the work of His Holy Spirit as we may be the instrument He uses and lives should be changed as a result of the movement of His Spirit on lives and/or situations.

Keep in mind, that so many other cultures do not have access to so many of the world's "Things" as we do in our culture so when you show up with your arms full of "Things" including money, there would be few that would not rush to you and quickly embrace your philosophy or whatever other hoop you might want them do to jump through in hope of having access to whatever you might offer. Just a few days ago, a young person was telling me how much she enjoyed a missionary trip to Mongolia, to provide things to these people was so thrilling but when I inquired if she knew if any one gave their heart to the Lord, her face became a blank, she thought for a minute then admitted that she was not aware of it if any did.

Good works of "righteousness" performed with either impure motives or outside the will of God are all good works as defined by our culture and even by our Church. They can elevate us in our standing or perception by the Community resulting in praise and goodwill from them, producing a sense of good feeling about ourselves, even pride in ourselves, but works without the power and demonstration of the Holy Spirit will add nothing to His kingdom. In many cases, they can harm the believer's walk with the Lord as they appease the flesh becoming as a narcotic to the believer. They can even have a negative effect on our testimony to the community.

We recently saw the approval of same sex marriages in our State. I suspect that it was approved at least in part, because well meaning, religious people included, voted approval as they didn't want to feel bad about the possibility of contributing to the unhappiness of other humans based on an entirely emotional argument that says, "the only reason you would oppose redefining marriage is if you don't want perverted people to be happy." Again; it appeals to their sense of "feeling Good" about themselves rather than feeling good about pleasing God by demanding that our culture adhere to His word, even if those who are addicted to their perversion are not pleased.

Jesus, in sending out His disciples, told them to preach this message: "The kingdom of heaven is near, (Matt. 10:8), heal the sick, raise the dead, cleanse those who have leprosy, drive out demons." These actions would necessitate the indwelling of the Holy Spirit in the messenger and reflect the dramatic demonstration of His power however, many changes can occur without necessarily such dramatic or obvious change. In all cases, lives should be touched by His Holy Spirit and not just by the human spirit of the messenger. A strong stand on both biblical doctrine and biblical morality go hand in hand.

Under no circumstances am I trying to say that acts of charity or goodness are wrong but only suggest the individual might address the motive. All resulting credit should be directed toward the Lord and/or His Holy Spirit in a manner that precludes making us look or feel religious.

I recently noticed a posting on Face Book calling attention to military action between Israel and the Palestinians and extolling the fact that innocent people were being injured and killed as a result. It also suggested that the Poster, who happened to be a Church leader, was going to make a time of prayer for peace over there and within about 2 minutes he had taken 68 hits from viewers who liked his post with some cheering him on. It sounded 'soooooooo' religious. Now taken lightly, it sounds like a very noble action, worthy of honor and praise, clearly, no one likes to think of human's beings harmed so concern would push it to the level of praying about it and letting others know of your decision could generate a considerable amount of positive image building. But if you seriously think about it, a dose of reality subdues you. This area has never had peace and the Bible suggest to those who know the Bible that there will never have peace in this area until the Prince of Peace arrives. You can pray until you are blue in the face, it will change nothing. I choose to leave it in His hands knowing He is in control even if no one living in that area appears to be.

Prayer might make you feel better just communing with the Lord. If you tell others what you are planning on doing, you may get positive feedback that can make you feel even better, even more religious or more Christian especially if you are in position over others but would not necessarily reflect the depth of your faith.

I must confess that when I read it, it came across to me as shouting to a group of cheerleaders and in return, receiving a considerable amount of image building while acknowledging that I may have misinterpreted the author's intention and only picked up on the response.

My point moves back to motive. Let us walk in a manner that brings glory and honor to Him. Let our actions and/or reactions be conditioned by the presence of His Holy Spirit in our lives. To a lot of people, the Holy Ghost is some made up thing. To some people the Holy Ghost is some cult idea. But if you ever felt in your life, you would realize that the Holy Ghost isn't just some made-up idea or thing, but it is the indispensable POWER of God manifested through us.

This same Facebook post drove out the following comment in response to the context depreciating through a number of unsolicited follow on post including the following one:

Ok Ivan, you want some proof that there is no God? I'll give you a live experience one. Once upon a time, I grew a pair & told the invisible man: "God, if you're real, let me go to Mexico with my youth this year for a Missionary Trip and let me have a face to face encounter with you like Moses had." and surely enough I did not go, so I just left church behind & I became an Atheist, because God has simply fed me over & if there's a God, I'll tell Him on my judgment day that He's not a just God at all. -- Now that I became a spiritual man, there's no need for me to discriminate against anybody at all! Bible is filled with it. Tuh Duh!!!:D

Now, no matter what anybody tells me about God, to convert back, I firmly know that there's no God and I bet we're on Earth for a much greater purpose than serve the invisible hollow man whose name is Santa (Satan) Claus. Lol ha-ha-ha, Igor.

Our sinful nature leads us to think we can determine truth apart from God, including the idea that, if we are "good enough," then God will let us in to heaven. Our independent spirit has led many to think that they can earn salvation by their good works and thereby escape the judgment of our holy God. But they are gravely mistaken. We can never conquer our greatest problem; sin!

Popular psychological teaching bolsters man's independent thinking by telling him that he is inherently good and can solve his problems on his own. However, the Bible teaches the opposite. Man's "heart is deceitful above all things, and desperately wicked; who can know it?" (Jeremiah 17:9). We pride ourselves on our solutions to the minor problems we encounter, but we can never conquer our greatest problem—sin—in our own strength.

We have all sinned and fall short of the glory of God (Rom 3:23). So, no matter how many "good" deeds we do (Isa 64:6), apart from Christ we will still face God's judgment for the sins we have committed. Good deeds do not wash away our sins; they only mask them in the eyes of others. However, God sees through our self-righteous veneer and knows every sin we have ever committed.

Thankfully, God sent His Son, Jesus Christ to earth. He is "the Lamb of God who takes away the sin of the world" (John 1:29). Jesus did not come so that we could tell cute nativity stories or so that we would think of Him as simply a good teacher. No, Jesus came to die an agonizing death on the Cross. He came to take our punishment on Himself. He died on the Cross, was buried, and then rose from the dead three days later, demonstrating that He has power over death, that He took the wrath of God for our sins, and that He has secured our hope of eternal life.

On the night before His Crucifixion, Jesus said, "I am the way, the truth, and the life. No one comes to the Father except through Me" (Jn 14:6). This statement directly contradicts the man-made religious concept that a person can earn his own salvation. His declaration is extremely offensive to the modern "tolerance" mindset which refuses to tolerate the exclusive claims of Jesus Christ. Jesus unequivocally declared that He is the only way to the Father.

This is why it is so important for us to learn to become dependent on Jesus Christ. If we truly want to be free, then we need to depend on Jesus Christ who said that "if the Son makes you free, you shall be free indeed" (Jn 8:36). This freedom is a freedom from the punishment of our sin and from the ungodly burdens of this world. Salvation from sin is available to all who turn from their sin (repent) and place their trust in the Lord Jesus Christ as their Savior and Lord.

We may cherish our independence and freedom in the

United States, but that independence and freedom is eroding and can be taken away. The further we drift from the authority of and obedience to God's Word in this nation, the less freedom and independence we will possess. The more we reject God's authority as a nation, the less godly we will become as a people, and the more laws will be required to govern our sinful behavior. We have witnessed the stripping away of personal freedoms in this nation and this directly corresponds to the loss of biblical authority in society.

We must depend on our Creator and Savior Jesus Christ for our salvation, for the strength to make it through each day, for the power to forgive and show grace to others, and for the ability to live a life that pleases Him. If you have never placed your faith in Jesus Christ and asked for His forgiveness, please repent of your sins and call on Him today.

Love of God

The common usage of the word love might suggest it is the most frivolous word in the English language. We hear people use it to describe their attachment to their pets, cars, houses, jobs, cities, clothes and just about everything else. People even "make love." It is used in such a frivolous manner that if you really think about it, it means nothing specific anymore. Its common usage is missing any reference to a meaningful relationship or the implication of reciprocal responsibility and its meaning is ambiguous.

It can be and is often confused with the word compassion which can include a form of caring without all the other things that the word love can conjure. Compassion may motivate action without necessarily requiring reciprocal commitment. Love, at its best, in as much as humans can comprehend, necessitates reciprocal commitments.

Whenever the subject of homosexuality comes up, invariably, someone wants to state that "God loves the homosexual but hates their sin." Let's look at that statement carefully.

It sounds very Christian, hence its appeal to well-meaning Christians and/or religious people but its message is ultimately from Satan. Not in its content, but in its subliminal intoxication and manipulation of perception, which has caused Christians to accept homosexuality or individual homosexuals, if not completely, at least philosophically and/or, at least decline to tell them the truth of God's expectations of man in contrast to popular belief about Him. This has managed to convene a virtual army of Christian leaders willing to overlook the deception of the homosexual argument for the sake of sounding politically correct, and while appearing as a form of righteousness actually doesn't rise above the level of filthy rags.

1 John 15-16; Do not love the world, or the things that are in the world. If any man loves the world, the love of the Father is not in him. For all that is in the world; the lust of the flesh, the lust of the eye and the pride of life, is not of the Father, but is of the world. This Scripture tells us that God's love is not in that person who refuses to exclude the things of the world or the lusts (addictions) of the physical body.

Some proudly proclaim that the Church they attend would warmly receive homosexuals and any other sinner and while that sounds so noble, I would suggest that any/all sinners attending a Church where the Spirit of God is moving would become immediately convicted of their sin and would either surrender their lives to God or immediately leave as they would become so uncomfortable.

Homosexuality, whether male or female, is detestable in God's sight. It comparable to the Asherah poles mentioned several times in 1st and 2nd Kings in the Bible and the stench of Sodom and Gomorrah found in the 18th and 19th chapters of Genesis.

Is it likely that God loved the people associated with these chapters? Absolutely! Or at least, He would have had a sense of compassion for them as His compassion extends to all mankind. Did He allow that sense of compassion to deter His punishment on them? Absolutely not! His judgment came upon them and destroyed them. Scripture doesn't indicate that He spent any time trying to influence them by reminding them that He loved them but just didn't like their behavior. His punishment was swift and complete without recourse. We can't presume to critique the morality of that punishment since our own sense of morality was created by Him and He exist outside of and above anything we can perceive. We are the created and He is the Creator. No matter how clever, creative or how much knowledge we think we have, it amounts to nothing beside His Majesty.

But the proponents of the love aspect quotes John 3:16; "For God so loved the world that He gave His only begotten Son that whosoever believes on Him shall not be destroyed but shall have ever lasting life". Usually they only quote the first part about Him loving the world and giving His Son but fail to notice the word world is used rather than mankind and usually don't get into the latter part of the verse where expectations are expressed as a condition to achieving the promised everlasting life. Although there is no condition for His sending His Son to die for the sins of the world, there is a condition to His love for individuals and by endorsing one's existence does not preclude His judging them for their sins. He has set terms for individuals to enter into His love. To suggest, as some do today, that God's love is "unconditional" is to mislead people into thinking that God will not judge them. The idea of "unconditional love" as expressed by Christian mystics is unbiblical. A parent may love a child, but that is no comfort if the child knows his choices keep him from the benefits of that love.

John 15:9-10; "As the Father has loved Me, I have loved you also. Abide in my love. If you keep my commandments you shall abide in my love, just as I have kept My Father's commandments and abide in His love. And John 16:26-27; "The Father Himself loves you because you have loved Me and have believed that I came out from the Father. These are the conditions to enter into God's love: love Jesus and keep His commandments.

Secular culture tries to explain away man's sin. The plagues of immorality and violence are attributed to poverty, social injustice and even genetics. The blame is placed everywhere except where it belongs; the sinful human heart. From the time of the early Church, many have wishfully speculated that all people will eventually, somehow, reach heaven. But God's Word clearly states that all mankind is lost unless or except they embrace/accept the substitutionary death of Christ as payment for their sins.

Our culture is increasingly oriented to the present. The demand for instant gratification dominates. Our perspective on life is naturally framed in time but God's perspective is eternal.

The word perishes in John 3:16 and 2 Peter 3:9 does not refer to physical death or even the end of existence, but rather torment that last forever.

God is eternal; without beginning or end. While all created beings have a beginning, God's Word indicates that once life begins, its existence never ends and each person will face a final lasting judgment. Whatever a person's destiny, it is eternal whether everlasting reward or punishment.

 Refusal to minister God's truth to those caught in sin. Particularly when they insist that God endorses their sin, is cowardice and is certainly not loving rather, it is pure pious nonsense.

1st Corinthians 6:9 (NIV) clearly states "Do you not know that the wicked will not inherit the kingdom of God? Do not be deceived: Neither the sexually immoral nor idolaters nor adulterers nor male prostitutes nor homosexual offenders.......... will inherit the kingdom of God.

1 Cor. 6:13; (NIV) the body is not meant for sexual immorality, but for the Lord.

1 Cor. 6:18 (NIV) Flee from sexual immorality. All other sins a man commits are outside his body, but he who sins sexually sins against his own body. (v19) Do you not know that your body is a temple of the Holy Spirit, who is in you, whom you have received from God? You are not your own; (v20) you were bought with a price. Therefore,

honor God with your body.

Perversion of any kind is an addiction of the physical body and while chemical, drug or alcoholic addictions can be and are broken and some even experience deliverance after surrendering their life to the Lord, sexual perversion can be impossible to separate from as it involves the mind as well as gratification of the flesh. Over the years, I have known a few who profess to have been delivered but in time they go back to it. There may have been some that I don't know about who maintained sustenance. The tendency now is to forget about deliverance but rather to find scriptures about the love of God and extrapolate those scripture into an excuse to cover their behavior while demanding Believers living in a "feel good" culture accept their behavior. But you say; God is Love (1 John 4:8, 4:16 NIV) therefore we should love everybody unconditionally and He does, but that's not all that He is, He is also Justice, Mercy, Longsuffering, Patient, He is Holy and He is Majestic and Awesome and much more. His sense of Justice demands retribution for the disobedient. Sin is a disease and God as well as His dwelling place is Holy, that is, clean of any disease or impurities. Sin cannot and will not enter there. Like a diseased plant that is pulled up and cast on the compost pile, if we want to kill the disease on the plant, we burn it instead.

Romans 2:22 NIV; "although they claimed to be wise, they became fools. (23) And exchanged the glory of the immortal God for images made to look like mortal man and birds and animals and reptiles. (24) Therefore, God gave them over in the sinful desires of their hearts to sexual impurity for the degrading of their bodies with one another. (25) They exchanged the truth of God for a lie and worshiped and served created things rather than the Creator; who is forever praised. Amen. (26) Because of this, God gave them over to shameful lust. Even their women exchanged natural relations for unnatural ones.

(27) In the same way the men also abandoned natural relations with women and were inflamed with lust for one another. Men committed indecent acts with other men and received in themselves the due penalty for their perversion. (28) Furthermore, since they did not think it worthwhile to retain knowledge of God, He gave them over to a depraved mind, to do what ought not to be done.

John 6:44 NIV "No one can come to me unless the Father who sent me draws him, and I will raise him up at the last day". It appears that a depraved mind is a mind (heart) that can no longer respond to nor even receive the drawing of the Holy Spirit. God would be aware that such person can no longer be reached or touched by His loving embrace, and in effect, would be cut off from possible salvation and as such would be subjected to the destruction of themselves.

Today, homosexuals demand legal marriage but don't be deceived, tomorrow, they will demand your family members as they did of Lot in Sodom. Their agenda is very aggressive and cannot be appeased by granting them what they demand. The nature of their perversion demands more and more with the promise of satisfying their craving tortured flesh, but ultimately, they never find that satisfaction so is driven further into deprivation. Recently; a local Catholic school dismissed a vice principal for marrying another man. The school is now a target of homosexual and hate groups demanding the Catholic Church alter their stand to accommodate the homosexual lifestyle as a means of imposing their lifestyle onto all others who differ from them. Even if the Catholic Church/Schools do, you think for a moment, the homosexual community will stop there? They will not stop until their lifestyle permeates or dominates our culture. It is a heady yet dangerous position in which to be when the world applauds you. The world hates God and loves its sin; it loves affirmation of its sick and sinful condition.

The argument has been made that all sin is of the same

gravity therefore if we judge the sin of the homosexual, we should threat all sin as its equal to include those generally accepted by the church as minor such as lying or boasting or, but as a young friend recently pointed out that those humans guilty of "lesser" sins have not tried to impose acceptance of their behavior on our culture whether we agree with them or not as the homosexual Community does and by doing so, requires the rest of us to make a judgment about their behavior.

Jude 7; "In a similar way, Sodom and Gomorrah and the surrounding towns gave themselves up to sexual immorality and perversion. They serve as an example of those who suffer the punishment of eternal fire."

When the question about homosexuality is posed, we must be able and willing to give a sound biblical response that leaves no room for ambiguity on the part of the questioner. Just answer the question in a straightforward and biblical manner. Psychological integration is among the greatest deceptions that has ever entered into a body of Believers. And while those who promotes the ungodly integration of man's false wisdom with the Scriptures may think they are ministering to the spiritual and temporal needs of their listeners, in truth they are leading them astray by convincing them the Lord loves them as they are.

Every advance in the homosexual agenda represents a setback for mankind and for sexual normalcy. A tragic level of sexual confusion exists in our culture. The fact that it's something that would be celebrated is a tragic indication of how far we have drifted from God's expectations. Sexual perversion in one form or another has become so prevalent that degrading misogynist images have become the wallpaper of our lives and they are robbing young people of a healthy sexuality that is a basic right to all humans as well as a requirement of our God.

So I say, live by the Spirit, and you will not gratify the

desires of the sinful nature. Galatians 5:16 NIV. The one who sows to please his sinful nature, from that nature will reap destruction; the one who sows to please the Spirit, from the Spirit will reap eternal life. Galatians 6:8 NIV

You adulterous people, don't you know that friendship with the world is hatred toward God? Anyone who chooses to be a friend of the world becomes an enemy of God. James 4:4 NIV

It is actually reported that there is sexual immorality among you, and of a kind that does not occur even among pagans: A man has his father's wife. **2** And you are proud! Shouldn't you rather have been filled with grief and have put out of your fellowship the man who did this? **3** Even though I am not physically present, I am with you in spirit. And I have already passed judgment on the one who did this, just as if I were present. **4** When you are assembled in the name of our Lord Jesus and I am with you in spirit, and the power of our Lord Jesus is present, **5** hand this man over to Satan, so that the sinful nature may be destroyed and his spirit saved on the day of the Lord. 1 Corinthians 1:5 NIV.

We often hear "We are not supposed to judge anybody!" yet Paul in the above scripture reference didn't seem to hesitate about making a judgment call concerning the member of the Roman Church congregation and encourage the members to make the same judgment with their actions. There are many similar references in scripture encouraging Believers to make a judgment call about testing the Spirit or evaluating other Believers and or Preachers/Teachers. Matthew 7:20 NIV "Thus, by their fruit you will recognize them" would require a decision/judgment.

We do, however, speak a message of wisdom among the mature, but not the wisdom of this age or of the rulers of this age, who are coming to nothing. 1 Corinthians 2:6 NIV

The Spirit clearly says that in later times some will abandon the faith and follow deceiving spirits and things taught by demons. 1 Timothy 4:1 NIV

Frequently I encounter a person who appears to have established their own ideas about what they think God expects of them or for that matter, doesn't expect of them, then proceed to find and isolate scripture to support their beliefs. It's sort of like a person standing with their nose against a 12-foot wall painting, seeing only that part of the painting that appears right in front of their eyes, then declaring a description of the whole picture based on what they see while ignoring the remainder of the picture. Likewise, you can't take an isolated scripture, usually even out of context, to support any belief unless you balance it against all other scriptures that might be pertinent to the subject, thereby, seeing the whole picture.

For certain men whose condemnation was written about long ago have secretly slipped in among you. They are godless men, who change the grace of our God into a license for immorality and deny Jesus Christ our only sovereign and Lord. Jude 1: 4 NIV

... "In the last times there will be scoffers who will follow their own ungodly desires. These are the men who divide you, who follow mere natural instincts and do not have the Spirit. Jude 1:18-19 NIV

Our secular culture tries to explain away man's sin. The plaques of immorality and violence are attributed to poverty, social injustice and even genetics. The blame is placed everywhere except where it belongs; the sinful human heart. Our culture is also increasingly oriented to the present. The demand for instant gratification dominates. Our perspective on life is naturally framed in time but God's perspective is eternal. Each person will face a final lasting judgment. Whatever a person's destiny, it is eternal, everlasting reward or punishment waits for every person on earth. Even though contemporary culture seems to have designated tolerance as a primary moral virtue and promotes the idea that being nice will gain you Spiritual reward, it remains that trying to be nice to someone might appeal to the nature of our narcissistic character, but it could also condemn a soul to an eternity of torment if we fail to tell him what he must hear to challenge him to change. 2nd Timothy 4:3 (NIV) "For the time will come when men will not put up with sound doctrine. Instead, to suit their own desires, they will gather around themselves a great number of teachers to say what their itching ears want to hear. We need a strategy that recognizes the sin of lust and calls it by its name, rather than pretending that we have no agency beyond reacting to environmental stressors or psychological difficulties. We must treat lust like other sins; not a way we act out as a consequence of other problems in our lives, but as a sin requiring us to learn the discipline of self-control that we must master if we ever hope to be the person God made us to be.

Ephesians 5: 3; "But among you there must not be even a hint of sexual immorality, or of any kind of impurity, or of greed, because these are improper for God. (5) For this you can be sure: No immoral, Impure or greedy person; such a man is an idolater; has any inheritance in the kingdom of Christ and of God. (6) Let no man deceive you with empty words, for because of such things God's wrath comes on those who are disobedient. (7) Therefore, do not be partners with them.

I was recently accosted by a young lady who was begging for money. When she asked me for a contribution, I asked her why she thought I might give her money. She replied that most people do and that is how she takes care of herself. I suggested to her that maybe as long as people gave her money, she might never develop the incentive or the ability to go get a job and take care of herself and life is such that it is extremely important for her to learn to do that. I suggested that people supporting her might not be good for her in the long run and if they were really concerned, they shouldn't try to help in that manner. She showed surprise that someone would verbalize such thoughts. That goes counter to what today's culture tries to pressure onto us. It would suggest "Be nice, please don't hurt the person's feeling as that wouldn't be nice, to avoid hurting her or laying a guilt trip on her, just don't tell her what she needs to hear that might cause her to take control of her life and would bring about change, besides, I could walk away feeling 'sooooooo' good inside that I was able to help support this poor girl, why, she might have it tough if I hadn't helped her.

No matter what a Father might expect of his children, they will and must walk through life on their own and make their own decisions about their life. There will be times and for some of them, perhaps many times, when they will break Father's heart. Some Fathers have seen their own children whom they love dearly, destroy themselves and the parent can do little more than wring his hands and/or pray. Doesn't mean the Father's love is withdrawn or he loves the child less, it means the child can become unreachable and unaffected by that love.

My father was a loving parent, and I always knew he would take care of me, but my happiness was almost completely contingent upon my obedience to his directives. When I had done what he had assigned, I looked forward to seeing him; but when I had disobeyed him, I did my best to avoid him. "Loving" God as a mere mental focus does not make us happy, but love expressed through obedience brings lasting happiness

Likewise, every parent holds expectations of their children dear to their heart, rightly so, but they cannot force their ideas onto them. The child must and will develop their own. Their hope is that the child will make the right choices knowing that many of their choices will be wrong and will bring hurt to themselves and concern to you. If the child is foolish and decides to jump from a cliff and destroy himself, the parent will cry but at last, can do nothing. The Father can love the child with everything that is in him but the child holds his own future in his own hands. It's his decision.

Picture a surgeon and his medical team as they prepare to operate on a child who has cancer. The surgeon knows if the tumor is not removed, the child will die. For that reason, he'll use every measure to get the cancer out of the child's body, no matter the pain it causes. He knows his surgical work is going to bring deep hurt. And now, as he prepares to cut, a tear forms in his eye. It is an especially painful moment for him because the child is his. But to get to this surgery, it takes the patient's (son's) willingness to accept/embrace by faith the idea that his Father can/will do it. Had the child refused treatment, he would die as a result of that decision and there would be nothing the Father can do about it.

Understand that our Father is in a special place and there are some things that it is impossible to get into/or take there. A couple of those things are sin and anything with physical dimensions. Physical because His place is outside of the physical world. Sin because it would be the same as taking a dread disease there that would quickly spread all over as it has in the physical world. That means you have to be washed and/or cured from that disease else there is no future place for you with Him so you would wind up going to the same place where all other diseased ones go. To be washed means you have to agree and/or submit to the treatment but as it was your son's agreement to the surgery, you would not hold him down and cut him even though you might know that the surgery is necessary or you will lose him.

End of the Age, An Admonition

I am writing this today as I feel a compulsion to share with others something that is troubling my spirit, the challenge of living a righteous life with the Lord or settling for passing glory and worldly popularity among peers.

I need also to say that we live in the time just preceding the "end of the age" that our Lord referred to in the 20th chapter of Luke and that phase is actually found several other places in the Bible.

Many are familiar with the 3 beasts referred to in both Daniel and Revelations. Ervin Baxter, from the TV program "End of the Age" does a very good job of providing supporting and convincing argument suggesting the 3 beasts, the Bear, the Leopard and the Lion represent Countries or Political systems that exist today. The Bear represents Russia who displays it as their mascot, the leopard represents Germany and the Lion represents England. The Bible also suggests the Lion will be given a voice to speak for the other two beasts and today, the English language is spoken in most Countries around the world. Russian young people are rushing to learn English like never before and of course, most Europeans speak English. The Bible states that from out of the back of the Lion, an Eagles wings will sprout and we know that the original United States came from England and our mascot is the Eagle. Those readers who would like to review this subject further, I would recommend obtaining Ervin Baxter set of DVDs'.

You will see in your time many terrible things happen in the World and specifically in our own Country as the world changes to accommodate events spoken of as happening just before His return. Be very careful that you don't become focused on these events rather than focused on Him and His sustaining power. Recently, while observing things happening in our Culture that I could not have even dreamed of it happening a few years ago, "I said to myself, My God, what is this world coming to?" I wasn't really speaking to Him, but He heard me anyway and spoke back, "wait a minute, what you just said implies that I am not in control, I am, but the things you see happening must happen in order to usher in last day events" He said, "You will see many, many things that will make you shudder inside before I come, but it must happen, just keep your focus on me" He gave me an illustration. As a young boy, I used to swim in the river and He showed me that if I keep my eye on the other side, I can reach there, but if I focus instead on all the debris floating in the water, I can wind up going upstream or downstream or around and around. I will never reach the other side. As we encounter rough water in the last days, we must keep focused on Him and know in our hearts that He will take care of us, no matter.

I believe with all my heart that your generation will face and see things happen to this Country and the world, that was not even imagined previously. When it happens, you will remember my words and take heart that the Lord's coming is near and I want to encourage you to trust the Lord, no matter what you see happening. Establish in your heart that He is in control regardless. I see so many ominous signs on the horizon today but the blunt force will hit your generation and especially your children's time frame. I will go before you but it is my heart's desire that you follow me later. It will be your responsibility to establish in your children's heart the solidarity of their belief, the conviction that provides determination to trust Him no matter what and the necessary perseverance to live among the filth and rot of the coming age without being defiled by what's around them even as Lot was considered "good" by God even though he lived in the most depraved City, no doubt, in history. Those who persevere to the end will be lifted out of it. Keep the strong faith no matter what ideas people will try to feed you, no matter the pressure to conform. You may at times feel that you are standing alone or all by yourself as you see people of God surrender and fall around you, but you must stand. No matter what comes your way, until He takes you home. Keep in mind that those who are set apart by Him are as aliens in this world, we wait for a better place as our home. As one of my sons once stated, "when the devil reminds me of my past, I will remind him of his future"

Artificial Intelligence (AI) will be developed to the extent that we can't even imagine at this time. Time magazine, (January 15, 2018) carried an article by Lili Cheng, VP, Microsoft AI Research in which the author outlined expectations stating " recent breakthroughs in AI, based on computers' ability to understand speech and language, and have vision, have given rise to our technology alter ego, a personal guide that knows your habits and communication preferences, and helps schedule your time, motivate your team to do their best work, or be, say, a better parent" I have also seen recently on the internet articles touting man's ability to design robots that will incorporate AI to function as humans. In the near future, as this technology increases very sharply, humans, at least in the cultures impacted by it, will become more dependent on it to provide their basic needs to include those needs that are primarily psychological in nature such as satisfying the need for worship. As that happens, their dependency on and recognition of God, the Creator, will decline quickly. They confidence will be in their technology and their own ability, resorting to their sinful nature but they will not be aware that in their spirit, they have said Who needs a God? Daniel (Dan 12:4) speaking of the last days states that "many will go here and there

THE GOD THAT DOES NOT FAIL

to increase knowledge"

It's interesting that in the Genesis account (Gen. 11) of the Tower of Babel, God confused the tongue of man to retard the flow of knowledge because He said (v. 9) "nothing they (man) plan to do would be impossible for them to do". Yet today, when it seems man is many times more intelligent than then, yet God seemingly, is not concerned about it, at least not yet. I suspect that God would have known at that time, if He didn't do something, mankind would advance in intellect to the point that His plan for mankind would be drastically altered. Today; He knows we are near the very end of His plan for the end of the age, that He will let it unfold as we move rapidly toward that point. Except for the chosen ones, man will separate himself further and further from their creator as they build a reliance on their own created. The chosen ones will discover themselves under such tremendous stress to accept status quo that they will pray, even so, come Lord Jesus and/or slip into the sewer.

Already, I see numerous attacks against the scripture and traditionally accepted understanding of what should be expected by those who profess to be "Christian" or those "Church" people. The Church is under attack as never before that I recall, and the method of attack is insidious in that like a cancer, much of it coming from within the Church, rendering it powerless, stroking the religious, feel good side of humanity but not changing lives, reducing itself to nothing more than a social club and/or a business. Many boldly proclaim, "Give us your money and God will prosper you in return!" suggesting prosperity a motive for attending Church and hundreds of thousands sat in the pews, drawn there by greed. Many leaders lavish themselves in lush multi-million-dollar homes, profitable business, private Airplanes or Helicopters. You must learn to trust Him simply because of who He is whether or not He ever provides material gain for you.

Many "Church" leaders, Church businessmen and

"Christian" Community leaders are such poor role models themselves, with good intentions, embrace and project to their young people role models such as the Seattle Seahawks players or the such as Michael Jackson, who was both a pervert and a drug addict, that many are trying to emulate individuals with harmful at best, evil at worst, lifestyles that will destroy them. Others project a lifestyle that distorts what they claim to be, from what they really are, young people, who seem to have built in antenna's and can spot a phony a mile away, turn away from them. I often hear young people say, "I can't hear what they are saying because of what they are doing" thus reducing them from role model to nothing more than role-playing. I've often told folks that I don't want to hear what you are, let me see what you are.

I recently attended a church meeting where I counted nearly 50 folks wearing Seattle Seahawks Shirts, including the assistant Pastor, in the house of our Lord and the Pastor bragging on game players from the pulpit to a favorable response from the attendees far exceeding any reference to the Lord Jesus Christ. I was nearly overcome with the feeling that I was among Ashtaroth poles which the Bible states that God hates. The poles usually contained a symbol representing the heathen god known as Balaam (Baal) and while we today know the poles represented no god but we also know the Seahawk does not represent a real creature, it doesn't matter, for much of the year, you can see people going crazy over the symbol as if it was a real god, far exceeding any response to the name of the real God or His symbol of the cross. In the scenario above, there was one young person who was wearing a shirt that stated "Jesus" across the front so I just had to meet him afterwards and compliment him. He also mentioned that he was bothered by so many Seahawks shirts present.

In an attempt to attract young people, the Church has succumbed to acceptance of rock music, sports events and/or sports figures/players and body mutilations including body tattoos, not realizing these practices have their origin in primitive cultures which historically have been dominated by demons. I believe the institutional Church will and is experiencing a great falling away as the Bible said would happen in the last days, but that doesn't necessarily mean people physically leaving it but a significant amount of that body lacking any Spiritual experience that could carry them through the dark days coming on the world as we approach the end time and thereby, ultimately, being lost, falling away from their previous real experience with Him.

From outside the Church, there are so many indecent and morally decadent, corruptive challenges being pressed onto those who profess to be believers, yet the vast majority of believers seem to be either asleep or numb to what's happening and in even some cases, professing believers are accepting these ungodly and destructive lifestyles or philosophies and by doing so, fulfilling scriptural projections about last day events. If not outright accepting them, because the Church is asleep and blinded to what's happening around, they are encouraging broader acceptance of them by doing nothing. We currently live in a democratic Country where the Majority rules but it amazes me that the majority moves so quickly to appease a vocal minority thus suggesting the minority is actually calling the shots even if it requires significant change to accepted norms for the majority creating the illusion that the majority really stands for nothing. It would seem that all it would take to expose these fraudulent charades is basic common sense, the greatest enemy of "Political Correctness." Where today do you hear anything about "common sense"?

Be especially careful of internet chat rooms or the piles of other "stuff" that sounds so religious, pious or enlightened that is being dumped by the truck load into the internet. Remember that Mathew 24:24, Jesus said that in the last days, "false Christ's and false prophets will appear and perform great signs and miracles or profess to be so smart, to deceive even the elect, if that were possible." I believe many, who in the past, have demonstrated logic or clear thinking, will be, and are even now, being deceived by flattery and supposedly, by words implying enlightenment by divine discernment. This heresy will not be coming from those who come from the backside of the desert, rich in Spiritual understanding but the media will be and is being flooded by people who project themselves as having been enlightened. They project themselves as having new knowledge or a new way of looking at things and usually critical of historically acceptable forms of worship or traditional norms of Christian behavior. Paul in Acts 12:1-2, says, "Therefore, I urge you, brothers, in view of God's mercy, to offer your bodies as a living sacrifice, holy and pleasing to God. This is your spiritual act of worship. Do not conform any longer to the pattern of this world but be transformed to the renewing of your mind. Then you will be able to test and approve what God's will is, His good and pleasing and perfect will," including His will for your life on a daily basis.

Be aware of the effect of the media on mass man today. As the 80-20 rule suggest, only about 20% of people think at any given time while the other 80% usually are carried about by the prevailing winds of philosophy, also known as the Parrado rule.

I remember Dr. Dan Pecota, Professor at Northwest College when I attended, giving a little pep speech to the class before we started the semester, stating, "We will be discussing many things before this semester is over, but if I can just teach each of you to think, I will feel that I have accomplished something significant". The media will and is even now, pushing all kinds of agenda's and that 80% of the listeners will be buying into and/or accepting everything, most without even doing any in depth thinking. The Obama Presidential election was basically an election by media and it appears today the media may be the leader in pushing anything unwholesome and/or indecent.

It has been said that, except for intuitive knowledge, everything you know and accept, has been told to you by somebody else, who had it told to them, who had it told to them since the beginning. Educators have even tested you to make sure you got it their way. That's not to say they were wrong but to lay it out that way, it can be scary. We must be able to listen carefully, but afterwards, carefully analyze everything. Those things that we can't accept, don't necessarily throw it out but put it on a shelf somewhere in our mind until or unless we can get some additional verification and there is a lot of religious "stuff" out there that can confuse the mind and anesthetize you to the truth if you buy into it too quickly.

These things are just a few of the many destructive thrusts infiltrating both the institutional Church as well as the Church of believers. They are insidious and deceptive. Many people don't even realize they have moved away from a vibrant walk with the Lord until their knowledge of Him has become so twisted or maligned that by the time they do realize their lives have changed, they will have so fully embraced the change that they can never regain their previous position in Him nor for that matter, may never realize where they have moved to or often, using certain verses from the Bible, build cases to justify the change in their life. It will get worse as the world moves closer to the end.

If I measure the future with the rapidity of my past and since it seems that all my past life happened only yesterday, I can say with some certainty that my homecoming with occur fairly soon even if the Lord lengthened my life span and in saying that, I want to exhort you to be very diligent with your walk with the Lord after I have gone to my real home. I pray for you that even if I am not around to exhort you, the Lord Himself, by His Holy Spirit, will nudge you or send you someone that may assist you to keep your feet on the right track so that all who know Him may later be reunited and enjoy eternity together. I urge you to use the good common sense that the Lord provided you with and when everything around you fail, let it go but stand for Him and wait out His return for you.